P9-DIB-465

100 GREATEST
U.S. MODERN COINS

Scott Schechter and Jeff Garrett

Forewords by Kenneth Bressett and Q. David Bowers

www.whitman**books**.com

Whitman Publishing, LLC
Atlanta, GA

100 GREATEST U.S. MODERN COINS

www.whitman**books**.com

© 2011 Whitman Publishing, LLC
3101 Clairmont Road · Suite G · Atlanta, GA 30329

100 GREATEST is a registered trademark of Whitman Publishing, LLC.

All rights reserved, including duplication of any kind and storage in electronic or visual retrieval systems. Permission is granted for writers to use a reasonable number of brief excerpts and quotations in printed reviews and articles, provided credit is given to the title of the work and the authors. Written permission from the publisher is required for other uses of text, illustrations, and other content, including in books and electronic or other media.

Correspondence concerning this book may be directed to the publisher,
Attn: 100 Greatest U.S. Modern Coins, at the address above.

ISBN: 0794832563
Printed in China

Disclaimer: No warranty or representation of any kind is made concerning the accuracy or completeness of the information presented, or its usefulness in numismatic purchases or sales. The opinions of others may vary. The authors may buy, sell, and sometimes hold certain of the items discussed in this book.

Caveat: The price estimates given are subject to variation and differences of opinion. Especially rare coins trade infrequently, and an estimate or past auction price may have little relevance to future transactions. Before making decisions to buy or sell, consult the latest information. Grading of coins is subject to wide interpretation, and opinions can differ. Past performance of any item in the market is not necessarily an indication of future performance, as the future is unknown.

Advertisements within this book: Whitman Publishing, LLC, does not endorse, warrant, or guarantee any of the products or services of its advertisers. All warranties and guarantees are the sole responsibility of the advertiser.

If you enjoy the fascinating history and color images of the *100 Greatest U.S. Modern Coins*, you will also enjoy the other books in this collection, including *100 Greatest U.S. Coins*, *100 Greatest Ancient Coins*, *100 Greatest American Currency Notes*, *100 Greatest American Medals and Tokens*, *100 Greatest U.S. Error Coins*, and *100 Greatest American Stamps*.

For a complete catalog of numismatic reference books, supplies, and storage products,
visit Whitman Publishing online at www.WhitmanBooks.com

Read book reviews, hobby articles, guest columns, Q&A, and more, in *The Whitman Review*,
online at www.WhitmanReview.com

Whitman®

CONTENTS

In the 1950s and early '60s, Americans could still find older coins in circulation —as well as the occasional commemorative that slipped into pocket change. These coins disappeared with the advent of the modern era.

BY KENNETH BRESSETT

Regardless of what date is chosen as the beginning of "modern" coinage, or what constitutes a "great" coin, it is all a matter of personal preference. The turn of the last century, 1934, 1982, or almost any other date might be a valid choice. The authors of this work have targeted 1964, and in my mind that is not just an arbitrary starting date, but a very valid transitional year for a number of significant reasons.

The world was in a state of flux at that time. It had just been turned upside down by the tragic assassination of President John F. Kennedy. The placid times of the past were soon to change and never return, and coin collecting as many of us knew it then was to change forever. It all began the following year with the removal of silver from our national coinage, and the curtailment of precious-metal coins all over the world.

The official medal of the 1966 U.S. Assay Commission, which counted Kenneth Bressett among its members.

It was a time I remember well, for in 1966 I was appointed by President Lyndon B. Johnson as a member of the United States Assay Commission and assigned to check on the quality of coins minted in 1965. The annual assay was a tradition going back to the beginning of U.S. coinage, but effectively ending with the last of the silver coins being minted that year. Probably one of the most famous coins of this time was the silver dollar made in 1964 at the Denver Mint. It was an ill-fated venture that never progressed beyond the striking of a limited number of coins before the order came to abandon the project and destroy the entire output.

The mid-1960s were an exciting time for collectors. It was a time when the old silver coins still saw limited circulation, and even scarce dates could sometimes be culled from pocket change. It was also a time of great expectations, when new types of coins were being planned for introduction into circulation. Few had ever seen or heard of "clad" coins. They quickly became known as "sandwich" coins because of the unusual red streak of copper showing along the outer edge. During the early transition from silver to clad coins astute collectors could easily gather the older coins and sell them to smelters, sometimes for up to double their face value.

The 1964 transition was clearly a time of change not only for the hobby but for the entire nation. The changes touched off by the assassination of President Kennedy were echoed around the world and reflected by a universal interest in all of the many commemorative items associated with him. The new half dollars with his image were wildly popular everywhere, and notice was taken when the composition was changed from silver to copper-nickel. It was an event that seemed to herald similar changes in coinage throughout the world. In an instant our long-held perceptions of the character of coinage, and how it should look and function, were changed forever.

Collector interest in all U.S. coins was growing in the late 1960s. Everything—from great rarities to circulated coins and even rolls of new coins—was in demand. There never seemed

(Top) The assassination of President Kennedy was one of many events in a decade of upheaval.

1964 Kennedy half dollar, variety with Accented Hair.

to be enough new issues or interesting items to satisfy collectors' appetites. Oh, how we wished that the Mint would resume making commemorative coins, or give us a voice in advising what would be good for the hobby; or that there could be some better way of protecting and grading coins, or making them more understandable and secure investments for the "outsiders" who were beginning to enter the market. We even wished that the price of gold would be normalized so we could once again openly collect those old coins, or perhaps that the government could make new issues for us. We really did not think to "be careful of what we wished for"!

In time, all those wishes came true, as collectors of modern coins now know. Some of the changes came about because of pressures by hobby leaders; some were a natural economic evolution.

Examples of "non-circulating legal tender." The Austrian and Australian coins are shown with certificates of authenticity, which are commonly provided with such items.

Much of the numismatic world as we know it today is a result of the worldwide change from hard money (paper and checks) to electronic and card transfers. The new order, it seems, is on the way to a cashless society, and mints everywhere are struggling to create new products to keep their presses running. I remember wondering what we should call those new coin issues from around the world that were intended solely for sale to collectors and not for commerce. To resolve the issue, a quiet conference of numismatic publishers convened to address the subject; we agreed to name them NCLT, "non-circulating legal tender." It is a term that now appropriately applies to a large percentage of coins throughout the world—coins of every ilk that display images of everything from octopi to mustachioed old presidents, but are rarely seen outside coin collections.

An offshoot of this is the nearly overwhelming array of enticing offerings each year of U.S. coins with new designs, new finishes, new packaging, and novel metals. At the beginning of the "modern" era of numismatics, buying a set of all U.S. coins each year cost a whopping $6.50: $2.50 for the Proof set and $4 for the Mint set. Today the vast array of choices—which include bullion, commemorative issues, and other items that will never see circulation—would cost well over $10,000. We have at last been given more than everything that was wished for in the past.

Among the vast array of numismatic treats we have been blessed with are numerous unusual, rare, and "great" coins. These are the pieces described by authors Jeff Garrett and Scott Schechter in this compelling book. You will be not only fascinated by the coins, but also thrilled to know that some can actually be found in your pocket change. They disprove the axiom that all the good coins are gone from circulation, and give inspiration for all to continue the search while enjoying the numismatic hobby on whichever level appeals to each of us.

By Q. David Bowers

Numismatist: A collector of *old* coins. A quick definition that leaves out a great deal, it nonetheless covers the basics. Numismatists seek 1793 cents with our country's name abbreviated as "AMERI." on the reverse; they look for 1785 Vermont copper coins with the sun-over-mountains design; and if they specialize in Morgan silver dollars minted from 1878 to 1921, their Holy Grail is a nice 1893-CC.

Many numismatists focus on rare older coins like colonial and early American coppers and 19th-century silver dollars. The panoply of modern coinage is equally rich.

When I discovered the world's greatest hobby in 1952 and began dealing in coins in a small way shortly thereafter, these *old* coins were of necessity the main things to collect. United States coinage offered few modern issues—just routine releases of the Lincoln cent, Jefferson nickel, Roosevelt dime, Washington quarter, and Franklin half each year, both for circulation and in Proof sets. No variation here except for a change of date. (To be sure, Carver-Washington commemorative half dollars were still being issued, but most collectors found them unattractive, and to this day I have never met anyone who has focused on them.)

This scenario changed, and dramatically so, in 1982, with the issuance of the first modern-era commemorative: a half dollar designed by Elizabeth Jones, chief sculptor and engraver at the Mint, and honoring the 250th anniversary of George Washington's birth. This opened the floodgates, and since that time there have been dozens of new commemorative issues—the good, the bad, and the ugly, commemorating important anniversaries and people (most of us like baseball star Jackie Robinson) as well as the illogical (such as a silver dollar for the 38th anniversary of the Korean War—the thirty-*eighth?* Give us a break!).

"The design [of the 1991 Korean War Memorial silver dollar] has been criticized as being cluttered," notes the *Guide Book of United States Coins*, "and the occasion no more than a fund-raising opportunity for the creation of a national monument in Washington."

Oddities notwithstanding, today, the many new U.S. Mint products—from commemoratives to bullion coins to special strikings of quarter dollars, and more—have opened up a wonderful new panorama of opportunity. While some such coins have become scarce in their context (the aforementioned Jackie Robinson commemorative being an example), most are readily available and quite affordable. One can pick and choose favorites, or endeavor to acquire one of everything. A few years ago, in connection with an exhibit, I bought one of every commemorative, regular, and bullion coin minted during the administration of President Ronald Reagan (1981–1989). What I thought would be a piece of cake actually took more than a month and cost more than $10,000. I was surprised to realize that there were so many things.

In this book, Jeff Garrett and Scott Schechter compile the all-time favorites—the "greatest"—of modern coins. Contemplating the voters' choices will undoubtedly ignite in you a desire to possess some of the items featured. As mentioned earlier, traditional numismatist might seek out a 1793 cent or 1785 Vermont copper—coins for which circulated Fine or Very Fine is an acceptable grade, Extremely Fine is exceptional, and gem Mint State is impossible. Not so with the majority of the 100 Greatest *modern* coins, for which grades such as Mint State and Proof 68 to 70 are the rule, not the exception.

The "mother" of all unusual coins made since I started collecting is the 1955 doubled-die Lincoln cent. Strictly speaking, it is too old for inclusion in the present compilation of modern coins, which commences with the year 1964; however, a mention of it here is worthwhile, for it started the (very modern) passion for unusual die varieties, a great many of which are included in this book. Back in 1955, Jim Ruddy, who later became my business partner, operated his coin business in Johnson City, New York. It was one of three major centers of release of the 1955

doubled-die cents, the other two being greater Boston and an area of western Massachusetts near Pittsfield. Jim made it known that he would pay 25¢ each for these coins, but soon he had dozens, had no resale customers for them, and stopped buying! (In those days, unusual die varieties of modern coins had no following. Collecting them became popular in the early 1960s with the help of New Jersey numismatist Frank G. Spadone; and interest went into really high gear when Bill Fivaz and J.T. Stanton produced their *Cherrypickers' Guide to Rare Die Varieties*.) Today one of those 1955 doubled-die cents is worth thousands of dollars. I wish I had kept some!

The 1955 doubled-die Lincoln cent—a precursor to today's popularly collected varieties.

A personal favorite—or rather, two such favorites—among the coins you'll read about in these pages are the 2004-D Wisconsin statehood quarters with curious leaves. In January 2005 I was at the Florida United Numismatists show tending a bourse table with Christine Karstedt and other American Numismatic Rarities staffers. Dennis Tucker, who had recently signed with Whitman as publisher, came by, and we were chatting about upcoming books. Well-known Arizona coin dealer Rick Snow stopped by the table with two unusual Wisconsin quarters, each with a leaf that did not belong on the design. Dennis and I were intrigued. I motioned to David Hall, the founder of PCGS, and he came over and was amazed as well. I bought the two pieces from Rick and gave them to David, and the two coins became the first pair to be certified. "What should they be called?" we wondered. We discussed this and agreed that Extra Leaf High and Extra Leaf Low would be ideal descriptors. These modern-day varieties would later be featured in the *Guide Book of United States Coins* (the annual "Red Book").

As I perused the galleys of *The 100 Greatest U.S. Modern Coins* I enjoyed reading about my own favorites, but also came to appreciate many varieties I had overlooked. Authors Schechter and Garrett have done an excellent job tracking down the histories of these pieces, delving into their availabilities, and presenting the coins in an interesting and authoritative manner. When my copy of this book arrives, I'll stop everything and read it again. I expect it will become one of the favorites in *your* numismatic library, as well.

CREDITS AND ACKNOWLEDGMENTS

ACKNOWLEDGMENTS

I would like to thank my wife, Sonia, whose love and support truly made this book possible.

–Scott Schechter

I want to thank my wife, Mary Lynn, and my daughter, Morgan, for allowing me to take the time away from my family required to write these books.

–Jeff Garrett

CREDITS

Images were provided by Numismatic Guaranty Corporation photographers Terry Shank and Donnell Hagan, and researcher Max Spiegel; Mid-American Numismatic Rarities photographer Tom Mulvaney; Heritage Auction Galleries; *Coin World* (www.CoinWorld.com); and Library of Congress.

Charles Moore and Heather Grant provided research and other assistance. Mark Salzberg, Richard S. Montgomery, David W. Lange, and David J. Camire were all very helpful sounding boards for concepts and arguments presented in the text. Steven Eichenbaum graciously made special accommodations that contributed to the book's timely completion.

The following books in the Whitman library were also valuable resources for images, data, and other information: *A Guide Book of United States Coins*, 65th ed. (Atlanta: Whitman Publishing, 2011); *A Guide Book of United States Coins, Professional Edition*, 2nd ed. (Whitman, 2011); *Cherrypickers' Guide to Rare Die Varieties of United States Coins*, 4th ed., vol. 2, and 5th ed., vol. 1 (Bill Fivaz and J.T. Stanton; Whitman, 2006 and 2009); *100 Greatest U.S. Error Coins* (Nicholas P. Brown, David J. Camire, and Fred Weinberg; Whitman, 2010); *A Guide Book of Franklin and Kennedy Half Dollars* (Rick Tomaska; Whitman, 2010); *A Guide Book of United States Commemorative Coins* (Q. David Bowers; Whitman, 2008); *A Guide Book of Lincoln Cents* (Q. David Bowers; Whitman, 2008); and *A Guide Book of Modern U.S. Proof Coin Sets* (David W. Lange; Whitman, 2010).

WHAT ARE MODERN COINS?

There is a very simple definition of modern U.S. coinage, which is a good starting point: modern U.S. coins are those struck from 1964 to date. All the coins described in *100 Greatest U.S. Modern Coins* fall within this time period. The reader need go no further to have a very serviceable and accurate definition.

As with many things that seem simple on the surface, a deeper look reveals complexity. For example, it would be easy to mischaracterize the above definition as "coins of relatively recent vintage." This, of course, implies that the definition is a moving target, subject to change over time. In truth, it is not. Just as *modern art* defines a period of artistic production and connects works based on their content and character, *modern coinage* is more than a date range.

Coins minted in 1964 hint at this complexity. The date 1964 is hugely significant in American numismatics. It is the last year that U.S. coins struck for circulation contained 90% silver. It marks the end of a metallic composition that had been in use since the Mint Act of 1792 first established the standards for U.S. coinage. From 1965 forward, the formerly silver dimes and quarters struck for circulation would be sandwiches of copper and nickel. (For a short period, the post-1964 half dollar continued to be made with silver in its outer layer, but by 1971 no circulation issues would contain any silver.)

1964-D Washington quarter, Reverse of 1965.

Not all Mint products from 1964 should be considered modern. In the *100 Greatest U.S. Modern Coins*, there are three entries from this year. One is the 1964 Special Mint Set—a set of coins with an unusual finish that replaced the Proof finish on coinage sets made for collectors from 1965 through 1967. The Proof set was put on hiatus while the Mint put all its attention on the production of new-composition coinage. Another is the 1964, Reverse of 1965, Washington quarter, a coin that shows early use of a modified design created to suit the upcoming clad coinage. The third is the 1964 Accented Hair Kennedy half dollar, a first-year variety of a new, distinctly modern coinage series. All of these coins relate directly to the changes that were coming to the new coinage, and are modern for that reason. They are coins not entirely stuck in the context of pre-1964 issues.

So the era of modern coinage began with the Mint figuring out how to smoothly transition away from the silver issues of previous years. For years after the change, coin design remained stagnant, playing on the collective memory of past silver circulating coinage. Even when the Eisenhower dollar was introduced in 1971, a non-circulating version containing silver was also released, helping to create the still vitally important association between a coin's face value and its intrinsic worth. Not until 1979, nearly 10 years later, was this connection severed when a small-sized copper-nickel-clad dollar coin was issued replacing the original silver dollar of memory.

Subsequent new coinage programs similarly recalled the past before heading in a new modern path. In 1982, the U.S. commemorative coinage program re-launched (the last U.S. commemoratives had been struck in the 1950s). The first coin was a silver half dollar, as nearly all the classic commemoratives issues had been. When Olympic commemorative three-coin dollar sets were sold in 1983, they were each comprised of a Philadelphia, Denver, and San Francisco Mint issue, as the original commemorative P-D-S sets had been. At that time a new $10 commemorative coin followed, something novel enough to begin breaking ties with the commemorative coins of the past. In 1986, the first U.S. bullion coins were issued, in a program that had no historical antecedents in the United States. Even still, at this late date, designs were recycled from classic coinage issues for the obverses of both the gold and silver eagles.

1982 George Washington half dollar. With this coin, the United States' modern commemorative coinage program began after a nearly 30-year hiatus.

Eventually, these gradual changes gave way to dramatic experimentation. By 1999, the era of modern coinage at last had hit its stride. New designs were introduced five times every year on the state quarters issued from 1999 through 2008. A brand-new-composition dollar coin was introduced in 2000. Only faint connections can be drawn to earlier coinage. There is no doubt that these latter series are singularly modern.

The modern era has brought many new reverse designs for the Washington quarter—states, territories, and national parks have been honored in several popular series.

The Mint introduced a new "golden" dollar composition in 2000.

Throughout the modern era of coinage, a significant consideration has loomed in the background: every coin's design and composition needs to meet the demands of mass production. Modern coinage production is not an artisanal process. Instead, all modern coins are produced using very powerful, high-speed coinage presses in a refined mechanical process designed to create as many coins as needed. Technology and its limitations, therefore, also play a role in the story of modern coinage. No country produces nearly as many coins as the United States. The huge demand for coinage has been keenly felt throughout the era of modern coinage as the U.S. Mint has tested the upper limits of what is possible.

METHODS OF MANUFACTURE

Describing the way that modern coins are made is not as straightforward as it might seem. It requires that we delve into the jargon of numismatics. When we do, we encounter terms that are polysemes, single words that have multiple meanings. Initially, this creates a confusing mess. It is helpful to be aware of this at the outset.

The Mint formally divides the coins it produces into three categories: circulation coins, numismatic coins, and bullion coins.

Circulation coins are coins produced to be used as money. Other common names for this category of coins are *business strikes* and *currency issues*. These coins receive a single strike from dies that the Mint hopes will, under the best of circumstances, make more than a million coins each. Coins are ejected from the coinage press into large bins and packed into enormous ballistic bags before being wrapped into rolls. Circulation-issue coins may have numerous contact marks from exposure to other coins and Mint equipment. They may be weakly struck, or struck from late-state or fatigued dies, which imparts a mushy impression of the design. Additionally, these coins are struck on planchets that have received no special care to preserve high quality. Roughness or abrasion on the planchets may still be evident on the final coins.

As a result, the process of producing coins for circulation does not necessarily yield an attractive specimen for collectors, and circulation-issue coins can be challenging to find in the highest states of preservation. This is true even of very recent issues.

For years, standard-issue coins were packaged into Mint sets (annual sets of coins sold by the Mint). Starting in 2005, the Mint replaced standard-issue coins in Mint sets with satin-finish examples that have a light matte-textured finish and are usually found in much better condition than standard circulation examples.

Numismatic coins are coins that are struck at the Mint specifically for sale to collectors. These include special presentation versions of the circulating coins, issued annually in Proof sets. Since 1992, the Mint has also sold silver Proof sets that contain (in addition to other coins) a dime, quarter, and half dollar struck in 90%

Mint sets have been issued since the 1940s, specially packaged by the government for sale as collectibles.

silver. The category of numismatic coins also includes commemorative, thematic coins that serve the dual purposes of honoring an event, person, place, or organization as well as raising money for a specific purpose in the form of surcharges assessed by the Mint at the time of sale. The coins themselves, as with all U.S. coins, must be authorized by act of Congress, which selects their themes, sets mintage limits, designates the benefactor, and can even inform their designs.

Proofs and commemoratives are designated by the Mint as *numismatic coins*, as opposed to bullion coins and coins struck for circulation.

All numismatic coins receive extraordinary levels of special handling during the minting process. These coins are sold to collectors at a premium. Collectors—being a finicky bunch—demand quality. Numismatic coins are struck twice from fresh dies on planchets treated to yield the highest quality. The coins often are hand-packed into custom presentation cases. The Mint offers two finishes of numismatic coins: Proof and Uncirculated. Proof coins have mirrored areas that contrast with frosted portions of their design, a visual achieved by alternating polishing with sandblasting on different areas of the die. Uncirculated numismatic coins have an even, matte-like finish, an effect created by sandblasting, acid etching, or laser-cutting the entire die. (Starting in 2009, these finishes have been achieved by laser-cutting the dies rather than sandblasting or etching them.) Confusion, of course, results from the use of the term *Uncirculated* as a surface finish. Uncirculated is more commonly a grading term used to describe coins that show no metal loss from circulation. In *100 Greatest U.S. Modern Coins*, we have observed the Mint's convention of describing these coins with the terms *Uncirculated finish* or *Uncirculated issue*. The potential for confusion, however, is noted here.

The last category of coins produced by the Mint is *bullion coins*. Bullion is simply precious metal in coin form. Although bullion coins have a denominated face value, they actually trade based on their metal content. Scarce issues have become collectibles and can have a numismatic premium in addition to their bullion value. Normally, bullion coins have a matte-like or Uncirculated finish (in the Mint's parlance), but less care is taken in their production than for numismatic coins. Although they are always well struck from relatively new or fresh dies, they can have contact marks and hairlines. Bullion coins are quickly packed into tubes, and the tubes are placed in "monster boxes" of 500 ounces. This packaging is designed for the convenience of precious-metal transactions and not for coin preservation. Additionally, planchet preparation for bullion coins is not as meticulous as for numismatic coins. Often, planchets used to strike these coins are poorly rinsed, which later causes coins to spot or stain, especially on American silver eagles.

Bullion coins are produced for investors and do not have mint-marks. The Mint does make collector versions in Proof format with mintmarks (and special designs in the case of American eagle platinum coins). From 2006 through 2008, the Mint even made Uncirculated versions of the American eagles for direct sale to collectors. They are very similar in appearance to regular bullion coins except they include the W mintmark for West Point, New York, where they were all struck. These coins did receive some extra attention during production, as their coin blanks were burnished at the Mint. This treatment is not visible in the final prod-

uct except with respect to spotting and staining, which seems to be less prevalent in Mint-burnished coins. Additionally, these coins were individually packaged in capsules, and therefore tend to be comparatively devoid of contact marks.

VARIETIES VS. ERRORS

An area of perpetual confusion involves the differences between these two related but distinct terms: *variety* and *error*. There are a number of varieties included within the 100 Greatest U.S. Modern Coins, along with a handful of error coins. It's fair to say that this is an important distinction to understand.

Variety is short for die variety. A die physically imparts a coin with its design by striking a coin planchet with great force. The die contains the inverted design of the coin. If something unusual occurred to that die when it was created, resulting in an unusual attribute such as a doubled legend, it will pass that attribute onto all the coins that it strikes. A number of coins will be produced with this exact same feature. If the feature is prominent and interesting, it can become collectible. These are varieties.

For example: in 1995, a Lincoln cent obverse die mistakenly received two misaligned impressions of the coin's design. All the coins struck from this die had a doubled image, like a two-color document printed with bad registration. This is a very popular type of variety called a *doubled die*, and the specific coin described here is the 1995 Doubled-Die Obverse Lincoln cent.

The 1995 Doubled-Die Obverse Lincoln cent—a popular variety.

Because varieties are the result of a flaw or feature on a single die, they are said to be die specific. Sometimes, the same type of error will occur multiple times in the same year. For example, in 1972, the Mint produced a number of doubled-die obverse Lincoln cents. Some are quite minor, while one is very prominent and very famous. Each individual die variety is cataloged and assigned a unique reference number. A popular guide for collectible varieties is the *Cherrypickers' Guide to Die Varieties*, which illustrates and catalogs these coins. When you buy variety coins, it's important to know if there are multiple varieties for a year and exactly which one it is that you're purchasing. Major varieties can trade for huge premiums, while minor varieties often carry little or no premium. The most popular and coveted of all die varieties are those listed in the *Guide Book of United States Coins* (the annually issued reference known by coin collectors as the "Red Book").

A Mint error, in contrast to a die variety, results when a mistake occurs during the production of a single coin. One common type

The U.S. Mint launched its bullion coinage program in 1986, and has introduced several expansions and innovations in recent years.

of Mint error is an off-center coin. Such errors are created when a planchet is fed partway into the coinage press. When the hammer die comes to strike the coin, only a portion of the planchet receives an impression. This error is coin-specific—only that single coin is affected. The preceding coin and the following coin might be perfectly normal, well within the Mint's tolerances for acceptable production. This coin is an error because it falls outside those tolerances.

A remarkable error coin: an off-center 1976 Eisenhower dollar struck on a 1976 Lincoln cent. This unique piece was ranked No. 16 among the *100 Greatest U.S. Error Coins* (Brown, Camire, and Weinberg).

Even though an error results from a manufacturing mistake during the production of a single coin, some mistakes are repeated frequently. For example, minor off-center errors like those described above are common for most modern series even though they are created one-by-one when a single planchet is misfed into the coinage press. Occasionally, an error is repeated frequently enough to become a collectable adjunct to the standard set. One of the best examples occurred in 2007. The new Presidential dollar coins had a lettered edge. This feature is applied by a separate edge-lettering machine after the obverse and reverse of the coin are struck. For the first issue in this series, the George Washington dollar, several hundred thousand examples missed this step entirely and have blank edges. Although technically an error coin and not part of the regular series, the George Washington Missing Edge Lettering dollars are widely collected by Presidential dollar enthusiasts.

Both die varieties and Mint errors are the result of mistakes, and this can be a source of confusion. To draw the distinction between them it is important to know *where* during production the mistake occurred. If the Mint makes an error during die production, a variety coin is created. If the Mint makes an error producing a single coin, an error coin is created. This is the simple litmus test to determine whether a coin is a die variety or an error.

GRADING MODERN COINS

While grading modern coins is certainly similar to and related to grading classic coins, there are many specialized factors that come into play.

Grading is the art of condition analysis. Since the late 1940s, numismatists have used a 70-point numerical scale to describe coins' conditions. This system is called the Sheldon scale, after its originator, large-cent specialist Dr. William Sheldon. By analyz-

ing the surface, luster, strike, and eye appeal of a coin, a grader assigns it an alphanumeric grade. Grades above 60 are reserved for coins that have no wear or evidence of circulation. These are called Uncirculated or Mint State coins. The grade of 70 is the highest grade assigned.

A single-point differential on the Sheldon scale can translate to a considerable difference in value between two examples of the same coin. (For example, a 1972 Type II Eisenhower dollar in MS-64 might trade for $300, while an MS-65 trades for more than $2,000.) For that reason, collectors, investors, and dealers employ independent grading services that apply consistent standards and offer grade guarantees to draw these distinctions between grades. The most popular such services are Numismatic Guaranty Corporation of America (NGC) and Professional Coin Grading Service (PCGS). Both services assign grades on the 70-point scale and then encapsulate coins in sealed, tamper-evident holders with a grading certificate enclosed.

Independent third-party services grade and encapsulate coins for a fee. Because they are neither buyer nor seller, and because they have experience examining millions of coins, these services are highly trusted for their grading opinions.

One distinction of modern coinage is that many numismatic and bullion issues are collectible in the 70 grade, the highest grade assigned. In 2001, NGC formalized the description of this grade as describing "a coin having no post-production imperfections at 5x magnification," a definition which has since been adopted industry-wide. Only special-issue coins such as Proofs, commemoratives, and precious-metal issues are regularly available in the 70 grade. Circulation- or business-strike coins on this list can be found in Choice Uncirculated (MS-63) and Gem Uncirculated (MS-65) conditions. These coins will have some surface marks but no evidence of circulation. Learning to discern the differences between these grades requires years of experience but is a worthwhile pursuit for all collectors.

In addition to a numerical grade, some modern coins receive an extra designation indicating how well they are struck. Coins that have crisp, full details are said to be well struck. On Roosevelt dimes, graders will examine the horizontal bands on the coin's reverse, calling them Full Torch (FT) or Full Bands (FB) if these bands are clearly split. On Jefferson nickels, graders will actually count the number of steps present on Monticello, designating well-struck coins as having either five or six Full Steps (5FS or 6FS) or declaring them "Full Steps" if a certain threshold number of steps are present. Circulation-issue coins struck from highly polished dies are often called prooflike (PL).

A particularly important strike characteristic is used when grading Proof coins. Modern Proof coins have mirrored fields surrounding frosted design elements. The first coins struck from a Proof die will show the highest degree of contrast between these elements. Contrast gradually fades over the life of a die. Coins with heavy contrast are the most desirable, and in addition to receiving a number grade, they are said to be either Cameo or Ultra Cameo (also called Deep Cameo), based on the depth of their contrast. Coins lacking contrast do not receive any special designator. Some Proof coins from the late 1960s and early 1970s are very scarce (and therefore coveted) with the Ultra Cameo designation. By the mid-1970s, Proof coins were, at minimum, predominantly Cameo in appearance, while since the early 1980s almost all U.S. Proof coins are Ultra Cameo.

HOW THE 100 GREATEST U.S. MODERN COINS WERE CHOSEN AND RANKED

Since relatively few books have been written about modern coinage, it wasn't entirely clear what the list of 100 Greatest U.S. Modern Coins would look like once complete. When the idea for the book was first proposed, fundamental questions loomed. For example, how collectible would the coins on the list be? Would they represent a broad cross-section of coinage types, or would they be mostly obscure issues and elusive die varieties? The answers to these questions would help determine whether such a book could be of general interest.

So the authors compiled an initial list of coins as a proof of concept. Coins were chosen based on the authors' experience as professional numismatists. Both authors were well aware of the trading values of these coins, the number of collectors actively adding them to their collections, and the buzz that certain coins had created in the community. For each coin selected, the authors also wrote a brief explanation of why it should be included. That first list quickly grew to include more than 150 coins. It was sorted chronologically, without ranking, and was still by no means complete.

At this stage, the authors recognized two things. First, it was immediately clear that the *100 Greatest U.S. Modern Coins* would be an engaging book for collectors of all levels. Second, it would serve as the first real jumping-off point for meaningful discussion about modern numismatics. This grouping of coins had not previously been presented in this way, and, unlike in classic coinage, there were no undisputed "kings of coins" like the 1804 Draped Bust Dollar and 1913 Liberty Head Nickel.

Any ranking reflects a degree of personal opinion and is subject to debate. To cultivate a more universal view of the greatest modern coins, the authors consulted experts in the field. A draft of the list was discussed with leading dealers including Bill Gale, David Hendrickson, Robert Lecce, John Maben, and Lee Minshull. With information from these numismatists, the list became more focused, and an initial sequence was devised.

The next phase of ranking involved a survey of published works: books, specialized journals, numismatic periodicals, and Internet publications. While these sources are often-used tools of the authors, previously no efforts had been made to quantify the frequency with which certain coins were mentioned and how much attention was devoted to them. Books evaluated include works by researchers and dealers Bill Fivaz, Kevin Flynn, Ken Potter, J.T. Stanton, Rick Tomaska, and John Wexler. Web search engines and Internet-based news archives proved invaluable for determining how much attention had been given to various coins, allowing the authors to more accurately and objectively rank recent issues. As the manuscript was being prepared, numismatists David W. Lange and Richard S. Montgomery were consulted to add further refinement and nuance to the ranking.

The authors firmly believe that the coins in this list as it stands today represent the most significant numismatic properties of the modern era. New information and dialogue will certainly continue to shape perspectives of these coins. With this list now available, future opportunities exist for an expert panel or even open judging to impart a still greater level of impartiality and accuracy to the ranking. In the final analysis, modern coinage will always be the most dynamic area of numismatics.

100 GREATEST
U.S. MODERN COINS

Designed by Victor David Brenner (obverse) and Frank Gasparro (reverse). The obverse continues the design of 1909. The reverse shows a frontal view of the Lincoln Memorial with UNITED STATES OF AMERICA and E PLURIBUS UNUM appearing above and ONE CENT below.

Weight: 3.11 grams. *Composition:* 95% copper and 5% tin and zinc. *Diameter:* 19 mm. *Edge:* Plain.

Pick-up point: Date.

On October 3, 2007, Michigan collector Michael Tremonti made what is probably the greatest find from a Lincoln cent roll ever: a near-gem, fully red 1969-S Doubled-Die Obverse Lincoln cent. Soon after, it was recognized by variety expert Ken Potter as the finest example known. It was auctioned three months later for $126,500.

This example reignited interest in this coin, which is now considered the king of all Lincoln cent varieties. It is definitely the most valuable Lincoln cent variety and among the most rare. With one of the more dramatic and visually splendid doubled dies on U.S. coinage, it shows clear separation between the letters throughout the obverse legends. Perhaps because only a few dozen are known, over the years this coin had been less widely publicized than some of the other doubled-die Lincoln cents. It has one of the most fascinating stories of any 20th-century coin.

The overall rarity and mystique of this coin give the king of the Lincoln cent varieties a comfortable seat among the greatest modern U.S. coins.

When the variety was first discovered in mid-1970, the U.S. Secret Service declared it a counterfeit, and even seized the first of these coins that were discovered. Based on where and how the coins were found, numismatists objected—but the Secret Service held their position. The confusion surrounding the variety arose because two counterfeiters, Roy Gray and Mort Goodman, had created fake 1969 doubled-die cents, without mintmarks, to defraud collectors. When everything was sorted out, the Secret Service reversed their position and declared the 1969-S cent to be genuine, and returned the seized coins.

Over the years since then, finds of this coin remained scant. Freshly found examples were almost always circulated and did not retain their original Mint red color. Before Tremonti's discovery, no full-red examples had been graded by a major certification service, and only a couple examples were Uncirculated.

The coin is one that is also notoriously frustrating to hunt for. *Die doubling* occurs when the design of the coin is duplicated on the die that strikes a coin, and the position of the doubling is exactly identical on all the coins that it strikes. Not all doubled dies are valuable, but when there is good separation between the design details, the variety is very desirable. Unfortunately, the relatively common and worthless occurrence of *strike doubling* can sometimes resemble die doubling. Strike doubling occurs when the die bounces on the surface of the coin during striking, creating a shelf-like shadow of the design that resembles die doubling. Strike doubling is especially common on 1969-S Lincoln cents. As Ken Potter notes on his website, "It is *hard* to find a roll of cents for any of these dates without finding pieces exhibiting this affliction."

When looking for authentic 1969-S Lincoln cents, the searcher will find countless pretenders. Their abundance calls all stories of discovery into doubt until they can be verified by an expert. Nonetheless, recent auction transactions have intensified the hunt. The sale of Tremonti's coin was bookended by three others of slightly lower grade coins that all traded in the $60,000 to $80,000 range. Doubtless, more examples will become known to collectors, but the overall rarity and mystique of this coin give the king of the Lincoln cent varieties a comfortable seat among the greatest modern U.S. coins.

	Total Certified Population	Most Commonly Certified	
		Grade	No. in Grade
NGC	11	AU-55 BN	4
PCGS	29	AU-58 BN	8

Mintage: fraction of 544,375,000

Retail value in most common certified grade (AU-58 BN): $35,000

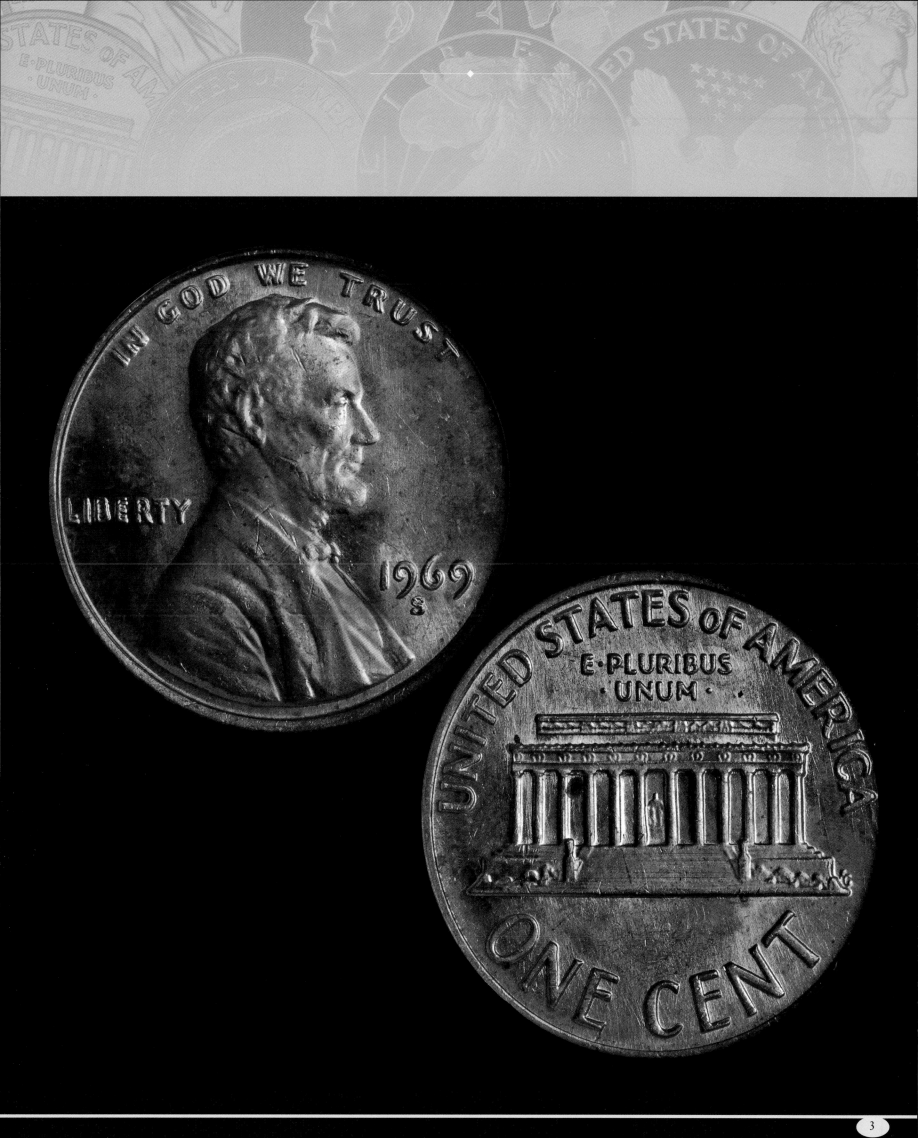

Designed by Glenna Goodacre (obverse) and Thomas D. Rogers (reverse). The obverse features the Indian guide Sacagawea and her infant son. LIBERTY appears above her head; IN GOD WE TRUST appears to the left, and the date is found on the right side. The reverse features an eagle in flight surrounded by 13 stars. UNITED STATES OF AMERICA arcs around the upper reverse; ONE DOLLAR arcs around the bottom. E PLURIBUS UNUM appears in small letters in the left field.

Weight: 8.1 grams. *Composition:* Outer layers of 77% copper, 12% zinc, 7% manganese, and 4% nickel over a core of pure copper. *Diameter:* 26.5 mm. *Edge:* Plain.

In late May of 2000, collector Frank Wallis, of Mountain Home, Arkansas, made an astonishing discovery. While searching a roll of new Sacagawea dollar coins he had acquired from the First National Bank & Trust, he found a single example that was different. The size, weight, composition, and reverse design were all correct for a Sacagawea dollar; the exciting discovery was that the obverse (which should have featured Sacagawea) was that of a statehood Washington quarter.

At the time of its discovery, this coin was the only known mule of a U.S. circulating coin—the first in 208 years of U.S. coinage production.

During striking of this particular coin, a die for the Sacagawea dollar had been used for the reverse, and a statehood-quarter die was accidentally used for the obverse. Error coins that combine parts of different coins are called *mules*—and mules of two different denominations are exceptionally rare and valuable. They are so rare, in fact, that at the time of its discovery, this coin was the only known mule of a U.S. circulating coin—the first in 208 years of U.S. coinage production.

The discovery coin wasn't unique for long. A second example, dispensed in change by a Philadelphia post office stamp-vending machine, was found soon after in June, and yet another Philadelphia area discovery followed. The finds garnered widespread media attention, including feature showings on television news. The U.S. Mint acknowledged that the error was legitimate, and that, even though they'd known the mules had been created, a small, unknown number had been released. Media attention gained additional steam when the second of the newly found coins was placed on eBay for sale by prominent coin dealer Delaware Valley Rare Coin Company. The eBay auction ended on July 7, 2000, with a final bid of $41,395. Details of the auction circulated so widely that the transaction helped to legitimize eBay as a viable venue for coin sales. Today more than one billion dollars' worth of transactions occur each year in eBay's coin category.

In spite of the excitement, many saw the auction price as staggering. As with any circulating rarity, there was concern during the first blush of discovery that more would come to light and compromise the value of the coin. Ultimately, the concern about unknown caches of coins proved unnecessary. Since August 2001, no new specimens have been found, and today only 10 Sacagawea dollar / statehood quarter mules are known. Their value has continued to escalate, with a handful of reported transactions in the low six figures.

For its rarity and influence, this is among the most important of the 100 Greatest U.S. Modern Coins. It may have helped publicize the brand-new Sacagawea dollar that was first released at the end of January 2000. The coin is distinctly modern as it combines the new-composition Sacagawea dollar and the obverse of the statehood quarter, two highly important, seminal coin series of the new millennium. Its first sale established eBay as a legitimate marketplace for coins in the eyes of many dealers. And, of course, it is among the most valuable of all modern U.S. coins and U.S. error coins of any era.

	Total Certified Population	Most Commonly Certified	
		Grade	No. in Grade
NGC	—	—	—
PCGS	—	—	—
Mintage: unknown			
Retail value in most common certified grade (MS-66): $250,000			

Designed by John R. Sinnock. On the obverse, the head of Franklin Roosevelt faces left. LIBERTY appears in large letters along the left rim; IN GOD WE TRUST appears in small letters at the lower left, and the date appears at the bottom right. The reverse features a lit torch flanked by sprigs of olive and oak. UNITED STATES OF AMERICA arcs above, ONE DIME arcs below, and the motto E PLURIBUS UNUM runs in a straight line through the bottoms of the sprigs and torch.

Weight: 2.27 grams. *Composition:* Pure copper core sandwiched between outer layers of 75% copper and 25% nickel. *Diameter:* 17.9 mm. *Edge:* Reeded.

While the United States transitioned from circulating silver to copper-nickel-clad coins between 1965 and 1967, no mintmarks appeared on U.S. coinage. Mint officials and politicians blamed the hoarding activities of collectors and speculators for coinage shortages around the nation. It was thought that removal of these distinguishing marks, which indicated where a coin was made, would give the public fewer reasons to hoard, and coins would circulate more freely. Also at this time, and with a related rationale, no Proof sets or Mint sets were issued. Instead, only a simplified single release of Special Mint Sets having some prooflike characteristics was available to collectors.

Proof coins missing their mintmark are aggressively sought-after. They vary in their rarity, and the 1968 No S dime is among the rarest.

Finally, in 1968, these dictums were lifted and the tradition of including mintmarks on coins and the production of Proof coinage both returned. From the time the first coins were issued in the United States until 1964, all presentation issues for sale to collec-tors had been made at the Mint in Philadelphia. The only note-worthy deviation from this had taken place from 1965 to 1967, when the production of Special Mint Set coinage occurred at San Francisco, but there was little fanfare or notice because these coins did not bear mintmarks. When Proof coinage returned, produc-tion remained in San Francisco and, for the first time, in 1968, Proof coins bore the S mintmark.

At some point during the production of 1968 Proof coinage, an unusual error occurred. Dimes were struck from an obverse die that lacked the S mintmark. It's easy to see how this error could have occurred. All dies are made at a single die shop in Philadelphia and then shipped to the branch mints where the dies are used in pro-duction. Coinage of this year was the first time that this missing-mintmark error could have occurred on a U.S. Proof coin because this was the first year that these coins had mintmarks. The great irony of the 1968 No S Proof dime is that it is missing the very feature that distinguishes 1968 Proof coinage from the Proof coin-age of all previous years!

Any error in the manufacture of a Proof coin is noteworthy because of the considerable amount of special care that is taken in their production. Indeed, Proof-coinage errors are rare across the board. Proof coins missing their mintmark, several of which appear in this book, are an especially desirable category of coinage and they are aggressively sought-after. They vary in their rarity, and the 1968 No S dime is among the rarest. Even as late as 1988, noted historian Walter Breen knew of only six examples. Because of this, it is widely believed that the mistake was discovered by the Mint. Subsequently, almost all the mintmark-less coins were pulled from release, and only a handful escaped. New estimates suggest that as many as two dozen examples are in collectors' hands, and the finest examples can trade for as much as $50,000.

	Total Certified Population	Most Commonly Certified	
		Grade	No. in Grade
NGC	4	PF-66 CAM	1
PCGS	18	PF-68	5
Mintage: fraction of 3,041, 506			
Retail value in most common certified grade (PF-68): $32,500			

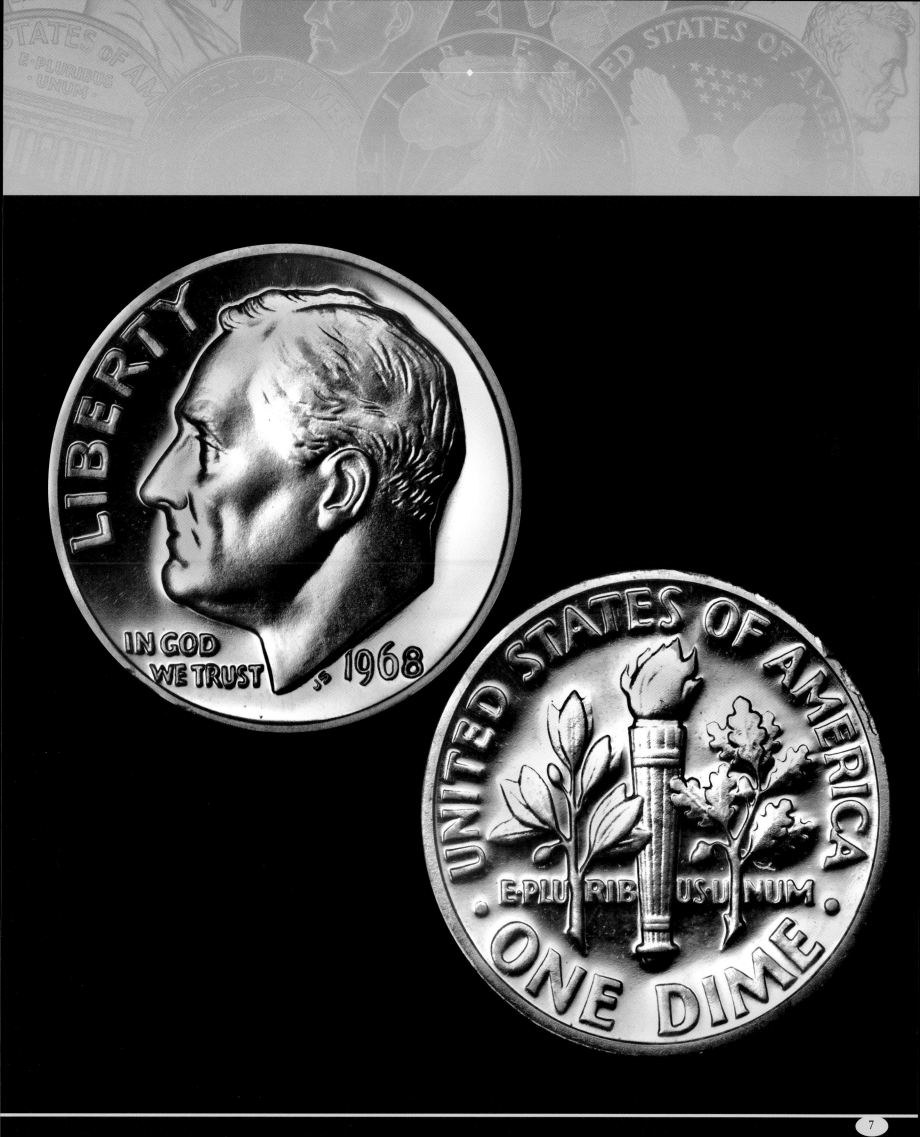

Designed by Adolph A. Weinman (obverse) and John Mercanti (reverse). The obverse features Weinman's Liberty Walking design used on half dollars from 1916 through 1947. Weinman's initials are on the hem of the gown. The reverse design is a rendition of a heraldic eagle by John Mercanti.

Weight: 31.101 grams. *Composition:* 99.93% silver and .07% copper (net weight 1 ounce pure silver). *Diameter:* 40.6 mm. *Edge:* Reeded.

The king of the silver eagles, the 1995-W silver eagle is one of the most coveted and important of all modern U.S. coins. It is also among the most controversial. As a result of a surcharge placed on these coins by the U.S. Mint, Proof silver eagles have been money-makers for the Mint since they were first issued in 1986. Roughly 500,000 of them were sold to collectors each year, making them a cash cow. Although Proof gold eagles were also offered during the same period, their higher cost meant that their total sales volume would amount to only 10 percent of the number of Proof silver coins that sold each year.

The king of the silver eagles is one of the most coveted and important of all modern U.S. coins. It is also among the most controversial.

These 1995 coins were the first Proof silver eagles ever struck at West Point and the first to have the W mintmark. During the 10th year of the American Eagle Bullion program, the U.S. Mint created a 10th-anniversary set of five Proof coins. All four denominations of the 1995 gold eagle were included: the $5 coin (1/10-ounce), the $10 coin (1/4-ounce), the $25 coin (1/2-ounce), and the $50 coin (1-ounce). As with all Proof gold eagles from that year, each coin was struck at West Point and bore the W mintmark. Also

included in the set, as the fifth coin, was a Proof 1995 silver eagle. To match the others, it too was struck at West Point.

Previous Proof issues had been struck in either San Francisco or Philadelphia, with an S or P mintmark, respectively. In 1995, however, Proof silver eagles were struck in both West Point and Philadelphia. If collectors ordered the coin for the issue price of $23 without the set, they received a 1995-P. The only way to get the 1995-W coin was to shell out the $999 for the complete anniversary set.

When the sales period for the 10th-Anniversary Proof Bullion Coinage Set ended, a total of 30,125 had been sold. This figure constitutes the entire mintage of the Proof 1995-W silver eagle, making it tremendously rare. By contrast, more than 400,000 of the Proof 1995-P silver eagle were sold.

Collectors were outraged. They accused the Mint of profiteering by forcing their loyal silver eagle customers to shell out a thousand dollars to get a rare issue. There were, after all, 10 times more collectors of Proof silver than Proof gold, making this a logical source of new customers for the Mint. Sales of the 1995-W in the secondary market did little to quell collectors' frustration. Immediately, the Proof 1995-W silver eagle was valued at a few hundred dollars, over 10 times more than previous issues. And as time passed, the price continued to climb. Collectors wrote to the Mint and even wrote open letters to numismatic publications announcing that they were no longer buying Proof silver eagles.

Their threats proved idle, and collectors never abandoned the series en masse. Even as early as January 1997, U.S. Mint Director Philip N. Diehl noted the growth of the program in a U.S. Mint press release: "Despite the controversy and criticism surrounding the issue of the 'W' Mint mark Silver Proof Eagle and predictions in the numismatic community that customers would desert the coin wholesale, sales rebounded and rose 15 percent."

The mystique and desirability of this coin have only grown over time. To say that the 1995-W is the "key" to the series is an understatement. Its small mintage of 30,125 is dwarfed by that of every other Proof silver eagle in the series. Its value is nearly equal to that of all the other coins in the series combined. By any measure, the Proof silver eagle program is more popular today than at any point in its past, which only continues to bolster demand for its king rarity, the 1995-W.

	Total Certified Population	Most Commonly Certified	
		Grade	No. in Grade
NGC	2,190	PF-69 UC	1,858
PCGS	1,991	PF-69 DC	1,298

Mintage: 30,125

Retail value in most common certified grade (PF-69 UC): $3,500

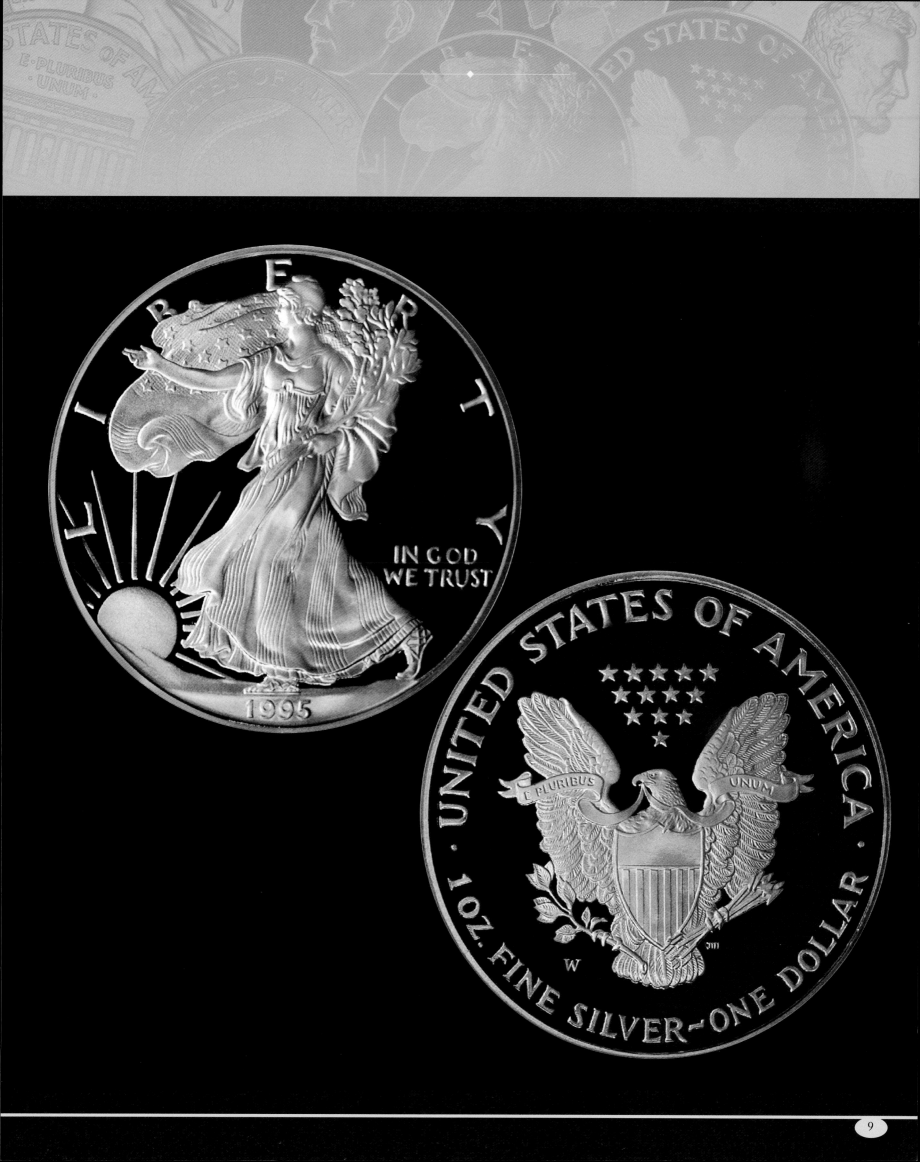

Designed by William C. Cousins (obverse) and James Peed (reverse). The obverse depicts a portrait of Jackie Robinson in his later years as a civil-rights and political activist. The reverse shows the detail of the seams on a baseball, Robinson's 1919–1972 life dates, and the inscription "Legacy of Courage."

Weight: 8.359 grams. *Composition:* 90% gold and 10% copper (net weight .2418 ounces pure gold). *Diameter:* 21.6 mm. *Edge:* Reeded.

This coin is the best example of one of the many paths taken by coins in this book to earn their positions on the list of the 100 Greatest U.S. Modern Coins: "What is not desirable initially can become coveted in time." When the Jackie Robinson $5 gold commemorative went on sale on August 16, 1997, there was little interest. Congress had authorized that a maximum of 100,000 examples could be struck and that the sales period could extend for one year. By August 16, 1998, less than 30,000 had sold, divided between Proof and Mint State versions of the coin. Only 5,174 of them were of the Mint State, or Uncirculated, type, making it by far the lowest-mintage modern commemorative coin ever issued to that point.

The Robinson commemorative's low mintage makes it the key to the series, and it is now among the most desirable commemorative coins.

The coin's poor sales record has survived, and it is still far and away the lowest-mintage modern commemorative, followed by the 2001-W Capitol Visitors Center $5 Uncirculated coin at 6,761 minted (see number 40). Although few were attracted to the coin at the time of issue, the Robinson commemorative's low mintage makes it the key to the series and it is now among the most-desirable coins in the series; it commands the highest price of any gold commemorative, trading for more than $5,000.

Thematically, this coin is interesting. Jackie Robinson's head is shown on the obverse in three-quarters profile, and the reverse shows a baseball inscribed with the dates of his life, 1919–1972, and the phrase "Legacy of Courage." It is a stark and modern design, if plain, but also singularly American. Robinson himself is an inspiring figure, the first black player in Major League Baseball when he joined the Brooklyn Dodgers in 1947, and should have generated widespread appeal.

So what accounted for the commemorative's infamous unpopularity? Primarily, two things are to blame: the overabundance of commemorative issues and the falling price of gold. In 1995, the U.S. Mint had sold three $5 gold commemoratives: one commemorating the end of the Civil War and two Atlanta Olympic commemoratives. Two more Olympic commemorative $5 coins followed in 1996, along with the Smithsonian coin discussed later, at number 56 on this list. In 1997, there was a Franklin Delano Roosevelt $5 coin issued just a couple of months before the Robinson coin. This meant the avid collector had already purchased seven different gold commemorative issues in the last three years when the Robinson coin came to market. This high a number of gold coins had never been offered to the modern coin collector in such a short time period before.

During that same time period, gold decreased in value by 25 percent. Throughout much of 1995, gold had teetered above the $400-per-ounce level, but then fell steadily, month after month, to $300 per ounce by mid-1998. Collectors were seeing commemorative coins trading at discounts to the original offering price in the secondary market, often by as much as $100 less than what they had paid. Frustrated by both the number of issues and the falling prices, collectors simply waited on the sidelines.

Despite the atrocious sales record, no one ever doubted the merit of this coin or the quality of the Mint's execution. Instead, it was acknowledged that too many coins had been issued in too short a time. Beginning in 1998, Congress limited the number of commemorative programs to two per year and also limited the number of coins that could be made under those programs. These steps have prevented a repeat of the poor sales performance of the 1997 Jackie Robinson $5 commemorative, and have cemented its place as the series key. What no one wanted in 1997 is now the most sought-after issue in the current market.

	Total Certified Population	Most Commonly Certified	
		Grade	No. in Grade
NGC	577	MS-69	370
PCGS	840	MS-69	762

Distribution: 5,174

Retail value in most common certified grade (MS-69): $3,750

1974 ALUMINUM LINCOLN CENT

Designed by Victor David Brenner (obverse) and Frank Gasparro (reverse). The obverse continues the design of 1909. The reverse shows a frontal view of the Lincoln Memorial with UNITED STATES OF AMERICA and E PLURIBUS UNUM appearing above and ONE CENT below.

Weight: 3.11 grams. *Composition:* Aluminum.
Diameter: 19 mm. *Edge:* Plain.

The 1974 aluminum Lincoln cent has three major things going for it: a wonderful story, incredibly rarity, and a visually exciting appearance. First, the story.

Throughout the 1960s, the average annual value of copper ticked upwards from 30 to 40 cents per pound, spiking to 58 cents in 1970 and 77 cents in 1974. By 1973, the production and raw material cost of the bronze cent exceeded its value. That same year, Treasury Secretary George Schultz circulated draft legislation proposing that the metal composition of the cent be changed so as to lower costs. Although a number of different compositions were considered, it ultimately appeared that an alloy of 96 percent aluminum would be the best candidate. Late in 1973, the Mint struck more than 1.5 million aluminum cents dated 1974 in anticipation of their release the following year. A small number of these coins were given to members of Congress and to staff members of the Senate and House banking committees for inspection. Mint Director Mary Brooks also distributed a small number of coins. No precise records of their distribution were retained.

Both the copper-mining industry and the vending-machine industry lobbied successfully against a change to the cent's composition, and Congress did not press forward with the change. With no aluminum coin coming, the Mint destroyed the coins it was holding and asked for the return of the coins that had already been distributed. Most, but not all, came back, and it is thought that as many as a dozen may exist in private hands; the whereabouts of all but two are unknown. One resides in the Smithsonian's National Numismatic Collection, and another, which has been graded by an independent certification service, remains in a private collection. The surviving 1974 aluminum cents are among the most coveted of all 20th century coins. None have ever traded publicly.

An aluminum cent looks completely different from a bronze cent. Not only is its color whitish-silver, but it weighs only 0.9 grams, while a regular cent of the era weighs more than three times that at 3.1 grams. The considerable variance in weight makes it easy to spot plated examples pretending to be of rare aluminum composition. A scale isn't even necessary to tell the difference.

A standout, it falls somewhere between a pattern coin and a cancelled (or recalled) issue, giving it a special status shared by few other coins.

No aluminum coins have ever been issued for circulation in the United States, and this coin is as close as one has ever gotten. The price of copper jumped to more than a dollar per pound in late 1979, and Congress was ultimately forced to act to change the cent's composition, settling on copper-plated zinc in 1982. Other trial coinages, including brass-coated steel coins dated 1974, were struck. But the 1974 aluminum cent is a standout—a coin that captured the fancy of collectors. It falls somewhere between a pattern coin and a cancelled (or recalled) issue, giving it a special status shared by few other coins.

	Total Certified Population	Most Commonly Certified	
		Grade	No. in Grade
NGC	—	—	—
PCGS	—	—	—

Mintage: unknown

Retail value cannot be speculated, given the extreme rarity of this variety.

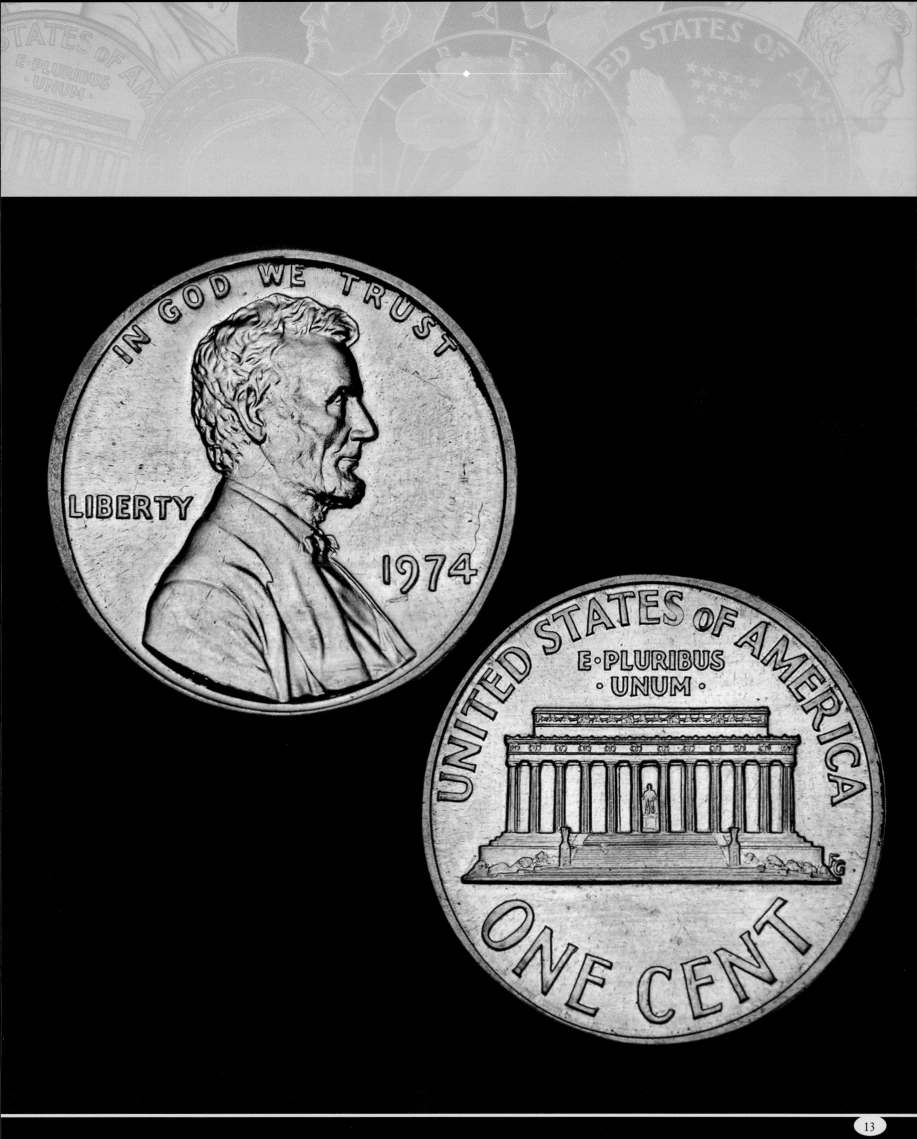

2006-W $50 AMERICAN GOLD EAGLE, REVERSE PROOF

Designed by Augustus Saint-Gaudens (obverse) and Miley Busiek (reverse). The obverse features a modified rendition of the Augustus Saint-Gaudens design used on U.S. $20 gold pieces from 1907 until 1933. The reverse displays a "family of eagles" motif.

Weight: 33.931 grams. *Composition:* 91.67% gold, 3% silver, and 5.33% copper (net weight 1 ounce pure gold). *Diameter:* 32.7 mm. *Edge:* Reeded.

The $50 gold eagle is the workhorse of the U.S. gold bullion program. This one-ounce coin is the largest gold coin in the series and accounts for the vast majority of gold units sold. Its obverse design is based on Augustus Saint-Gaudens's original design for the $20 gold coin that circulated from 1907 to 1933. The reverse is a more-contemporary arrangement by sculptor Miley Busiek and shows a male eagle returning to a nest containing a female eagle and hatchlings. Since it was first issued in 1986, this sequence has perennially been among the most popular bullion-coinage issues in the world.

To celebrate the 20th anniversary of the American Eagle Bullion program, the Mint offered three different 20th-Anniversary Sets. The most expensive option was the three-coin gold set, which featured a 2006-W Proof American eagle, a 2006-W Uncirculated eagle, and, for the first time ever, a 2006-W Reverse Proof American eagle; the set sold for $2,610. The offering was limited to 10,000 sets.

Normal Proof eagles have frosted designs surrounded by mirrored fields. When this arrangement is inverted, and the fields of the coins are frosted while the design portion, including the lettering, is mirror-like and reflective, the coin is said to be a *Reverse Proof*. It's an unusual surface finish that can be both striking and exotic, especially when employed on a familiar coin-type for the first time, as it was with the 20th-anniversary eagles.

The announcement of the Reverse Proof gold eagle was made nine days before the coin went on sale, and it was immediately clear that it would be something special. It was the only coin of its kind in the American gold eagle series, the most popular gold bullion-coinage sequence in history. Further, its mintage was limited to just 10,000 coins—far below what was then the lowest Proof one-ounce gold eagle mintage, the 24,555 pieces of the 2001 issue. As expected, the coin was a quick and complete sellout (accounting for returns, the net mintage is now reported as 9,996). Prices doubled in the secondary market, and the coins have retained their post-release premium while the value of gold has doubled.

The obvious question is why did the Mint produce only 10,000 coins? If the coin was so successful, why not make more? First, the Mint wanted to be sure that it would sell out. They produce collector versions of bullion coins only when production will not interfere with demand for bullion issues and when they can do so without creating expenses for taxpayers. A small program is more likely to sell out and easier to manage. Reverse Proof coins require special handling and die production; a much larger mintage would have made it difficult for the Mint to produce the coins.

It was the only coin of its kind in the American gold eagle series, the most popular gold bullion-coinage sequence in history.

Also, with gold valued at $617 per ounce on the initial sale date, the set of three gold eagles had an intrinsic metal value of $1,851. Thus, its issue-price of $2,610 represented a large premium to gold weight and placed it among the most expensive sets ever sold by the U.S. Mint. With such a high original issue price, perhaps the Mint felt that if they produced more coins they would not sell or that the price premium to gold would be unsustainable.

The net effect of what appears to be an example of extreme caution is a modern rarity that will seldom be available on the market in large supply. Its unique appearance makes it always desirable and a standout precious-metal coin among modern U.S. issues.

	Total Certified Population	Most Commonly Certified	
		Grade	No. in Grade
NGC	3,604	PF-70	2,448
PCGS	2,576	PF-70	1,469

Mintage: 9,996

Retail value in most common certified grade (PF-70): $3,750

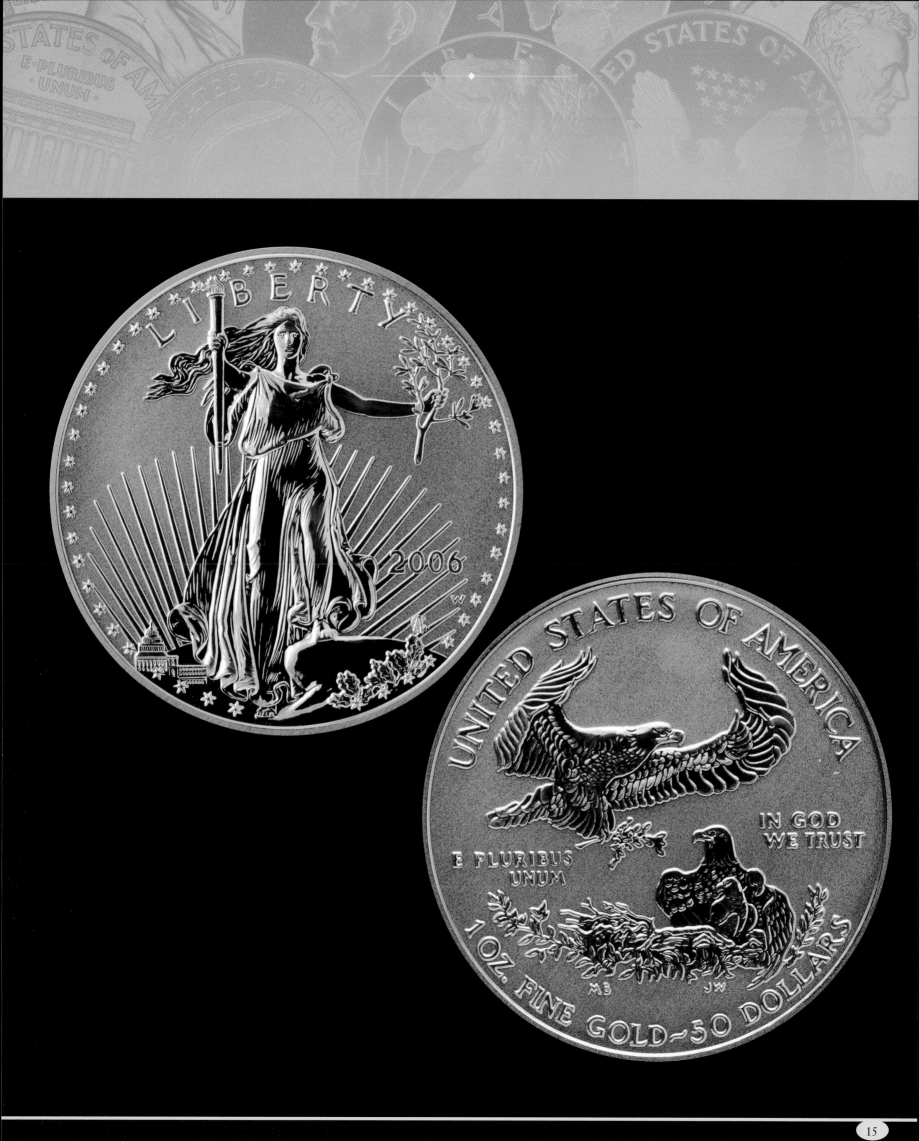

1976 NO S BICENTENNIAL EISENHOWER DOLLAR, PROOF

Designed by Frank Gasparro (obverse) and Dennis Williams (reverse). The obverse features the head of Dwight Eisenhower facing left. LIBERTY arcs around the top and the date reads 1776–1976. On the reverse, the Liberty Bell appears superimposed on the moon. The outer legends include UNITED STATES OF AMERICA above and ONE DOLLAR below. The motto E PLURIBUS UNUM appears in small letters to the lower right of the Liberty Bell.

Weight: 22.68 grams. *Composition:* Outer layers 75% copper and 25% nickel bonded to a core of pure copper. *Diameter:* 38.1 mm. *Edge:* Reeded.

This coin is as mysterious as it is rare—extremely so in both cases! A solitary example is known and a great deal of speculation surrounds its origins. Two things make this coin unique. First, it is the only Proof Type 2 Eisenhower dollar struck without an S mintmark. Second, it is the only Proof Type 2 Eisenhower struck on a 40 percent silver planchet; all others are copper-nickel-clad.

This particular Proof coin, already unique for not having a mintmark, is also struck on a silver flan, the only silver Proof Type 2 dollar.

The 1976 Eisenhower dollar was actually struck in both 1975 and 1976. No dollar coins dated 1975 were struck, but instead this special Bicentennial coin, dual-dated 1776–1976, was issued in both years. The design for the reverse was selected in a contest held in 1974, and the entry of sculpture student Dennis R. Williams was selected for the dollar. The coins issued in 1975 include the blocky letter style used in Williams's original design. These are called Type 1. In late 1975, the U.S. Mint announced that a slightly modified Eisenhower dollar would be introduced in 1976. The new design had a narrower letter style to match the obverse and is called Type 2. The difference is readily apparent.

When the first designs were selected, a handful of presentation examples of all the Bicentennial coins were struck at Philadelphia. One set was sent to be exhibited at a numismatic convention, while others were presented to government officials, including President Gerald Ford. These Type 1 coins did not include the S mintmark, and a few examples survive. The Type 1 dollar has been catalogued as a pattern in the standard reference, *United States Pattern Coins* by J. Hewitt Judd, and assigned the number J-2163. While the occasion for these Type 1 dollars to be struck is clearly documented, no similar event is recorded for the Type 2 dollar.

Proof Bicentennial Eisenhower dollars were struck in both silver-clad and copper-nickel-clad composition, but all silver coins were Type 1. This particular Proof coin, however, already unique for not having a mintmark, is also struck on a silver flan, the only silver Proof Type 2 dollar.

There are two popular theories as to why this coin was made. Many people assume that it was a test-striking of the new Type 2 design, and was created in mid-1975 to confirm that the new design was an aesthetic (or technical) improvement upon its predecessor. This coin is assigned a catalog number of J-2164 in the pattern reference, based upon the presumption that it is a trial coin. Others, however, speculate that, like the extant No S Type 1 coins, this piece was coined for presentation to statesmen or dignitaries.

The discovery of the coin might support the latter theory, because it's unlikely that a test-piece would leave the Mint. According to the *Coin World Comprehensive Catalog & Encyclopedia,* the unique coin was discovered in a cash register at a Washington, D.C., department store. The coin was last sold at auction in September 2002 and resides in a private collection. Research efforts are ongoing to uncover the true story of its origin.

	Total Certified Population	Most Commonly Certified	
		Grade	No. in Grade
NGC	—	—	—
PCGS	—	—	—
Mintage: unknown			
Retail value cannot be speculated, given the extreme rarity of this variety.			

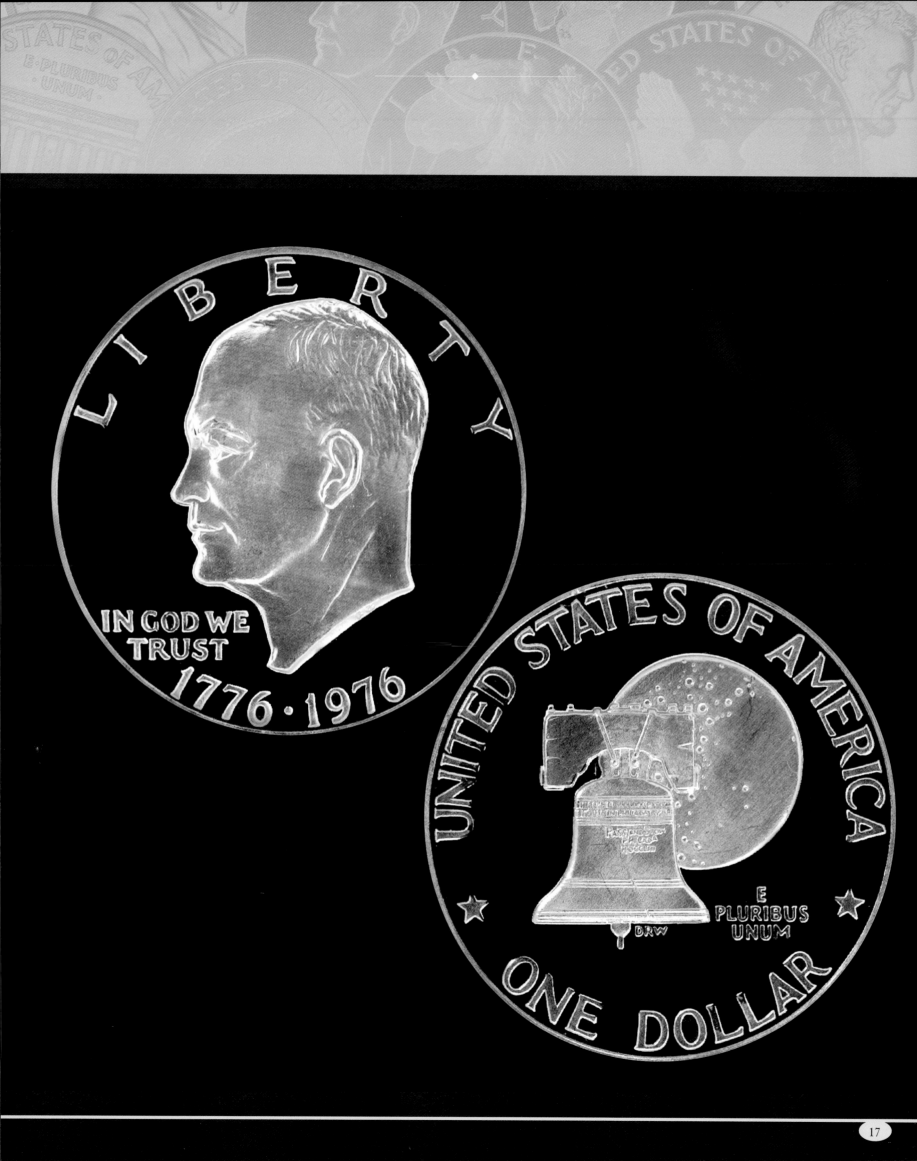

1999-S SILVER DELAWARE QUARTER, PROOF

Designed by John Flanagan, as modified by William C. Cousins (obverse), and Eddy Seger (reverse). The obverse depicting President George Washington was modified to include some of the wording previously used on the reverse. The reverse shows patriot Caesar Rodney on his historic 80-mile ride through terrible heat and thunderstorms to cast his vote in favor of Delaware signing the Declaration of Independence. Rodney's vote turned out to be the tie-breaker.

Weight: 6.25 grams. *Composition:* 90% silver and 10% copper. *Diameter:* 24.3 mm. *Edge:* Reeded.

Many hyperbolic claims surround the 50 State Quarters® Program. For example, it's often asserted that these new circulating coins turned 100 million Americans into collectors, as they sought to complete sets of quarters from change. If that statement seems overreaching, it's important to consider the facts of the state-quarter series. For starters, it was certainly the most ambitious commemorative-coinage program and the most aggressive coinage-design program in U.S. history. Additionally, it produced some of the most important collectible quarters of the era, the most prized of which can trade for a few thousand dollars—yes, that's right, a few thousand!

At the outset, 50 different coins were to be struck honoring each state in the nation over the course of a 10-year period. Coins for each state were issued in the order that they achieved statehood. The first state in the union is Delaware, and its coin came first. Coinage legislation required that each state's governor select the coinage theme design. For Delaware, it was decided that the coin would honor early statesman Caesar Rodney. In 1776, hearing that his fellow Delaware representatives were deadlocked in the vote over independence, Rodney rode 80 miles on horseback (at least partially) through a stormy night to arrive in Philadelphia in time to cast a deciding vote. Shortly thereafter, Rodney signed the Declaration of Independence.

As the first coin in the series, the Delaware quarter has some special cachet. But the silver Proof version is turning into a modern "classic." To begin with, the only way to get the Proof version at the time of issue was to purchase the complete silver nine-piece Proof set from the Mint, which included the cent and nickel, as well as 90 percent silver examples of the dime, half dollar, and all five 1999 quarters: the Delaware, Pennsylvania, New Jersey, Georgia, and Connecticut coins. The initial sales price for the set was $31.95, meaning that these coins were premium items from the start. Slightly more than 800,000 silver Proof sets sold and they were widely dispersed. Today, it is challenging to find more than a handful of the sets on the market, and their price can be as high as $400 per set.

As the first coin in the series, the Delaware quarter has some special cachet—but the silver Proof version is turning into a modern classic.

The packaging of 1999 statehood quarters Proof sets is different from that of subsequent years. The materials do little to protect the coins from toning, and most 1999 silver quarters are seen with a whitish haze. The Delaware quarter shows Caesar Rodney on horseback on an open field, with most of the margin of the coin flat and open. It may be this aspect of the coin that makes the Delaware quarter particularly prone to discoloration or spotting. As a result, it is far and away the hardest of the silver state quarters to find in the highest condition, Proof-70. There are fewer than half as many Delaware quarters graded at this level by the top grading services than for the next-scarcest quarter. In fact, the finest examples routinely trade for as high as $3,000 per coin!

The 50 State Quarters® Program started a trend in circulating-commemorative programs and caused many to take a closer look at their pocket change. There is no doubt that it contributed to a renaissance of coin collecting in the United States. It also produced one of the most coveted of all modern coins in the Proof silver 1999-S Delaware state quarter.

	Total Certified Population	Most Commonly Certified	
		Grade	No. in Grade
NGC	7,865	PF-69 DC	7,032
PCGS	5,665	PF-69 DC	5,124
Mintage: 804,565			
Retail value in most common certified grade (PF-69 UC): $125			

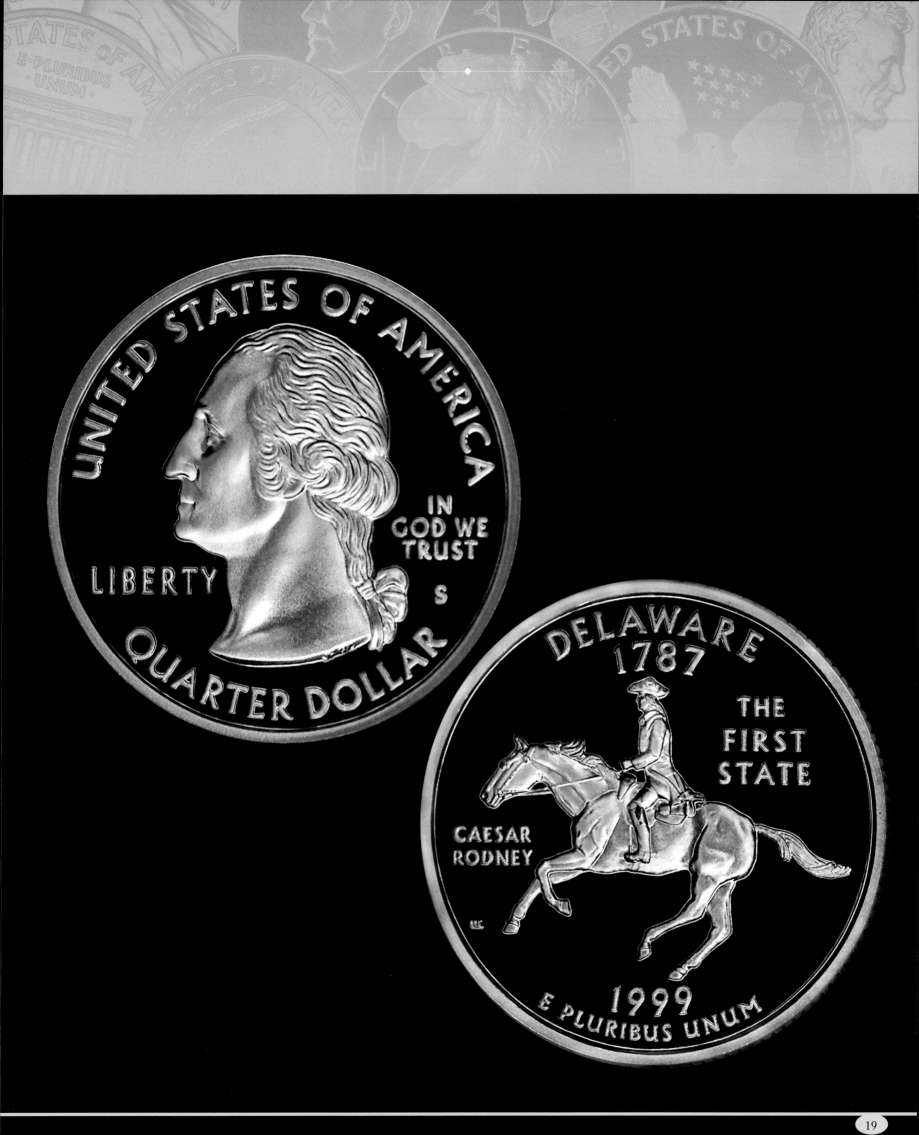

1972 DOUBLED-DIE OBVERSE LINCOLN CENT

Designed by Victor David Brenner (obverse) and Frank Gasparro (reverse). The obverse continues the design of 1909, featuring a bust of Lincoln facing right, the word LIBERTY to his left, and the date in the field in front of his coat. The legend IN GOD WE TRUST appears above his head. The reverse shows a frontal view of the Lincoln Memorial with UNITED STATES OF AMERICA and E PLURIBUS UNUM appearing above and ONE CENT below.

Weight: 3.11 grams. *Composition:* 95% copper and 5% tin and zinc. *Diameter:* 19 mm. *Edge:* Plain.

Pick-up points: Date, lettering.

This strongly doubled die is one of the most visually dramatic varieties in the Lincoln Memorial cent series. It caused a sensation when it was first discovered in 1972 and collector interest has never faded. The entire obverse is fully doubled, with the doubling clear both on the legends, IN GOD WE TRUST and LIBERTY, and on the date. Each element shows a slightly offset replication of itself. The variety was created when the die that struck the coins was produced, and it received two misaligned impressions of the design from the hub. The doubling was then struck on each coin in the same way.

One of the most visually dramatic Lincoln Memorial cent varieties, it caused a sensation in 1972, and collector interest has never faded.

The coin was first spotted in the Mid-Atlantic states in 1972. Examples were offered for sale by prominent Philadelphia dealer Harry Forman. Almost immediately after the discovery of the variety, the price per coin jumped up to $30, allowing anyone who found one to turn a tidy profit. Unsearched 1972 cent bags, still Mint-sewn with 5,000 coins inside, traded at premiums as well.

Because the coin couldn't be found outside Philadelphia, Atlanta-based dealer John Hamrick contacted Forman for coins. To induce Forman to sell him a 50-coin roll, then priced at $1,500, Hamrick also agreed to buy ten Mint-sewn bags. The bags sat for a couple of months until Hamrick and his colleagues had time to sort them. When the job was completed, Hamrick had found 40 rolls of 1972 Doubled-Die Lincoln cents. The price and interest in the coin had blossomed during the months that led to Hamrick's discovery. Coin dealer Fred Balmer was paying $3,500 per roll at the time and bought Hamrick's entire find. In today's market, this would be a million-dollar cache of Lincoln cents—at the time, it made Hamrick the primary market maker in 1972 Doubled-Die Lincoln cents through the early 1970s.

The 1972 Doubled-Die Lincoln cent is one of the most desirable coin varieties found in circulation, although they are tough to find today. The strong interest in this coin from the time of issue means that a number of examples were located for the numismatic community, so they can be purchased from dealers. Condition plays a major factor in determining the value of this coin. Staining and carbon spots are common and finding a visually appealing example is not a simple task.

This coin can be easily mistaken for other, similar varieties—and subtle variety differences can mean a huge difference in value. A footnote to the Lincoln cent, Memorial Reverse section of *A Guide Book of United States Coins* (the Red Book) includes an important caveat: "Other slightly doubled varieties (worth far less) exist." Because so much time was devoted to searching for 1972 Doubled-Die Lincoln cents, other varieties that have been found are collectible. Very specialized collectors will pursue as many as nine different doubled-die obverse coins, but the coin properly referred to as the 1972 Doubled-Die Lincoln cent is very prominently doubled, easy to recognize, and worth the big premium.

	Total Certified Population	Most Commonly Certified	
		Grade	No. in Grade
NGC	1,716	MS-64 RD	465
PCGS	3,119	MS-65 RD	1,197

Mintage: fraction of 2,933,255,000

Retail value in most common certified grade (MS-65 RD): $900

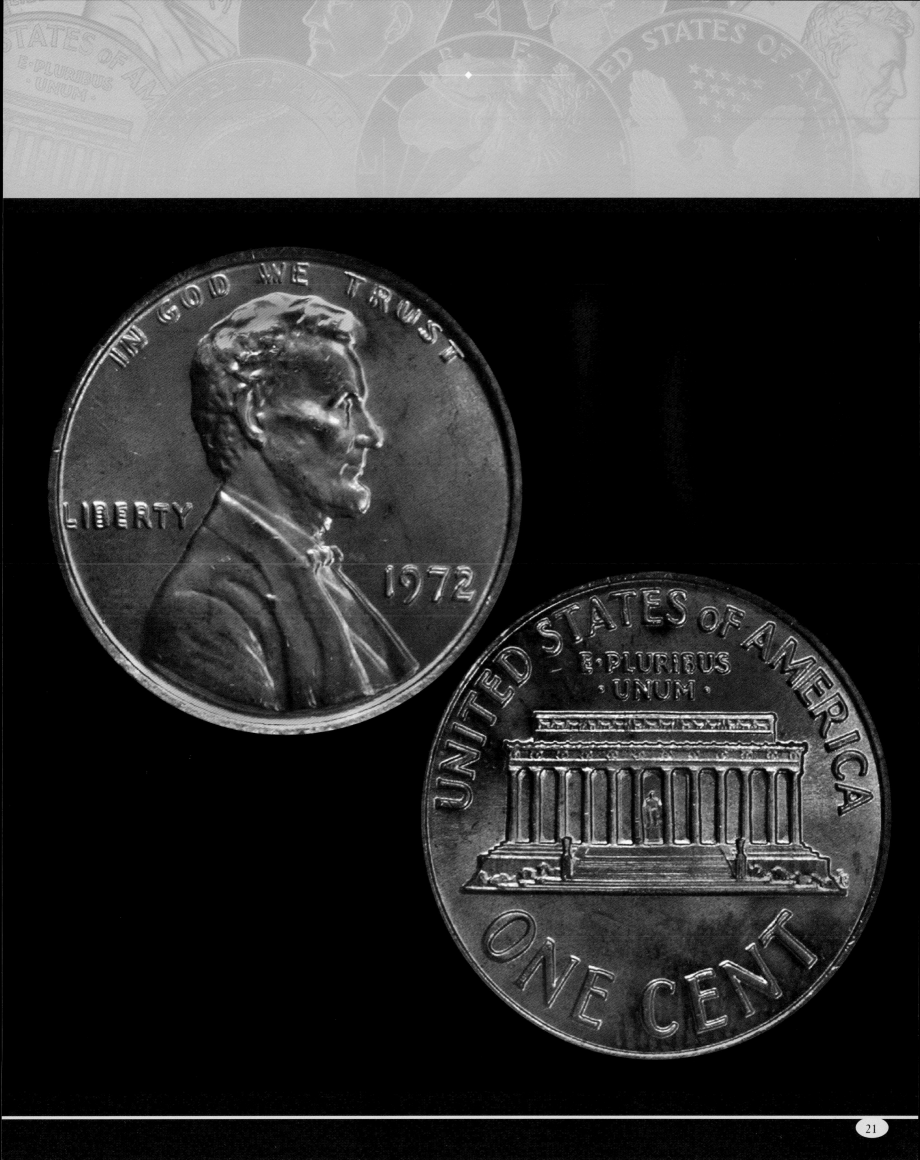

2006-P $1 AMERICAN SILVER EAGLE, REVERSE PROOF

Designed by Adolph A. Weinman (obverse) and John Mercanti (reverse). The obverse features Weinman's Liberty Walking design used on half dollars from 1916 through 1947. Weinman's initials are on the hem of the gown. The reverse design is a rendition of a heraldic eagle.

Weight: 31.101 grams. *Composition:* 99.93% silver and .07% copper (net weight 1 ounce pure silver). *Diameter:* 40.6 mm. *Edge:* Reeded.

On August 21, 2006, the U.S. Mint announced the 20th Anniversary Eagle Sets—special collector editions being sold to celebrate the 20th anniversary of the American Eagle Bullion Program. One of the options was a three-piece silver coin set, including a Proof coin, an uncirculated coin, and a Reverse Proof coin. The announcement described the Reverse Proof coins as featuring "a unique finish which results in a frosted field, or background, and a brilliant, mirror-like finish on the raised elements of the coin, including the design and inscriptions."

It's difficult to imagine exactly the environment into which this coin was released. Silver had roughly doubled in price, from $6 to $12 an ounce, in the two years leading up to this coin's release. There was a tremendous baseline of interest in the silver eagle generally. Add to that articles in the numismatic press and blogosphere, which were intimating that the Reverse Proof would be a successful coin—not only would it be the only Reverse Proof in the silver eagle series, but its mintage would be limited to 250,000.

With the exception of the Proof 1995-W (ranked at no. 4), this would be far and away the lowest-mintage silver eagle; the next closest was the Proof 1994-P silver eagle, with a mintage of 372,168.

Also in 2006, more-advanced and intricate finishes were appearing on foreign issues of silver and gold bullion coins. Mints in Australia, Canada, China, and Great Britain were all producing precious-metal Reverse Proof coinage for collectors (as well as holographic coins and privy-marked, limited-edition coinages). The U.S. Mint had, in prior years, used the Reverse Proof finish: platinum eagle bullion issues from 1997 through 2000 were struck with frosted fields and mirror-like devices. Nonetheless, in the context of 2006 and the silver eagle series, this felt like a very unique American silver coin, and the only way to get it was as part of the three-coin set.

Few collectors were willing to miss the opportunity. To defend against speculators, the U.S. Mint set an order limit of 10 sets per household. The issue price of the set was $100. A flood of orders began at noon on Wednesday, August 30, and the flurry of activity slowed the Mint's website to a halt. The Mint's toll-free order hotline reached a continuous busy signal. Devoted collectors, dealers, and speculators spent furious hours trying to complete their orders. After the maddening rush of orders, collectors waited two months before Reverse Proof silver eagles began to ship in earnest from the Mint. Those who received their coins in early October were already able to double their money and resell the sets for $200.

The price of Reverse Proof silver eagles continued to climb to the end of the year as they trickled out of the Mint and were absorbed into the marketplace. Prices and demand appear to have stabilized not far from those original post-release levels, keeping one of the key issues of the series within reach of collectors. Its look is so distinctive within the series that the Reverse Proof will always be a curious standout among silver eagles—but of course, other special anniversaries are ahead.

	Total Certified Population	Most Commonly Certified	
		Grade	No. in Grade
NGC	45,052	PF-69	36,127
PCGS	18,327	PF-69	14,650

Mintage: 248,875

Retail value in most common certified grade (PF-69): $225

1964 SPECIAL MINT SET

In 1993, an unusual set of coins appeared for auction in a sale conducted by the venerable coin auction house Stack's Rare Coins of New York. They offered a set of specimen coinage dated 1964. Each of the five coins in the set—the cent, nickel, dime, quarter, and half dollar—had razor-sharp strikes. Rather than the deep mirrorlike surface seen on Proof coins, these coins had a satin sheen, possessing none of the reflectivity seen on Proof coinage. Swirling die polish was evident throughout the coins' fields, indicating that the dies that struck them had received special treatment. In fact, these coins looked nothing like other known coins dated 1964—they looked most similar to the Special Mint Set coins of 1965!

The obvious speculation was that these coins were produced as a trial version of the Special Mint Set coins that were to come in the following year. In 1965, circulating silver coinage was to be replaced with copper-nickel; to manage the metal transition, the Mint was forced to produce an unprecedented number of coins. To aid them in their task, two noteworthy accommodations were made. First, all coins were to be struck without mintmark, as it was widely believed that this measure would limit hoarding of coins by collectors and speculators. Second, no Proof coins were to be struck until enough coins could be produced to meet the requirements of circulation.

In lieu of selling Proof and Mint sets, from 1965 to 1967 the Mint sold Special Mint Sets. The sets consisted of just five coins, all circulating denominations without mintmarks. Each coin had a special finish, often described as falling somewhere between Proof and Mint State coins. The dies that struck the coins received additional polishing, but the coins received only a single blow from the coinage die—true Proofs receive multiple strikes to more sharply impress the design. The issues of 1965 usually have a satin-like surface, but later issues from 1967 have a shallow, mirrored surface, more closely resembling Proofs. They are all readily distin-

guishable from circulation issues of the period and are available in high grades.

But there was no way to explain the existence of a 1964 Special Mint Set, as Proof coins were produced that year and no documentation concerning the creation of a 1964 Special Mint Set exists. Two theories predominate. The first is that there would have been a need to test the process of creating these Special Mint Set coins as a way of assessing their feasibility for production. To do this, a number of trial 1964 sets were made. Additionally, the examples that are known today are always found in high grade, a sign that they were preserved and maintained by their owners. That latter fact has led to a second possibility, that these coins were produced as special presentation sets, the last 90 percent silver coins. Whatever the case may be, either scenario contributes to their appeal.

When pressed about their origin, the auction house offering them for sale disclosed that the coins were from the estate of a coin dealer. Because of the timing of the sale, some speculate that these coins in fact came from the estate of former Mint director Eva Adams. She served as director from 1961 to 1969 and passed away at the age of 80 in 1991. The coins first appeared at auction two years after her death, and she would have had access to them during her tenure at the Mint.

Initially, it was reported that 15 sets were produced in total, but as more 1964 Special Mint Set coinage appears, that figure has since been revised upwards to 50. They are still seldom offered, though. Their unique appearance, the clear attention to their production quality, and their mysterious origin make them among the most coveted of all U.S. coinage sets.

		Total Certified Population	Most Commonly Certified	
			Grade	No. in Grade
CENT	NGC	11	SP-65 RD	5
	PCGS	22	SP-67 RD	5
NICKEL	NGC	5	SP-67	3
	PCGS	18	SP-67	9
DIME	NGC	1	SP-67	1
	PCGS	22	SP-67	13
QUARTER DOLLAR	NGC	1	SP-67	1
	PCGS	28	SP-67	12
HALF DOLLAR	NGC	6	SP-67	3
	PCGS	12	SP-67	6

Mintage: unknown

Cent—Retail value in most common certified grade (SP-67 RD): $4,000

Nickel—Retail value in most common certified grade (SP-67): $3,000

Dime—Retail value in most common certified grade (SP-67): $4,000

Quarter Dollar—Retail value in most common certified grade (SP-67): $6,500

Half Dollar—Retail value in most common certified grade (SP-67): $15,000

1990 NO S LINCOLN CENT, PROOF

Designed by Victor David Brenner (obverse) and Frank Gasparro (reverse). The obverse continues the design of 1909, featuring a bust of Lincoln facing right, the word LIBERTY to his left, and the date in the field in front of his coat. The legend IN GOD WE TRUST appears above his head. The reverse shows a frontal view of the Lincoln Memorial with UNITED STATES OF AMERICA and E PLURIBUS UNUM appearing above and ONE CENT below.

Weight: 2.5 grams. *Composition:* A core of 99.2% zinc and .8% copper, with a plating of pure copper. *Diameter:* 19 mm. *Edge:* Plain.

The 1990 No S Lincoln cent is a Proof coin struck at the San Francisco Mint missing the obligatory and otherwise standard S mintmark. This omission had occurred several times in the past, including at least three times on the Roosevelt dime and once on the Jefferson nickel. This issue is the sole Lincoln cent missing its mintmark and represents the last time to date that such an omission occurred on a Proof coin. The first detail makes this coin especially coveted, while the second tells a particularly fascinating story.

Lincoln cents are collected by a large and enthusiastic group, a fact that makes this coin, the only Lincoln cent of its kind, very desirable. All collectors of Proof Lincoln Memorial cents want one. It also turns out that the coin is very rare, much rarer than many expected (more on that to follow), which makes it rather expensive, trading for as much as $7,000 in the highest grades.

All of these cents were issued in Proof sets and Prestige Proof sets—versions of the Proof set that included a Proof 1990-P Eisenhower commemorative dollar. In 1990, a Proof die struck approximately 3,700 cents, which is the estimated mintage figure of the 1990 No S Lincoln cent. When this coin was discovered not long after the Proof sets were issued, the U.S. Mint confirmed the error and announced that they had recovered and destroyed 145 examples. For this reason, the net mintage figure of this variety is often reported as 3,555. The total number of Proof sets issued in 1990 was nearly 2.8 million. To date, only about 250 examples are known, less than 1/10 the number thought to be struck. The discovery rate is so low that some numismatists suggest that many fewer than 3,555 ever actually left the Mint.

The question remains as to how such a coin could have been produced in 1990. Preparing a Proof die requires that the die be chrome-plated, polished, and, in 1990, sandblasted by hand to create the frosted design elements. A number of Mint employees handled and inspected the die without, apparently, noticing the missing mintmark. Another detail adds more intrigue to the story of this coin, as, starting in 1985, the master dies used to make dies for Proof coins included the S mintmark. When such errors had occurred previously, most recently in 1983, mintmarks were still being added by hand to individual dies, making this type of error more likely. Furthermore, Lincoln cent dies without mintmarks in 1990 would all have been clearly intended for the production of circulating coinage. In the case of the 1990 No S cent, it appears that a die intended to strike circulating coinage was treated and used to strike Proof coins at San Francisco.

There are certainly still discoveries of these coins to be made. Most commonly, they are found in the Prestige Proof set, and the prize of finding one is significant. Additionally, a doubled-die nickel and a doubled-die quarter can be found in 1990 Proof sets (numbers 60 and 51 on this list, respectively). The prospect of finding one of three valuable varieties makes sets of this year irresistible to modern-coin specialists.

	Total Certified Population	Most Commonly Certified	
		Grade	No. in Grade
NGC	34	PF-68 UC	14
PCGS	116	PF-68 DC	66

Mintage: *100–250 (estimated)*

Retail value in most common certified grade (PF-68 DC): $4,250

Designed by Glenna Goodacre (obverse) and Thomas D. Rogers (reverse). The obverse features the Indian guide Sacagawea and her infant son. LIBERTY appears above her head; IN GOD WE TRUST appears to the left, and the date is found on the right side. The reverse features an eagle in flight surrounded by 13 stars. UNITED STATES OF AMERICA arcs around the upper reverse; ONE DOLLAR arcs around the bottom. E PLURIBUS UNUM appears in small letters in the left field.

Weight: 8.1 grams. *Composition:* Outer layers of 77% copper, 12% zinc, 7% manganese, and 4% nickel over a core of pure copper. *Diameter:* 26.5 mm. *Edge:* Plain.

Acknowledging the failed prior attempts at getting a dollar coin into circulation, the Mint in 2000 wanted to remove all the possible barriers to their latest effort at introducing such a coin. They initiated a widespread media blitz that included television commercials and enlisting Wal-Mart to provide the new dollar coins to customers as change. One of the more novel efforts was a coinage give-away conducted with General Mills, which pictured the coin on every box of Cheerios.

Billed as a millennium promotion, a single example of the first 10,000,000 Lincoln cents struck bearing the date 2000 was included inside each marked box of Cheerios that year. One in every 2,000 boxes included both a cent coin and a Sacagawea dollar. According to a General Mills promotional release, "during the month of January, the only place to get either coin [was] in a box of Cheerios." We know this is a true statement regarding the Sacagawea dollar, as it was not released to Federal Reserve banks until January 26, 2000, and Wal-Mart had agreed not to release them until January 30, 2000.

In order to have the dollar coins delivered to General Mills in time for its promotion, the Mint struck 5,500 coins in late summer or early fall of 1999. Full-scale production of the finalized Sacagawea dollar did not begin until more than a month later, on November 18, 1999. During the intervening time, tests of the design were still ongoing at the Mint. A design variation other than the final circulation version had been used to strike the coins delivered to General Mills.

The so-called "Cheerios" or Reverse of 1999 Sacagawea dollar is easy to distinguish from a circulation issue by examining its reverse. The eagle's wings and tail show intricate feather detail, including raised central feather shafts and numerous veins. These details are absent on the final adopted design, on which the central tail feather shows an incuse shaft. This same level of reverse detail is present on the 22-karat gold coins with the West Point mintmark that were struck in June 1999 and sent into space aboard the shuttle *Columbia*. Numismatic researcher Tom Delorey speculates that the same die that was used to strike the gold Sacagawea dollars may have also struck the coins delivered to General Mills.

The timeline and story of this coin were pieced together by noted numismatic researchers, including Delorey, David Lange, and David Camire. Collectors and hobbyists such as Pat Braddick and Mike Wallace also played a critical role in gathering information about this coin. But the discovery of this coin did not come until June 2005, five years after the coin was released. Two factors account for the late discovery of such an important coin. For one, the coin was mounted obverse-up in the holder, and the reverse with the extra tail-feather detail is not visible. Secondly, these coins were distributed in non-numismatic circles—to buyers of Cheerios—and few went to coin dealers. For years, no one wanted to remove them from their holders, thinking that it was the holder that imparted a small premium.

With only 5,500 examples extant and a wide distribution into mainstream commerce, this coin is a major rarity; there are fewer than a hundred examples in the numismatic marketplace. Discoveries are happening all the time, though, and these coins can turn up just about anywhere.

Pick-up point: Tail feathers (left, normal; right, boldly detailed).

	Total Certified Population	Most Commonly Certified	
		Grade	No. in Grade
NGC	31	MS-67	16
PCGS	48	MS-68	20

Mintage: 5,500

Retail value in most common certified grade (MS-68): $6,500

1997-P JEFFERSON NICKEL, MATTE "SPECIAL UNCIRCULATED"

Designed by Felix Schlag. The obverse features a bust of Thomas Jefferson facing left. IN GOD WE TRUST appears inside the left edge, and LIBERTY and the date appear inside the right edge. On the reverse, Jefferson's home, Monticello, appears as the central device. E PLURIBUS UNUM arcs above. The word MONTICELLO captions the building, and the words FIVE CENTS and the legend UNITED STATES OF AMERICA appear below.

Weight: 5.00 grams. *Composition:* 75% copper and 25% nickel. *Diameter:* 21.2 mm. *Edge:* Plain.

The 1997 U.S. Botanic Garden commemorative dollar was a coin that held a special interest for lawmakers. The museum and conservatory were created by an act of Congress in 1820, and together they are the oldest continuously operated garden in the nation. Although the U.S. Botanic Garden is little known outside of Washington, D.C., it sits at the foot of Capitol Hill and its trustees are Washington's elite. Given that the U.S. commemorative-coinage program was foundering under a swelling number of issues in the late 1990s, Congress intentionally acted to bring attention to this commemorative dollar in order to raise money for the National Fund for the U.S. Botanic Garden.

The Jackie Robinson commemorative coins (number five on this list) were scheduled to go on sale later that same year. One senator was so concerned about the competition caused by that coin that he took action. Senator J. Bennett Johnston, a Louisiana Democrat

whose wife, Mary, was a vice chairwoman of the National Fund for the U.S. Botanic Garden, intended to block the Jackie Robinson coin unless a portion of the proceeds were diverted from the Robinson coins' surcharges to support the Botanic Garden. Instead of raising money for the Jackie Robinson Foundation, which gives college scholarships to poor inner-city youths, sales supported the garden. Needless to say, this was controversial and did not improve the image of the suffering U.S. commemorative-coinage program.

In a rare bit of irony, the Botanic Garden coin sold better than the Robinson coin. One reason was the 1997-P Jefferson nickel Matte "Special Uncirculated" coin. In an effort to spur sales, as they had done for the 1993 Thomas Jefferson dollar, the U.S. Mint offered a coinage and currency set that included a specially struck Jefferson nickel with a matte finish, minted in Philadelphia and bearing a P mintmark. Thomas Jefferson, along with other founding fathers, had championed the concept of a botanic garden on the National Mall, so there was some historical relevance. Just 25,000 examples of the set were to be sold and the pre-issue price was $36. The only way to get the special-finish Jefferson nickel was in the set and the small premium over the $30 pre-issue price for the commemorative alone made the coin an unbelievable deal. Everyone predicted a sellout, and everyone was right.

It's easy to make an argument that the 1997-P Jefferson nickel Matte Finish coin was born of a special interest to boost the sales of another coin favored by Washington insiders, but that doesn't diminish its appeal. Within the context of the Jefferson nickel set, it is a standout key coin. Its mintage is a mere 25,000 pieces, the lowest of any U.S. coin belonging to a regular series since 1942. It is visually dramatic, with a sharp, Proof-quality strike but monotone dull surface shared in the series only by the 1994-P nickel Matte "Special Uncirculated"—yet this coin is nearly seven times scarcer.

Because it was issued in a commemorative set, almost all of these coins are well-preserved and high grade. It is not unusual to find examples that have toned to a golden hue. Untoned examples of the highest grade, 70 out of 70 on the Sheldon grading scale, command a premium and are highly sought-after.

	Total Certified Population	Most Commonly Certified	
		Grade	No. in Grade
NGC	339	SP-69	223
PCGS	48	MS-69	40
Mintage: 25,000			
Retail value in most common certified grade (SP-69): $125			

Designed by Augustus Saint-Gaudens. This is a modern version of the famous U.S. 1907 Ultra High Relief double eagle gold pattern, and was made as a tour de force to demonstrate how technical advances in the minting process can now accommodate manufacturing such a coin. The 2009 version was made in a slightly smaller diameter and composed of 24-karat gold, thus making it easier to strike and maintain the fidelity of the design. The date was changed to MMIX, and four additional stars were added to represent the current 50 states. Also included was the inscription IN GOD WE TRUST, which was not used on the 1907 version.

Weight: 31.1035 grams. *Composition:* 99.99% gold
(one ounce pure gold). *Diameter:* 27 mm. *Edge:* Lettered.

This coin is the most recently released issue of all the coins in this top-100 list. The coin was announced just as the U.S. Mint was affirming a commitment to creating coins of the highest level of artistic excellence. This coin was a demonstration of that goal.

When President Theodore Roosevelt sought to redesign U.S. coinage during his presidency, he enlisted the services of Augustus Saint-Gaudens, one of the preeminent sculptors of the era. Beginning with the $20 gold piece in 1907, Saint-Gaudens produced a phenomenal design to be rendered in high relief. It was agreed that the coins were magnificent, but they were impractical for production because they required many, repeated strikes from coinage dies to show full detail.

During one experimental attempt to produce high-relief coinage, the diameter of the $20 coin was reduced from 34 to 27 millimeters, the size of a $10 gold piece, and its thickness was doubled.

It was soon discovered, though, that for this reduced-diameter version to enter production, Congress would need to legislate a change to the $20 coin's specifications. Testing along these lines was abandoned, and ultimately the coin was issued in lowered relief. Two of these reduced-diameter 1907 Ultra High Relief $20 gold coins were retained and are now in the National Numismatic Collection at the Smithsonian Institution.

In 2008, new Mint Director Edmund Moy wished to bring this coin back as a bullion issue to display the capabilities of today's modern mints, as this early 20th-century work was widely considered the high-water mark of U.S. coinage design. The plan was announced in early 2008: a pure gold, .9999 fine version of the double-thick Ultra High Relief would be issued as part of the American Eagle Bullion program. There was to be no cap on the coin's mintage.

Step by step throughout the year, the Mint reported on its progress. In a series of feasibility tests, they discovered that the coin could be struck with just two blows of the coinage dies. Test pieces were displayed amidst much fanfare at the 2008 American Numismatic Association's World's Fair of Money, and the exhibit became an interactive feature on the U.S. Mint's Web site.

At noon on January 22, 2009, the coins went on sale. In a soaring bullion market, the one-ounce gold coin was priced at $1,189, with a limit of just one coin per household. The Mint would later announce that first-day sales alone totaled $33.7 million. In early February, the coins began to trickle out from the Mint and dribbled into the marketplace throughout the year. Significant back orders and fulfillment issues meant that customers didn't know when the coin they ordered would be received. Dealers wanting to make an active secondary market in the issue were hampered by the one-coin-per-customer order limit. It was a challenge to get any kind of quantity of the coin. Even though speculator buzz quelled, the coin remained the most-talked-about issue of 2009, more so than even the redesigned Lincoln cent.

By the end of the year, 115,178 had been sold. As a stand-alone $20 coinage issue and as a bit of an outcast from the rest of the American gold eagle series, the future prospects for this coin seem unclear. If eagle and modern commemorative collectors both embrace it, though, there is no doubt it will become a classic.

	Total Certified Population	Most Commonly Certified	
		Grade	No. in Grade
NGC	10,988	MS-70	6,003
PCGS	11,793	MS-70	6,840
Mintage: *115,178 (estimated)*			
Retail value in most common certified grade (MS-70): $2,750			

2008-W $1 AMERICAN SILVER EAGLE, REVERSE OF 2007

Designed by Adolph A. Weinman (obverse) and John Mercanti (reverse). The obverse features Weinman's Liberty Walking design used on half dollars from 1916 through 1947. Weinman's initials are on the hem of the gown. The reverse design is a rendition of a heraldic eagle.

Weight: 31.101 grams. *Composition:* 99.93% silver and .07% copper (net weight 1 ounce pure silver). *Diameter:* 40.6 mm. *Edge:* Reeded.

Not long after the first 2008 silver eagles came out, it was reported that the coins had been "re-hubbed." A hub is used to make dies, which in turn strike coins. *Re-hubbing*, therefore, meant that a new design template was being used to create all the dies that struck these coins. While the major design elements of the coin had not changed, subtle alterations had been made to the lettering and elsewhere. This change was consistent across the entire silver eagle production of 2008, including bullion, Proof, and Uncirculated versions of the coin.

In the course of producing modern coinage, these types of subtle changes occur over time. Technical aspects of minting, including attempts to prolong die-life and improve the clarity with which the design renders on the coin, find their way into the design process. According to the U.S. Mint, the changes seen on the 2008 silver eagles were made because of the adoption of digital engraving in the production of silver eagle dies. This was a more efficient and cost-effective method of production.

To accommodate this new process, a handful of modest changes were made to the coin. The most noticeable change occurred on the style of a single letter. In 2008, the U had a spur or foot on its right side, while on all previous issues the spur was absent—the old U was a simple bowl shape. Even though it affected just a single, small letter, this change was the tell-tale diagnostic that allowed

the reverse hub of 2008 to be distinguished instantaneously from that used in previous years.

In mid-April 2008, only a couple of weeks after the first 2008-W silver eagles were sold, collector John Nanney of Georgia noticed that a small number of coins had the old reverse style of 2007. This immediately ignited a search among collectors, and interest in this curious variety began to grow. When the variety was confirmed by the grading services, the search became a frenzy, and a number of collectors placed additional orders for coins from the Mint.

Numerous inquiries were directed to the U.S. Mint. The Mint responded quickly, acknowledging that during three production shifts for the 2008 coins, dies originally crafted for 2007-W silver eagle production were used inadvertently. Approximately 47,000 silver eagles had been struck with the reverse style of 2007. This type of variety is called *transitional* because it is a hybrid that combines the styles of coins used in two consecutive years. The 2008-W Reverse of 2007 silver eagle is the only significant die-variety in the entire silver eagle series, and it is collected by enthusiasts as a required coin in the complete set.

The coins were crafted from designs by A.A. Weinman and John Mercanti. Weinman, who is responsible for the obverse design, originally created this composition for the Liberty Walking half dollar first released in 1916. It shows Liberty striding amidst the rising sun, and the design was long considered to be the most attractive ever used on a U.S. silver coin. The reverse heraldic eagle composition was designed and engraved by Mercanti.

Reverse lettering styles: (left) 1986–2007, with smooth curve at bottom right of U; (right) 2008 to date, with spur at bottom right of U.

	Total Certified Population	Most Commonly Certified	
		Grade	No. in Grade
NGC	15,014	MS-69	7,978
PCGS	3,719	MS-69	3,322

Mintage: *47,000 (estimated)*

Retail value in most common certified grade (MS-69): $450

2004-D WISCONSIN QUARTER, EXTRA LEAF HIGH

Designed by John Flanagan, as modified by William C. Cousins (obverse), and Alfred Maletsky (reverse). The obverse depicting President George Washington was modified to include some of the wording previously used on the reverse. The reverse features an agricultural theme: the head of a cow, a round of cheese, and an ear of corn, along with the motto FORWARD on a banner.

Weight: 5.67 grams. *Composition:* Outer layers of 75% copper and 25% nickel bonded to an inner core of pure copper. *Diameter:* 24.3 mm. *Edge:* Reeded.

At the time of its inception, the 50 State Quarters® Program was universally hailed as exciting and innovative, but by 2004, it was becoming old news. The program was already more than five years old and had passed its halfway-point. The coin market had certainly benefited from a rush of new collectors who entered the field by assembling quarter sets from pocket change; for the first time in a long time, Americans were looking at circulating coins. But outside of the design selection process, which made headlines in their respective states, these coins weren't a front-page story anymore.

The 30th coin in the set would change everything. First released on October 25, 2004, the agriculturally themed Wisconsin quarter was well received. Shortly after the Wisconsin quarter's release, though, a Tucson, Arizona, collector named Bob Ford found a handful of the newly struck coins that were clearly something different.

For more than a decade, Ford had searched through circulating coins, looking for errors and varieties. On December 11, 2004, he noticed, unexpectedly, that some Wisconsin quarters appeared to have an extra leaf placed beneath the left leaf on the ear of corn, one of the central elements of the coin's design. This "extra leaf"

could be found in two distinct varieties. One showed a thin extra leaf that ran from the base of the ear and connected with the larger, curved leaf above. The other variety showed a thicker leaf that came out of the ear at a lower angle, never touching the leaf above.

Ford shared his find with coin dealer Rob Weiss of Old Pueblo Coin in Tucson. They realized that this was indeed something highly unusual and alerted the numismatic press. The extra leaves caused a flurry of speculation about their origin, and almost immediately "extra leaf" Wisconsin quarters were trading for hundreds of dollars. Quick on the uptake, collectors in Western states demanded rolls of Denver Mint Wisconsin quarters from their local banks, hoping to strike it rich. The story soon spread to the mainstream media. By mid-January 2005, it was front-page news on the *Arizona Daily Star*, and less than a month later it was reported in *USA Today*.

Questions regarding the irregularity remain unresolved. It is clearly the result of a *die-gouge*, an impression in the die that creates a raised element on the struck coin. Some people speculate that the gouge was created purposefully, to create an embellishment and stimulate waning collector interest. Other compelling evidence suggests that a misaligned die clash may have transposed elements of Washington's hair curls, which in radius and size resemble the shapes of the leaves. The exact cause of these varieties is unknown and certainly ranks among the most intriguing mysteries of modern coinage.

Of the two varieties, the Extra Leaf High is a bit scarcer than the so-called Extra Leaf Low (number 19 on this list), and therefore rates higher on the top-100 list. Among experts, the estimate of the number of coins struck varies widely from 10,000 to 25,000.

Pick-up point: Corn on reverse.

	Total Certified Population	Most Commonly Certified	
		Grade	No. in Grade
NGC	4,282	MS-65	1,652
PCGS	2,773	MS-64	1,190
Mintage: fraction of 226,800,000			
Retail value in most common certified grade (MS-65): $250			

2004-D WISCONSIN QUARTER, EXTRA LEAF LOW

Designed by John Flanagan, as modified by William C. Cousins (obverse), and Alfred Maletsky (reverse). The obverse depicting President George Washington was modified to include some of the wording previously used on the reverse. The reverse features an agricultural theme: the head of a cow, a round of cheese, and an ear of corn, along with the motto FORWARD on a banner.

Weight: 5.67 grams. *Composition:* Outer layers of 75% copper and 25% nickel bonded to an inner core of pure copper. *Diameter:* 24.3 mm. *Edge:* Reeded.

This variety is slightly more common than the related Extra Leaf High variant, although it is also more dramatic in appearance. The story of its recovery is recounted under its sibling coin, which was discovered simultaneously: the 2004-D Extra Leaf High Wisconsin state quarter. It appears on this list of the 100 Greatest U.S. Modern Coins as number 18.

The Wisconsin quarter design was the first in the entire state-quarter series to display an agricultural theme. It's certainly fitting, as Wisconsin is among the leading dairy-producing states. More than 350 different cheeses come from Wisconsin, more varieties than are produced in any other state. Wisconsin is also the fifth-largest producer of corn, and, for numismatists, fortunately so. It is a variation on the ear of corn depicted on this coin that was to inflame collectors' passions.

In a clean arrangement, the Wisconsin quarter design depicts the head and neck of a dairy cow. Beside the cow is a round of cheese, with an ear of corn above and behind. The corn ear is unfurled, with a single leaf sweeping out to either side. The design also bears an inscription of the state motto, FORWARD, on a pennant. Each component is well-proportioned and precisely detailed, sitting on an empty, flat field. The precise spacing of the elements provides a perfect canvas for this unusual variety. About two months after the coin was originally released, an astute collec-tor in Tucson, Arizona, discovered that an extra leaf, in two different varieties, could be seen beneath the left leaf on the ear of corn. Its unexplained appearance excited collectors around the country.

On the Extra Leaf Low variety, the added leaf is broad and appears to have two symmetrical sides. Its shape complements the curve of the leaf above it. Although this design element was clearly not part of the coin's intended design, and is in fact absent on the vast majority of Wisconsin state quarters, it seemed too perfect and too deliberate to simply be a random die-gouge. Its apparent precision caused many to believe that this was an intentional creation by a Mint employee.

According to data from a Freedom of Information Act request made by *USA Today* and released in January 2006, approximately 50,000 coins displaying blemishes were struck on a Friday night in November 2004. Presumably, this figure includes both the Extra Leaf High and Extra Leaf Low varieties. In this same statement, the Treasury Department's Office of Inspector General stated that the errors "were most likely produced as a result of machine or product deficiencies, not as a result of an intentional act." Even though these coins had been detected by Denver Mint employees, they had already been bagged and prepared for shipment. Quite simply, it would have been too costly to separate them from regular coins, and thus they were released into circulation.

Although collectors around the country searched for these coins, most of their efforts were in vain. Their distribution appears to have been localized, and nearly all significant finds were in the Tucson area. Seemingly about 20 to 25 percent more common than the Extra Leaf High variety, the Extra Leaf Low variety is esti-mated to number somewhere between 12,500 and 30,000 pieces.

Pick-up point: Corn on reverse.

	Total Certified Population	Most Commonly Certified	
		Grade	No. in Grade
NGC	5,790	MS-65	2,348
PCGS	3,874	MS-64	1,857

Mintage: fraction of 226,800,000

Retail value in most common certified grade (MS-65): $250

Designed by Frank Gasparro. The head of Dwight Eisenhower faces left on the obverse. LIBERTY arcs around the top of the obverse, and the date appears below the head. IN GOD WE TRUST appears at the lower left. On the reverse, an eagle with an olive branch in its talons alights upon the surface of the moon. A tiny earth can be seen in the background, and 13 small stars surround the eagle. UNITED STATES OF AMERICA and E PLURIBUS UNUM appear above the eagle; ONE DOLLAR appears below.

Weight: 22.68 grams. *Composition:* Outer layers of 75% copper and 25% nickel bonded to an inner core of pure copper. *Diameter:* 38.1 mm. *Edge:* Reeded.

This elusive and desirable coin demonstrates that testing and experimentation were components of the Mint's process to meet the demands of modern coinage production. Little more than a hundred years before this coin was struck, dies were individually handcrafted. The need for greater output and a focus on consistency and uniformity meant that the die-creation process also became mechanized. Errors that occurred during the mechanized process, such as doubled-dies, account for some of the most compelling entries among this top-100 list. But there are also instances where the involvement of artists and craftsmen contributed to make an important modern coin. The 1972 Type 2 Eisenhower dollar is the best example of this.

When the Mint was testing Eisenhower dollar dies, it was clear that the design as proposed was too high in relief to meet the challenges of production. To enable the large-scale minting of a dollar-sized copper-nickel coin, the U.S. Mint re-rendered the design in low relief. The higher-relief design was retained for production of Proof coinage, and a lower-relief version was used for circulating coins. This change allowed the Philadelphia and Denver Mints to strike more than 115 million circulation Eisenhower dollars in

1971, but the compromise was evident. The coins were very flat and otherwise poorly detailed.

The Proof coins, by contrast, were struck with the original, higher-relief design, and its effect and appearance were far superior. Herein lay the problem, however: a Proof die was used for only 4,000 strikes (or for making 2,000 coins, each of which got two blows from a die), while a circulation die struck 100,000 to 200,000 coins. How could the design be improved while still meeting enormous production demands?

In 1972, at the Denver Mint, the original, low-relief dies were used to strike all 92 million coins made there that year. At Philadelphia, however, the tinkering began. Of the 75 million coins produced there that year, an estimated 50 million are of the original, low-relief design, called Type 1. Enthusiasts speculate that a single die-pair of the high-relief design normally used to make Proofs was prepared to make business strikes, testing the design and performance. This is the so-called Type 2 variety. Based on die life, some 100,000 to 200,000 coins were presumably struck in this variety. Later in the year, a modified design was introduced, called Type 3, which was used for all Proofs and business strikes of this design at all Mints in subsequent years. According to estimates, 25 million or so of the Type 3 variety were struck.

The best way to tell the three varieties apart is to look at the earth as depicted on the reverse of the coin. On Type 1 coins, the earth shown on the reverse of the coin is not round, but rather is flattened in its upper-left from 9:00 to 11:00. Additionally, the islands beneath Florida are all directly underneath it or to the right. None are to the left of it. On the Type 2 examples, the earth is round and there are no islands beneath Florida. Instead, delicate inset lines strengthen the outlines of the continents. On the Type 3 coins, the earth is again round, but three islands are visible beneath Florida and extend well to the west of the state into the Gulf of Mexico.

In the realm of modern coinage, these details distinguishing the various types constitute dramatic and deliberate design changes. The Type 2 Eisenhower dollar is legitimately scarce, and adding to its allure is its absolute rarity in high grade—it is so elusive that gem examples trade for thousands of dollars when they can be found.

	Total Certified Population	Most Commonly Certified	
		Grade	No. in Grade
NGC	283	MS-64	99
PCGS	1,309	MS-63	424

Mintage: fraction of 75,890,000

Retail value in most common certified grade (MS-63): $400

1996-W ROOSEVELT DIME

Designed by John R. Sinnock. On the obverse, the head of Franklin Roosevelt faces left. LIBERTY appears in large letters along the left rim; IN GOD WE TRUST appears in small letters at the lower left, and the date appears at the bottom right. The reverse features a lit torch flanked by sprigs of olive and oak. UNITED STATES OF AMERICA arcs above, ONE DIME arcs below, and the motto E PLURIBUS UNUM runs in a straight line through the bottoms of the sprigs and torch.

Weight: 2.27 grams. *Composition:* Pure copper core sandwiched between outer layers of 75% copper and 25% nickel. *Diameter:* 17.9 mm. *Edge:* Reeded.

It may not always be recognized as an important milestone, but the United States has often observed the 50th anniversary of a coin's design. The best such example is, of course, the Lincoln cent. First issued in 1909, the Lincoln wheat cent got an update in 1959 on the occasion of its 50th anniversary. In that year, a reverse design featuring the Lincoln Memorial was first released. When the Lincoln cent had aged another 50 years, in 2009, it got another update, this time with four new reverse designs featuring snapshots of Lincoln's life.

The Roosevelt dime was similarly honored on the occasion of its 50th anniversary. First issued in 1946, the Roosevelt dime hon-

ored President Franklin Delano Roosevelt, who had died in 1945 while serving his fourth consecutive term as president. The dime was an especially fitting tribute to Roosevelt, as in his adult life he had been a leader of the March of Dimes' fundraising efforts to combat polio. Although originally issued in silver, the dime underwent no significant design changes throughout its entire 50 years of workman-like service. The only noteworthy design change was the movement of the mintmark to the coin's obverse in 1968.

In 1996, to celebrate the 50th anniversary of the Roosevelt dime, the West Point Mint was chosen to strike a special dime issue. The coin of course shows its usual austere design, except the W mintmark sits just above the numeral 6 in the date. It is the only dime to bear the West Point mintmark. This coin was not released into circulation, but instead was included as part of the 1996 Mint set, the Uncirculated coinage set sold by the U.S. Mint. The only way to get this coin was as part of the Mint set. A total of 1,457,000 sets were sold, which is correspondingly also the mintage figure of the 1996-W Roosevelt dime.

This low mintage figure gives the 1996-W Roosevelt dime the lowest mintage of any Mint State Roosevelt, including the 1946 to 1964 silver issues. In fact, the so-called key date of the silver series, the 1949-S, has a mintage of more than 13 million pieces! But the 1996-W Roosevelt dime is an anomaly in many ways. It is the only coin struck in copper-nickel-clad composition to bear the W mintmark. All other coins with this mintmark are precious-metal coins struck in silver, gold, or platinum. It is also the only commemorative dime ever issued in the United States.

Like most Mint set coins of the era, these dimes received very modest special handling and therefore can show contact marks from knocking against other coins and machine-sorting and packaging. Although most are gem Uncirculated, a disparity of quality does exist among them.

	Total Certified Population	Most Commonly Certified	
		Grade	No. in Grade
NGC	1,011	MS-67	434
PCGS	2,733	MS-67	1,056

Mintage: 1,457,000

Retail value in most common certified grade (MS-67): $100

Designed by Gilroy Roberts (obverse) and Frank Gasparro (reverse). On the obverse, the head of John F. Kennedy faces left. LIBERTY arcs across the top of the obverse; the date arcs along the bottom of the obverse and IN GOD WE TRUST runs in a straight line beneath Kennedy's head. The reverse features a heraldic eagle, similar to that seen on the 1801 through 1807 and 1892 through 1915 half dollars, within a circle of 50 stars. UNITED STATES arcs around the top and HALF DOLLAR arcs along the bottom of the reverse.

Weight: 12.50 grams. *Composition:* 90% silver and 10% copper. *Diameter:* 30.6 mm. *Edge:* Reeded.

By the late 1990s, the U.S. Mint was under pressure to boost commemorative coin sales. Coins for the 1994 World Cup and the 1996 Olympics had performed miserably and drowned sales of surrounding issues. Although today's collectors salivate when they see the low mintage figures of commemoratives from this era—making them among the most desirable of all the issues—at the time it was disastrous for the Mint. Millions of dollars were lost. For example, the U.S. Mint paid nearly $9 million to the World Cup Organizing Committee from collected surcharges on the sale of the 1994 commemorative coins, even though the Mint itself netted a loss of $5 million on the coins.

To boost sales, the Mint tried new things. In one experiment, special versions of circulating coins were paired with other Mint products. This was done to great effect in 1998, when the Uncirculated Robert F. Kennedy silver dollar was paired with a silver John F. Kennedy half dollar from the San Francisco Mint. Sold in the "Brothers Set," this Kennedy half dollar is a significant coin for many reasons. To match the appearance of the commemorative dollar it was paired with, the Kennedy half dollar was given a dull matte surface, the first time that this finish had ever been used on a Kennedy. Further, unlike circulating coins, the Kennedy half dollar issued in this set is 90 percent silver. Although 90 percent silver Kennedy half dollars had been sold since 1992 in special Proof sets, this was the first Kennedy of this composition since 1964 that wasn't strictly a Proof. Along these same lines, it is the only San Francisco Mint Kennedy half dollar that's not a Proof.

Adding another unusual element, the Brothers Set was only offered for sale during a six-week window. Rather than limiting the number of sets that could be produced, the Mint limited the sales period and therefore did not need to strike coins until it knew exactly how many were sold. Referring specifically to this facet of the program in the U.S. Mint's Annual Report, Director Philip N. Diehl wrote, "[The six-week sales window] created urgency among collectors and brought us cost and production benefits from knowing how many coins to produce. This innovation served us and the hobby, and it's a win-win option for the future. The program will close profitably on December 31, 1998."

A profitable commemorative program was indeed something to celebrate in 1998. But the program's success may have had more to do with the convenient thematic relationship of two siblings on coins combined with the rather high issue price of $59.95 for the set—a lofty $30 premium for the silver half dollar—than anything else. Despite the success, this type of initiative has not been repeated by the Mint.

The $30 spent on the coin back in 1998 has generated a nice return, as this coin is worth several hundred dollars today. Its mintage of approximately 62,000 is very low for the series and the unique attributes of the coin give it a broad base of appeal. Issued in special sets and created with extra care, the coin frequently survives in pristine condition, making this a key date than can be acquired in the very highest grades.

	Total Certified Population	Most Commonly Certified	
		Grade	No. in Grade
NGC	1,247	SP-69	909
PCGS	2,221	SP-69	1,183
Mintage: unknown			
Retail value in most common certified grade (SP-69): $200			

1982 NO MINTMARK ROOSEVELT DIME

Designed by John R. Sinnock. On the obverse, the head of Franklin Roosevelt faces left. LIBERTY appears in large letters along the left rim; IN GOD WE TRUST appears in small letters at the lower left, and the date appears at the bottom right. The reverse features a lit torch flanked by sprigs of olive and oak. UNITED STATES OF AMERICA arcs above, ONE DIME arcs below, and the motto E PLURIBUS UNUM runs in a straight line through the bottoms of the sprigs and torch.

Weight: 2.27 grams. *Composition:* Pure copper core sandwiched between outer layers of 75% copper and 25% nickel. *Diameter:* 17.9 mm. *Edge:* Reeded.

While, historically, coins made at the Philadelphia Mint did not have mintmarks, a change began in 1979. When the newly issued Susan B. Anthony dollars came out that year, they all had a mintmark, including those struck at Philadelphia, which were branded with a P. In 1980, this practice extended to all coins except for the cent. Just two years after this practice began, the first inadvertent omission occurred. In 1982, an obverse die without a mintmark was put into use, creating the 1982 No Mintmark dime.

Because dimes were struck for circulation at both Philadelphia and Denver, the missing mintmark could be either a P or a D. The uncertainty leads to the more general name "No Mintmark." In the early 1980s, coinage hubs did not include mintmarks. All dies were made in Philadelphia, and mintmarks were added before the dies were put into use or shipped to a branch mint for use elsewhere. This hand process accounts for the variations in mark sizes, positioning, and, as in this case, omissions.

Overwhelming evidence, however, suggests that the coins were, in fact, struck in Philadelphia, and thus this variety is also called the 1982 No P dime. Examples were first discovered in late 1982 in northern Ohio. A cache thought to number several thousand coins funneled from local banks through a coin shop in Toledo, Ohio, according to researcher and author Walter Breen. A subsequent discovery in Pennsylvania added a few thousand more coins to the total number available to collectors.

Numismatists distinguish between strong and weak varieties of the 1982 No Mintmark dime. The strong is properly struck and essentially fully detailed. The weak variety shows soft detail and, diagnostically, the 2 in the date is indistinct and melds with the rim of the coin. The same dies were used to strike both varieties, and the weak is variously attributed by researchers to either misaligned dies or weak striking pressure. Even though it is less common than the strong variety, the weak trades for much less, and price guides usually report only the price for the strong. Grading services do distinguish between the varieties.

The number of 1982 No Mintmark dimes produced is not known precisely. It is estimated that a single obverse dime-die produces as many as 150,000 coins. Roughly 10,000 examples are known to collectors, a sizable percentage of the original mintage for a circulation-issue variety. No other mintmark omission of any kind occurred on a circulating coin until 2007, and during the 25- year interlude, the 1982 No Mintmark dime grew in status. This coin is much sought-after and especially elusive in high grades, making it a key to the long-running Roosevelt dime series.

1982 No Mintmark dime (left, Strong Strike; right, Weak Strike).

	Total Certified Population	Most Commonly Certified	
		Grade	No. in Grade
NGC	297	MS-65	79
PCGS	1,973	MS-65	699

Mintage: fraction of 519,475,000

Retail value in most common certified grade (MS-65): $400

Designed by Augustus Saint-Gaudens (obverse) and Miley Busiek (reverse). The obverse features a modified rendition of the Augustus Saint-Gaudens design used on U.S. $20 gold pieces from 1907 until 1933. The reverse displays a "family of eagles" motif.

Weight: 8.483 grams. *Composition:* 91.67% gold, 3% silver, and 5.33% copper (net weight 1/4 ounce pure gold). *Diameter:* 22 mm. *Edge:* Reeded.

This 1/4-ounce $10 gold eagle, along with a similar 1/10-ounce $5 counterpart, is the first business-strike U.S. bullion coin that bears the W mintmark. In 1999, all U.S. gold bullion coins were struck at the mint in West Point, New York, but only the Proof version of the coin, sold directly to collectors, includes a mintmark. The bullion version, sold through official distributors, was made for the purpose of offering a high-quality, U.S. government–made product to investors in precious metals. These bullion versions trade largely based on their intrinsic metal content. Bullion coins do not include a mintmark, while collectible versions of these coins do.

The dies that produce these coins are made in Philadelphia and then shipped to West Point to strike coins. It is thought that a die intended for the production of Proof coins did not receive the final finishing steps and was sent to West Point. Being virtually indistinguishable from a bullion-coin die, it was put into use and 1/4-ounce gold eagles bearing the W mintmark were produced. This variety is alternately called the 1999-W "With W" and the 1999-W Struck from Unpolished Proof Dies.

It is said that Proof dies are individually accounted for and a number of manual quality-control steps occur in the production of these coins. How, then, could such an error occur? The blame likely rests on the enormous number of gold bullion coins struck in 1999. Y2K fears contributed to a flight to tangible assets, and the gold eagle was one of the chief beneficiaries. In most years, only 70,000 to 80,000 1/4-ounce $10 gold eagle bullion coins are struck. In 1999, however, a total of 564,232 were struck—a number that mintage figures have not approached since. Mintage levels have not even come within 400,000 coins of this figure since then. The die-production facilities and the quality-control processes were so overworked that it's easy to understand how such an error may have been created.

Approximately 6,000 1/4-ounce gold eagles are struck from each die-pair. Because it's widely thought that just one die with the W mintmark was used to create this coin, that figure is also the estimated mintage. Roughly 3,000 examples have been accounted for among the boxes of 1/4-ounce gold eagles. It is not unusual for these coins to trade hands still within the strapped boxes they were shipped in from the West Point Mint, and many pieces still remain to be discovered.

Interest in this coin grew in 2006, when the U.S. Mint offered Uncirculated versions of the American Eagle Bullion program coins directly to collectors. These coins made for direct sale to the public *did* include the W mintmark, and were issued in 2006, 2007, and 2008. To construct a complete set, collectors for the first time needed to acquire two different eagles: a coin with and a coin without the mintmark. The focus on mintmarks encouraged many collectors to take a second look at this coin, the first gold eagle $10 coin with a mintmark, but with only a few thousand in collectors' hands, it is a hot commodity.

	Total Certified Population	Most Commonly Certified	
		Grade	No. in Grade
NGC	11	AU-55	4
PCGS	6	MS-63 BN	3

Mintage: *10,000 (estimated)*

Retail value in most common certified grade (MS-69): $1,250

2000-W LIBRARY OF CONGRESS
$10 COMMEMORATIVE, BIMETALLIC

Designed by John Mercanti (obverse) and Thomas D. Rogers (reverse). The obverse features the hand of Minerva raising the torch of learning. The Library of Congress Jefferson Building's dome is visible in the background. The inscriptions around the ring state LIBERTY, 2000, and LIBRARY OF CONGRESS. The motto IN GOD WE TRUST appears in the platinum portion of the coin to the left of the hand and torch. The reverse features the seal of the Library of Congress surrounded by a laurel wreath. The outer ring carries the inscriptions UNITED STATES OF AMERICA and TEN DOLLARS. The motto E PLURIBUS UNUM appears in the platinum center below the eagle.

Weight: 16.2590 grams. *Composition:* 48% gold, 48% platinum, and 4 % alloy. *Diameter:* 27.00 mm. *Edge:* Reeded.

One sentence inserted into the authorizing legislation for this commemorative yielded one of the most intriguing coins made by the U.S. Mint. According to the law, the secretary of the Treasury was given the option of producing a $5 gold commemorative that conformed to the specifications of previous commemorative issues or, instead, could produce a $10 bimetallic gold-and-platinum commemorative. Thankfully for collectors, the Treasury elected to make the bimetallic coin.

The reasons for this selection are not entirely known, but there are a few likely causes. For one, the $10 platinum coin would be sold at a higher surcharge of $50 per coin compared with $35 for the alternative gold issue, and it was likely that this would raise more money for the Library of Congress Trust Fund Board, which supports outreach programs for the Library. More likely, however, is awareness that this would be the first commemorative coin

issued in the new millennium and a desire to celebrate with a coinage "first" as well.

While the composition of the coin is unique, the design itself is relatively staid. The central portion of the obverse, in platinum, shows a hand holding a torch before the dome of the Library's Jefferson Building. The legend surrounds on a golden ring and, cleverly, the flame of the torch rests fully on the gold portion as well. The reverse shows a compact version of the Library's logo in platinum, with legends surrounding on the golden ring. The coin was issued in both Uncirculated and Proof versions.

This ambitious bimetallic concept was only attempted this one time. It's widely thought that production of this coin was a huge challenge because the gold and platinum parts did not meld together well during striking. Indeed, platinum-and-gold bimetallic coinage issues are very few in number. Despite the obviously complementary nature of the metals, the disparate densities of gold and platinum make them difficult to strike in concert. Indeed, on many specimens of the Library of Congress $10 commemorative, the inner platinum core can be heard rattling inside its golden ring. In the end, the Mint was spared from producing them in large numbers because the coin did not sell very well.

While a total of 200,000 examples were authorized to be struck, only 7,261 of the Uncirculated version and 27,455 of the Proof version were sold. Today, its low mintage makes the Uncirculated, Mint State coin one of the most sought-after issues in the commemorative series, and it commands the second highest price of any modern commemorative, trailing after only the Uncirculated version of the Jackie Robinson $5 coin.

The reason for the commemorative's unpopularity at the time of production really isn't clear either. Perhaps this issue did not resonate very well thematically because it commemorates the anniversary of an institution rather than a person or an event. The novelty of its composition doesn't appear to have been much help, either. Most likely, the issue price was just too high at nearly $400 per coin, when previous U.S. Mint offerings of $5 gold commemoratives were offered for little more than $200 per coin. As one of the keys to the series, their original issue price now seems like an absolute steal!

	Total Certified Population	Most Commonly Certified	
		Grade	No. in Grade
NGC	1,176	MS-70	769
PCGS	1,516	MS-69	1,196

Distribution: 7,261

Retail value in most common certified grade (MS-69): $4,000

Designed by John Mercanti (obverse) and Thomas D. Rogers (reverse). The obverse features a portrait of Lady Liberty. The reverse (bullion issues) features an eagle soaring above America.

Weight: 1.0005 ounces. *Composition:* 99.95% platinum.
Diameter: 32.7 mm. *Edge:* Reeded.

In 1996, legislators passed a minor amendment to section 5112 of Title 31, U.S. Code, which prescribes the legal requirements and specifications for all U.S. coinage. Added to the U.S. Code was the following, in full: "Secretary may mint and issue bullion and proof platinum coins in accordance with such specifications, designs, varieties, quantities, denominations, and inscriptions as the Secretary, in the Secretary's discretion, may prescribe from time to time. : *Provided,* That the Secretary is authorized to use Government platinum reserves stockpiled at the United States Mint as working inventory and shall ensure that reserves utilized are replaced by the Mint."

With those two sentences, the American platinum eagle was created. First issued from 1997 until 2008, the bullion coin had a new design. The obverse, created by then–U.S. Mint sculptor and engraver John Mercanti, features a portrait of Liberty reworked from the Statue of Liberty in clean, modern lines. The reverse,

conceived by U.S. Mint sculptor and engraver Thomas D. Rogers Sr., shows a composition named "Eagle Soaring Above America" and displays a gliding eagle with its wings fully outstretched above the sun's rays. This same design is used on all bullion issues, while collector versions of the coins (Proof and Uncirculated issues) have a different design that changes each year.

Like the American gold eagle, coins were available in one-ounce, 1/2-ounce, 1/4-ounce, and 1/10-ounce weights, but with a face value double that of their gold counterparts. This gave the one-ounce platinum coin a $100 face value, the highest of any U.S. coin ever issued. Also, like the other bullion issues, the coins were sold only though authorized distributors who, in turn, sold them to other dealers, investors, and collectors.

The first few years of the platinum eagle showed banner sales: more than 50,000 one-ounce coins sold in the first and third years, and a mind-boggling 133,002 coins sold in year two, among the highest mintage figures for any platinum coin. Bullion sales declined steadily thereafter, reaching a nadir of only 6,000 examples of the 2006 $100 platinum eagle bullion one-ounce coin, the single-lowest mintage figure for any U.S. bullion coin ever issued.

Why was there such a precipitous drop? One answer is that platinum increased in price, making these coins more expensive and therefore less obtainable by a broad spectrum of collectors. Throughout 2005, platinum flirted with the $1,000-per-ounce price level, but on January 9, 2006, it broke through and never looked back, spiking to more than $1,300 per ounce in May. More significantly, however, in 2006 the U.S. Mint issued the American Eagle Uncirculated Coins for collectors, and offered versions of these coins directly for sale to collectors. The Uncirculated coins have a different reverse design, as do the Proof issues. Only 3,068 of the 2006-W $100 platinum eagle Uncirculated coins were sold. Likely, this accounted for much of the collector demand for platinum and fewer units of the bullion counterpart were needed to meet the requirements of investors.

	Total Certified Population	Most Commonly Certified	
		Grade	No. in Grade
NGC	863	MS-70	674
PCGS	1,121	MS-69	725

Mintage: 6,000

Retail value in most common certified grade (MS-69): $2,000

2001-P AMERICAN BUFFALO DOLLAR COMMEMORATIVE

Designed by James Earle Fraser. The obverse and reverse designs are based on the original 1913 Buffalo nickel, with modified inscriptions on the reverse. The obverse features a portrait of a Native American facing right with the inscription LIBERTY in front and the date on the shoulder. The reverse features a full figure of the American bison, standing, facing left. The inscription reads UNITED STATES OF AMERICA, IN GOD WE TRUST, E PLURIBUS UNUM, and ONE DOLLAR.

Weight: 26.73 grams. *Composition:* 90% silver and 10% copper (net weight .77344 ounces pure silver). *Diameter:* 38.1 mm. *Edge:* Reeded.

One major characteristic of modern U.S. coinage is that it frequently borrows from previous coinage designs. The obverse of the gold and silver eagles recast, respectively, Saint-Gaudens's design from his eponymous $20 gold piece and Weinman's design for the Liberty Walking half dollar, both issued near the turn of the 19th century. The First Spouse series similarly depicts adaptations of Liberty from earlier coinages when a particular president was not married while in the White House. Following in this tradition, James Earle Fraser's Buffalo nickel design has been recast on a series of .9999 fine gold coins since 2006, but its first reuse came in 2001 on the American Buffalo commemorative coin.

The coin was sold to benefit the National Museum of the American Indian (NMAI), a new Smithsonian museum then under construction on the National Mall. The authorizing legislation stipulated that a $10-per-coin surcharge be used to supplement the new museum's endowment. It also stated that James Earle Fraser's design for the Buffalo nickel, "which portrays a profile representation of a Native American on the obverse side and a representation of an American buffalo on the reverse side, is a distinctive and appropriate model for a coin to commemorate the NMAI." The design of the new coin followed Fraser's original in near-replica, making adjustments for its different relief and size, and the addition of requisite legends left off the original.

Whether or not it was Congress' original intention, its design selection created a blockbuster. A new Fraser Buffalo coin proved incredibly popular, and the authorized mintage of 500,000 was a complete and rapid sell-out. Prices quickly escalated in the secondary market, with coins almost immediately selling for double and triple their issue price. So many people were shut out of the ordering process that legislators examined whether it would be feasible to authorize an increase to the mintage of an additional 500,000 pieces. After all, they reasoned, proceeds should benefit the NMAI and not market speculators who had purchased coins solely to quickly resell.

Others questioned whether such a move would be legal. Many had purchased the coin with an understanding that it was to be limited to 500,000 pieces. Would an increase in mintage constitute a misrepresentation of the edition size? The debate played out well in the numismatic press and added interest to the coin. Ultimately, no increase in the mintage was authorized and the number produced remained at half a million coins. The Proof version had proven slightly more popular, selling 272,869 examples versus 227,131 for the Uncirculated format. All controversy aside, this coin ranks among the most sought-after of all modern U.S. commemorative coins, being one of the highest-priced silver issues in the series.

	Total Certified Population	Most Commonly Certified	
		Grade	No. in Grade
NGC	10,933	PF-69 UC	9,367
PCGS	11,884	PF-69 DC	10,927
Distribution: 272,869			
Retail value in most common certified grade (PF-69 DC): $300			

Designed by Victor David Brenner (obverse) and Frank Gasparro (reverse). The obverse continues the design of 1909, featuring a bust of Lincoln facing right, the word LIBERTY to his left, and the date in the field in front of his coat. The legend IN GOD WE TRUST appears above his head. The reverse shows a frontal view of the Lincoln Memorial with UNITED STATES OF AMERICA and E PLURIBUS UNUM appearing above and ONE CENT below.

Weight: 2.5 grams. *Composition:* A core of 99.2% zinc and .8% copper, with a plating of pure copper. *Diameter:* 19 mm. *Edge:* Plain.

Rare and interesting coins that form a short, compact grouping are sometimes able to take on special significance. For instance, collectors of classic coinage refer to the four issues of Carson City Liberty Seated dollars minted from 1870 through 1873 with great affection. Similarly, during the four-year span from 1969 through 1972, collectors were gifted with the production of four exciting doubled-die Lincoln cents.

This four-coin run began with the 1969-S Doubled-Die Obverse, the "King of the Lincoln Cent Doubled Dies" and by far the most valuable (and number one on this list). Next is the 1970-S Large Date Doubled-Die Obverse, a dramatic coin that remains so elusive that it didn't make this edition of *100 Greatest U. S. Modern Coins*, though some predict it may one day overshadow the 1969-S in terms of value and desirability. Next is the best doubled-die Proof in the series, the 1971-S Doubled-Die Obverse (more on this coin, the focus of this entry, to follow). Finally, capping off this unbeatable sequence is the 1972 Doubled-Die Obverse, the most visually splendid doubled die of the entire Memorial cent series and number 10 on this list.

Proof-coin doubled dies are made in the same way as circulation issues. The working die that is used to strike coins receives unintentional, misaligned blows from the working hub that imparts

the coin's design. Because Proof dies receive so much special attention, as do the coins that they strike, dramatic varieties are relatively rare. There is, of course, a grand exception. In 1971, the San Francisco Mint released *three* different doubled-die obverse cents.

The first was discovered by Philadelphia coin dealer Harry Forman in 1975, and variety expert John Wexler discovered a second, but even more dramatic, variety in 1982. Both of these coins show strong doubling on the word LIBERTY. The first variety shows a small amount of doubling on the date, while the second shows no doubling on the date but good doubling on the motto, IN GOD WE TRUST. A third, minor doubled die was later discovered and is worth much less than the two major varieties described.

As with all Proof-coin varieties, these coins are found only in Proof sets. Approximately 2,300 coins were struck from each Proof Lincoln cent obverse die at this time, making that the presumed mintage of each of these coins. The second variety has proven more elusive than the first and carries a greater value today. While most references try to list varieties from most important to least important, this progression can be violated to follow discovery order. It's vital to consult references to make sure varieties are properly attributed and that their value and rarity are being related accurately.

Pick-up point: LIBERTY.

	Total Certified Population	Most Commonly Certified	
		Grade	No. in Grade
NGC	16,771	MS-67 RD	9,155
PCGS	11,104	MS-66 RD	4,332

Mintage: fraction of 3,220,733

Retail value in most common certified grade (MS-67 RD): $125

1983-P WASHINGTON QUARTER

Designed by John Flanagan. The obverse features the head of George Washington facing left, with LIBERTY above his head and the date below. The motto IN GOD WE TRUST appears in small letters in the left field. On the reverse, an eagle, with wings outspread, perches on a tight bundle of arrows. Two olive sprigs are joined beneath the eagle. The outer legends include UNITED STATES OF AMERICA above and QUARTER DOLLAR below. The motto E PLURIBUS UNUM appears in smaller letters above the eagle's head.

Weight: 5.67 grams. *Composition:* Outer layers of 75% copper and 25% nickel bonded to an inner core of pure copper. *Diameter:* 24.3 mm. *Edge:* Reeded.

The Mint was looking for ways to cut costs in the early 1980s, and one product that found itself on the chopping block in 1982 was the once-popular Mint set. Issued since 1947, Mint sets include an example of each coin struck for circulation at each mint. These sets have served as one of the primary sources of Uncirculated coins for collectors and they were enormously popular. More than two million sets were sold each year throughout the late 1970s through 1981.

In the absence of Mint sets, a number of private companies took up the challenge of supplying demand, and thus, for 1982 and 1983, privately issued sets can be found. The other source of Uncirculated Mint set coins is Souvenir sets. After receiving a tour of a Mint, it's not unusual that visitors should want examples of the coins struck there. The Souvenir set was designed to meet this demand. Sold primarily in Mint gift shops, it includes circulation examples of coins struck at a single mint. The problem with both

Souvenir sets and privately issued sets is that the coins included seldom match the quality of Mint set coins, and are often low end Uncirculated examples. They are also comparatively scarce. Just 15,000 Souvenir sets were made in Philadelphia in 1983 and 20,000 were made in Denver, compared to 2.9 million Mint sets in 1981.

Bags and rolls of 1983 Washington quarters were rarely saved by collectors, meaning that the other obvious source for these coins is circulation. Many album sets assembled by collectors include blank spaces for this date. Collectors seeking high-quality examples face a further challenge. The 1983 Washington quarters from the Philadelphia Mint in particular tend to be heavily abraded. Production quality was low (possibly further indicative of cost-cutting at the time), and most coins are struck from late-state, heavily fatigued dies that imparted weak, mushy detail. Contact-marks and other forms of abrasion, including die burn, are common. They are typically not attractive coins.

Widely known to be scarce, 1983-P quarters are worth many times the value of equivalent coins from years with Mint set examples. In fact, non-collectors are often surprised to discover that if a particularly nice Uncirculated example can be found in pocket change, it's easily worth a hundred times its face value. Fewer than a dozen superb gem Uncirculated (MS-67) examples have been professionally certified, and these carry a price-guide value in excess of $1,000—more than 5,000 times their face value.

The move to drop Mint sets was timed in concert with the re-launch of the commemorative-coinage program in 1982, which likely mitigated complaints from collectors at the time. But the complaints grew louder over time, and in response the Mint reversed their policy; they began issuing Mint sets once again in 1984 and have done so each year since. As the half dollar and dollar coin are seldom used in circulation, a few sets from subsequent years included coins that were struck for sets only and not for circulation. These inclusions, along with the role of the Mint set as the most convenient source of high-quality examples of circulating coins, have sustained the sets' popularity and collectibility as well as their secondary-market value.

	Total Certified Population	Most Commonly Certified	
		Grade	No. in Grade
NGC	146	MS-65	63
PCGS	353	MS-65	180
Mintage: 673,535,500			
Retail value in most common certified grade (MS-65): $85			

Designed by Felix Schlag. The obverse features a bust of Thomas Jefferson facing left. IN GOD WE TRUST appears inside the left edge, and LIBERTY and the date appear inside the right edge. On the reverse, Jefferson's home, Monticello, appears as the central device. E PLURIBUS UNUM arcs above. The word MONTICELLO captions the building, and the words FIVE CENTS and the legend UNITED STATES OF AMERICA appear below.

Weight: 5.00 grams. *Composition:* 75% copper
and 25% nickel. *Diameter:* 21.2 mm. *Edge:* Plain.

In 1971, all Proof coins were struck at the San Francisco Mint and included an S mintmark. All, that is, except for a small number of nickels that were mistakenly struck without mintmarks. According to the Mint Bureau, some 1,655 coins were struck and released without the S mintmark. This figure was released after the initial discovery in 1971 of examples of these nickels. To date, only about 400 are known. They were found among the 3.2 million Proof sets issued that year.

Proof coinage is made with special care and attention, which makes No S Proof issues fascinating to collectors. They find a wide following, stretching well beyond collectors who specialize in a series. There are only five No S Proof coins in existence: three dimes struck in 1968, 1970, and 1983; a cent struck in 1990; and the 1971 No S Jefferson nickel, the lone nickel on the list.

Designed by Felix Schlag, the winner of a design contest in 1938, the Jefferson nickel was issued continuously without a design change for 66 years. The design itself demonstrated public support for the portrayal of a president and a monument on coinage, a pattern that would be repeated on the Lincoln Memorial cent as well as a number of commemorative issues. Despite the success of the Jefferson nickel, it is Schlag's only coin design; he did, however, also design a number of medals. In 1966, the initials FS were added to this coin for the first time, and they remain on the reverse to this day (the current obverse design no longer belongs to Schlag).

The Jefferson nickel series includes more than one interesting issue for collectors of Proof coinage besides the 1971 No S variety. In 1942, when Proof coins were still struck in Philadelphia, the Jefferson nickel was the first U.S. Proof coin to include a P mintmark. A large P was added to silver-alloy nickels struck from 1942 to 1945 to distinguish them from their regular copper-nickel-alloy counterparts. Nickel was needed for the war effort and thus was removed from use in coinage. The key Proof coin of the series, however, is unquestionably the 1971 No S nickel.

This coin usually grades at least gem Proof and more often superb gem Proof. Significant premiums are paid for the highest-condition coins. Most often, these coins are *cameo*, exhibiting medium contrast between the design and the field area. Very deeply contrasted coins, sometimes called *ultra cameo*, are less common, as are coins with minimal contrast. The degree of contrast is normally greater on the obverse than the reverse. Certification is strongly advised when paying a premium for condition.

	Total Certified Population	Most Commonly Certified	
		Grade	No. in Grade
NGC	46	PF-68 CAM	13
PCGS	153	PF-68 CAM	48

Mintage: *1,655 (estimated)*

Retail value in most common certified grade (PF-68 CAM): $2,500

1983 DOUBLED-DIE REVERSE LINCOLN CENT

Designed by Victor David Brenner (obverse) and Frank Gasparro (reverse). The obverse continues the design of 1909, featuring a bust of Lincoln facing right, the word LIBERTY to his left, and the date in the field in front of his coat. The legend IN GOD WE TRUST appears above his head. The reverse shows a frontal view of the Lincoln Memorial with UNITED STATES OF AMERICA and E PLURIBUS UNUM appearing above and ONE CENT below.

Weight: 2.5 grams. *Composition:* A core of 99.2% zinc and .8% copper, with a plating of pure copper. *Diameter:* 19 mm. *Edge:* Plain.

Almost all of the important doubled-die Lincoln cents share a common feature: they were struck from doubled-obverse dies, meaning that the best features of the coin are present on the front. The major exception in the series is the 1983 Doubled-Die Reverse, which has prominent, well-separated doubling throughout all of the reverse legends. There is a second impression on all of the reverse wordings, shifted upwards, above the image below.

The 1983 Doubled-Die Reverse Lincoln cent is the most dramatic of any doubled-die reverse (DDR) in the entire Lincoln cent series. Even though it is of relatively recent vintage, it is comparatively scarce. Authors have reported that two caches of these coins were found, in Pennsylvania and Florida, but they likely amounted to only a few thousand coins in all, the estimated number available to collectors.

The obverse of this coin features heavy die-polishing, giving it a very characteristic appearance. This obverse has been found paired with two different reverse dies other than the doubled reverse, which suggests that the doubled die was removed from service before the end of its functioning life. Further evidence confirms this theory: correspondence quoted in an Associated Press story from June 3, 1984, quotes George Hunter, assistant director for technology at the Mint, as stating that the error was discov-

ered and the die destroyed before 50,000 total coins were struck, and that only 5,000 or so entered circulation.

In addition to contending with this coin's scarcity, collectors seeking it have another issue to deal with: condition. The transition from a solid bronze cent to a coin with a copper-coated zinc core had begun in 1982, and the Mint was still plagued by serious production difficulties. Tiny gas bubbles often became trapped beneath the surface of the plating, causing small blisters to appear throughout the coin and damaging its aesthetics. Because these flaws are "as made," they are present even in high-grade examples and do not affect a coin's value unless they are severe. In areas where plating is too thin or, in rare cases, where the zinc core became exposed during striking, coins can discolor or corrode and, unfortunately, these effects are irreversible. Fortunately, most other condition issues affecting early copper-coated zinc-core Lincoln cents are manifest on these coins by now, and as long as collectors exercise proper care in storing their coins, further extreme changes are unlikely to occur.

The relative rarity of this coin and the condition factors affecting coins of the highest grade make this coin comparatively expensive at the very highest end of the grade range. Mid-range Uncirculated examples can be purchased at more modest prices, making them a fairly good value for the best DDR in the series.

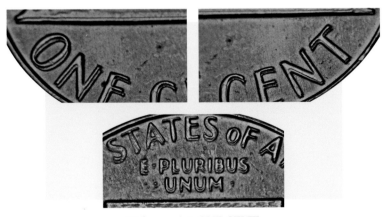

Pick-up point: ONE CENT.

	Total Certified Population	Most Commonly Certified	
		Grade	No. in Grade
NGC	507	MS-66 RD	184
PCGS	947	MS-65 RD	404
Mintage: 7,752,355,000			
Retail value in most common certified grade (MS-65 RD): $500			

Designed by John Mercanti (obverse) and Joel Iskowitz (reverse). The obverse features a portrait of Lady Liberty. The reverse depicts Justice, blindfolded and holding her scales aloft, in front of an eagle.

Weight: 1.0005 ounces. *Composition:* 99.95% platinum.
Diameter: 32.7 mm. *Edge:* Reeded.

Starting in 2006, the U.S. Mint began offering Uncirculated versions of the bullion American eagles for direct sale to collectors. Historically, bullion coins were sold only through dedicated distributors who purchased in bulk from the Mint. For collectors, Proof versions of the coins were offered at price premiums. The Uncirculated coins were meant to be sold at more modest prices than their Proof counterparts, a prospect that became more appealing as metal prices accelerated.

The Uncirculated versions differed from bullion coins in a few ways. First, Uncirculated coins had a W mintmark, for West Point, while bullion coins are issued without mintmark, even though they, too, are struck at West Point. Secondly, the Mint advertised that Uncirculated coins were struck on "specially burnished blanks," although the effects of this treatment, which occurs prior to striking, are not visible on the finished coins. Finally, for the platinum eagles, the reverse design is not the bullion version but rather the Proof design.

Each year, the Proof platinum eagle has a different reverse design, an element that makes this coin different from other coins

in the American eagle series. In 2006, the Mint began a three-year thematic sequence, creating reverse designs emblematic of the three branches of government, beginning with the Legislative Branch in 2006, followed by the Executive in 2007, and finishing with the Judicial in 2008. Sculpted and engraved by Mint designer Joel Iskowitz and Mint engraver Charles Vickers, the reverse for the 2008 coin shows a personified image of Justice holding a scale from her fingers to represent the balance of the law. She wields a sword to symbolize the power of reason, and a vigilant eagle, symbol of the nation, stands behind her as the protector of Justice.

Of all weights of the gold and platinum eagles, the 1/2-ounce and 1/4-ounce coins have always been the worst sellers. The lion's share of their sales comes from purchases of four-coin sets that include the one-ounce, 1/2-ounce, 1/4-ounce, and 1/10-ounce coins. In 2008, platinum metal was experiencing unprecedented price volatility, starting off the year at $1,500 per ounce and climbing to $2,100 per ounce at mid-year before settling back at $900 per ounce. When the 1/2-ounce 2008-W platinum eagle $50 Uncirculated coin went on sale on July 1, 2008, it was priced at $1,199.95, and the four-coin set was $4,289.95, among the most expensive products ever offered by the Mint. Platinum's price fluctuation worked against collector demand for these coins, as did the somewhat duplicative offerings of bullion, Proof, and Uncirculated versions.

These coins are produced to meet demand, and there is no pre-set order limit. Only 1,283 four-coin sets and 970 individual Uncirculated 2008-W platinum eagle $50 coins were sold, making a total mintage of 2,253. This figure is the lowest of *any* modern U.S. coin. In fact, to find a lower-mintage U.S. coin, one has to go back more than 70 years to 1939, to the Arkansas Centennial half dollar. Sales of the Uncirculated American eagles were deemed so poor that the Mint put the program on hiatus after 2008 and it's unclear if they will be offered again. Being the lowest-mintage regular-issue coin of its era, however, earns this coin a unique place in the mind of collectors.

	Total Certified Population	Most Commonly Certified	
		Grade	No. in Grade
NGC	3,632	MS-69	2,006
PCGS	420	MS-70	293

Mintage: 2,253

Retail value in most common certified grade (MS-69): $2,750

1964 KENNEDY HALF DOLLAR, ACCENTED HAIR, PROOF

Designed by Gilroy Roberts (obverse) and Frank Gasparro (reverse). On the obverse, the head of John F. Kennedy faces left. LIBERTY arcs across the top of the obverse; the date arcs along the bottom and IN GOD WE TRUST runs in a straight line beneath Kennedy's head. The reverse features a heraldic eagle, similar to that seen on the 1801 through 1807 and 1892 through 1915 half dollars, within a circle of 50 stars. UNITED STATES arcs around the top and HALF DOLLAR arcs along the bottom of the reverse.

Weight: 12.50 grams. *Composition:* 90% silver and 10% copper.
Diameter: 30.6 mm. *Edge:* Reeded.

Some of the most intriguing stories in numismatics involve major personalities (often politicians) who had the ability to influence coinage design with just a few words or pen strokes. There is such a tale about this coin, the Proof 1964 Kennedy half dollar Accented Hair variety.

After the president's assassination on November 22, 1963, discussion immediately began about how to commemorate his life with a circulating coin. Within only a few days of Kennedy's death, Mint Director Eva Adams contacted the Mint chief engraver, Gilroy Roberts, and told him to begin work on a design. Roberts quickly adopted his profile portrait for the Kennedy presidential medal. While this design work was ongoing, a new coinage bill was passed by Congress on December 30, 1963, allowing Kennedy to replace Benjamin Franklin on the circulating half dollar.

The first trial strikes were shown by Adams to the president's widow, Jacqueline Kennedy, and to his brother, Attorney General Robert F. Kennedy. They provided comments on the design and a modified version was prepared. It's this exchange, which took place less than a month after the president's death, that has implanted itself in the annals of numismatic lore. It is thought that Mrs. Kennedy objected to the heavily inscribed lines that showed the direction of the president's delicately coiffed hair, and that this

aspect of the design was changed because of her personal recommendation. In fact, this is a striking dissimilarity between the otherwise-parallel portraits used on this coin and Paul Manship's design of the Kennedy inaugural medal, in which the hair detail is only faintly hinted.

The very first examples struck were Proofs; the Mint rightly recognized that many would want the new coins as souvenirs, and nearly four million Proofs were struck. Two distinct varieties could be seen. One, known from only one Proof die, was the Accented Hair version, best distinguished by a series of accented hair lines in the area above Kennedy's ear. The other showed much-reduced detail and depth of lines in this area. Although not exactly rare, this Accented Hair variety accounts for fewer than 1 in 20 Kennedy half dollars struck in 1964 (less than five percent); many estimate that about 120,000 were struck. Clearly, some coins had been produced with this original feature still in place. Perhaps during the rush, dies for Proof coinage had already been prepared relying on Roberts's original design.

Although we do know that the Kennedys were consulted about the coin's design, any specific objection to this aspect of the coin, or how these Accented Hair examples came to be released, is left open to speculation. Numismatists, quite frankly, enjoy the good story. Another theory posits that the deeply incised grooves in the original version caused production problems, such as reduced die life, and the design was quickly changed so that the Mint would be better able to accommodate the aggressive demand for this coin in 1964.

Sometimes, spotting an Accented Hair Kennedy half dollar without another specimen for comparison can be tricky by looking at the hair detail alone. A tell-tale flaw at the bottom of the I in LIBERTY is the best diagnostic. On the Accented Hair variety, the lower-left serif will always be missing.

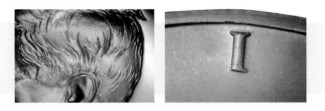

Pick-up points: Hair, I of LIBERTY.

	Total Certified Population	Most Commonly Certified	
		Grade	No. in Grade
NGC	3,695	PF-67	1,133
PCGS	3,125	PF-67	697

Mintage: 3,950,762

Retail value in most common certified grade (PF-67): $150

Designed by Augustus Saint-Gaudens (obverse) and Miley Busiek (reverse). The obverse features a modified rendition of the Augustus Saint-Gaudens design used on U.S. $20 gold pieces from 1907 until 1933. The reverse displays a "family of eagles" motif.

Weight: 3.393 grams. *Composition:* 91.67% gold, 3% silver, and 5.33% copper (net weight 1/10 ounce pure gold). *Diameter:* 16.5 mm. *Edge:* Reeded.

Peak production of 1/10-ounce gold eagles was realized in 1999, when a staggering 2.75 million examples were sold. To give some perspective, this figure is 10 times the typical number of sales; for example, in 2009 the net mintage was 270,000 coins. The reason for the considerable spike in sales was clearly known: Y2K.

Concerns about how computer systems would respond in the year 2000 was a constant and seemingly rational fear in 1999. Since a significant amount of software required only a two-digit date, the ramifications of a date recorded simply as "00" were unknown. Would computers, mistakenly programmed to operate as though it were 1900, fail to execute scheduled tasks in the year 2000, causing systems to go offline and financial markets to tumble? Whether or not an investor subscribed to this apocalyptic view, some financial investors recommended a move to hard assets.

As a result, all U.S. gold bullion coins had banner years in 1999. Every single denomination had by far its best sales to date, but the denomination that was most affected was the 1/10-ounce gold eagle with its $5 face value. The reason that this coin became so popular was because it was seen as the best hedge against the doomsday scenario. If electronic trading really were suspended and faith in governments truly rattled, gold would then become the principle medium of exchange. But paying for goods with a one-ounce gold coin, then worth $300, might prove impractical. Making change would also be difficult. On the other hand, a 1/10-ounce gold coin, a little bit smaller than a dime and worth about $30, would be an ideal unit for everyday commerce, and they sold like gangbusters!

Faced with the challenge of producing so many coins, the Mint had to make an enormous number of dies. Bullion-issue coins, which have a matte-like finish, are produced without mintmarks at West Point, while Proof coins do bear the W mintmark. In the course of producing these coins, apparently dies intended for the production of Proof coins were instead prepared for use and then struck bullion coins, creating the Mint State 1999-W "With W" $5 gold eagle. This variety is variously described either as "With W," to make sure that it is not confused with the Proof coin that rightly bears the W mintmark, or as being struck from unpolished (or unfinished) Proof dies. The coin was, however, distributed along with bullion coins, and simply a die with the W mintmark was used in error.

The Mint has reported that, on average, 6,000 1/10-ounce gold eagles are struck from a single die. Today, nearly that many are accounted for by the collecting community, and it's estimated that 15,000 or more 1999 $5 Mint State gold eagles were struck with the W mintmark. That figure suggests that more than one die was used to create these coins, and therefore that the mistake happened more than once! However unlikely that seems, it's worth noting that an identical error appears on the 1999 $10 1/4-ounce gold eagle (number 24 on this top-100 list). These two coins are the first Mint State American eagles ever issued with the W mintmark, a fact that puts them among the most desirable coins and key dates.

	Total Certified Population	Most Commonly Certified	
		Grade	No. in Grade
NGC	2,186	MS-69	1,818
PCGS	2,058	MS-69	1,646

Mintage: *14,500 (estimated)*

Retail value in most common certified grade (MS-69): $900

2008-W $50 AMERICAN PLATINUM EAGLE, PROOF

Designed by John Mercanti (obverse) and Joel Iskowitz (reverse). The obverse features a portrait of Lady Liberty. The reverse features the final design in the three-year series entitled "The Foundations of American Democracy," and celebrates our nation's Judicial Branch of government.

Weight: .5003 ounces. *Composition:* 99.95% platinum.
Diameter: 27 mm. *Edge:* Reeded.

In 2007, platinum tested new heights, briefly breaking through the $1,000-per-ounce price barrier. The year 2008 was even more volatile. The metal's value surged well past $2,000 per ounce and then tumbled back to $800 per ounce by the end of the year. This extreme volatility in its value was a reflection of global economics—the downturn in the stock market that year caused an aggressive flight to tangible assets. Sales doubled or tripled for almost all of the bullion versions of the silver, gold, and platinum American eagles in 2008 from their 2007 numbers.

Curiously, the exact opposite is true of the collector versions of these coins. The Proof and Uncirculated versions sold directly by the Mint to collectors almost all sold at half the level in 2008 that they had sold in 2007. This is very well illustrated by the 2007 and 2008 $100 platinum eagle one ounce coins. Sales of the bullion coins were 7,202 in 2007 and 21,800 units in 2008, while the Proof version declined from 8,363 in 2007 to only 4,769 in 2008.

There is a likely explanation. Investors sought exposure to precious metals, causing the surge of interest in bullion. Collectors, meanwhile, buying coins with discretionary money, were much more sensitive to price. In 2003, the price for the 1/2-ounce $50 platinum eagle Proof was $587. In 2007, the Mint offered the $50 platinum eagle Proof coin for $810, a leap of $223 in five years. When the next year's Proof coin went on sale on May 5, 2008, its price was $1,175, an increase of $365 in just one year. This aggressive pricing on collectibles in an uncertain economy discouraged collectors from buying.

There is also one more consideration. Of all the Proof American eagles, the single-lowest mintage has always been the $50 platinum eagle 1/2-ounce coin. In every year since its first offering in 1997, the 1/2-ounce Proof platinum eagle has been the lowest-selling issue, except in 2003 when 87 more units were sold than its platinum 1/4-ounce compatriot. In 2008, when collectors were skittish or unwilling to buy Proof platinum coins at platinum's new-found dizzying heights, the $50 platinum eagle was most affected. Being the lowest-mintage Proof American eagle in nearly every year meant that it found a new low of just 4,020 coins in 2008, the lowest mintage figure of a Proof American eagle in any weight or metal. With so few to go around, this coin is already seldom-found in the marketplace and is widely thought to be a major key issue.

	Total Certified Population	Most Commonly Certified	
		Grade	No. in Grade
NGC	970	PF-70 UC	862
PCGS	578	PF-69 DC	353

Mintage: 4,020

Retail value in most common certified grade (PF-70UC): $1,700

Designed by John R. Sinnock. On the obverse, the head of Franklin Roosevelt faces left. LIBERTY appears in large letters along the left rim; IN GOD WE TRUST appears in small letters at the lower left, and the date appears at the bottom right. The reverse features a lit torch flanked by sprigs of olive and oak. UNITED STATES OF AMERICA arcs above, ONE DIME arcs below, and the motto E PLURIBUS UNUM runs in a straight line through the bottoms of the sprigs and torch.

Weight: 2.27 grams. *Composition:* Pure copper core sandwiched between outer layers of 75% copper and 25% nickel. *Diameter:* 17.9 mm. *Edge:* Reeded.

When this coin was first discovered in a Proof set in mid-1983, it was widely believed that it would be more common than it has ultimately proved to be. Since its initial discovery, only a few hundred examples have been found, certainly fewer than 400 in all. This figure makes it a bit scarcer than the 1970 No S Roosevelt dime.

No S Proof coins are made when the S mintmark is omitted from the die. A number of steps are involved in the creation of Proof dies, during which they are inspected, or at least handled, by many different people in the process. It surprises many that this type of error can occur, and by 1983 it had happened at least three times already.

It is clear when this error occurred. In 1983, as in all previous years, dies were created from working hubs that did not contain a mintmark. The working dies themselves received an impression from a mintmark punch before being prepared to strike Proof coins—a very involved process.

To strike Proof coins, first the working dies are cleaned with solvents to remove grease, metal dust, and oil. Next, they are sandblasted. This task is performed by hand with the field areas marked off by tape, undoubtedly a tedious process. The field areas are then polished to a high shine. To increase die-life and retain the effects of the polish and sandblasting, dies are then chromium-plated. Every 500 to 1,000 strikes, they are examined and refreshed by reprocessing if needed; if they are too worn, they are discarded. Over the years, the exact sequence of preparation has varied. This overview of the process, though, has been in use for the production of U.S. coins since 1970, according to Proof-coinage specialist Rick Tomaska. Sandblasting was ultimately replaced in 2009 by laser-frosting.

Like most Proof coins of its era, the 1983 No S Roosevelt dime is almost always seen with a notable deep or ultra cameo contrast. It is clear that, as with regular Proof dimes, its obverse die was handled and inspected many times before and during the coinage process. To make the Proof 1983 No S Roosevelt dime, then, a number of individuals failed to note the omitted S mintmark. In fact, the nature of the oversight is what makes these coins so interesting to collectors, and the rarity of the error makes them valuable.

This coin is the most-recent issue of No S Proof dimes reported to date. To avoid mistakes like this in the future, starting in 1985, Proof dies were created from a production hub that included the mintmark. It is likely that this is the coin that led to the change in this process. While this change has prevented another No S dime from being made, a No S Lincoln cent was still produced in 1990, and is number 13 on this list.

	Total Certified Population	Most Commonly Certified	
		Grade	No. in Grade
NGC	70	PF-69 UC	51
PCGS	137	PF-69 DC	73

Mintage: fraction of 3,279,126

Retail value in most common certified grade (PF-69 DC): $2,000

2000-D SACAGAWEA DOLLAR, "MILLENNIUM" VARIETY

Designed by Glenna Goodacre (obverse) and Thomas D. Rogers (reverse). The obverse features the Indian guide Sacagawea and her infant son. LIBERTY appears above her head; IN GOD WE TRUST appears at the left, and the date appears on the right side. The reverse features an eagle in flight surrounded by 13 stars. UNITED STATES OF AMERICA arcs around the upper reverse; ONE DOLLAR arcs around the bottom. E PLURIBUS UNUM appears in small letters in the left field.

Weight: 8.1 grams. *Composition:* Outer layers of 77% copper, 12% zinc, 7% manganese, and 4% nickel over a pure copper core. *Diameter:* 26.5 mm. *Edge:* Plain.

Among the product offerings included in the U.S. Mint's 2000 Holiday Catalog was a novel grouping called the United States Millennium Coinage and Currency Set. The set included a 2000-D Sacagawea dollar, a 2000 silver eagle, and a $1 note with the first four digits of its serial number being "2000." The edition was limited to 75,000 sets. Combining these items into a single set may have been thematically important to the Mint because the silver dollar and the dollar bill are clearly the most recognizable dollars. Now joining the ranks in the new millennium was the golden-colored Sacagawea dollar. Regardless of the intent or the message, there wasn't too much collector interest in the set—until the sets started arriving in collectors' hands, that is.

When buyers received the sets, they saw that the 2000-D Sacagawea dollar in the set was deeply reflective. It had clearly received special handling from the Mint, having been struck on polished planchets and from polished dies. This fact had not been promoted in the Mint's literature when they were offered for sale, and the presence of "prooflike" Sacagawea coins ignited a frenzy among collectors. The sets then quickly sold out from the Mint.

These coins are referred to as "prooflike" because they have some of the attributes of Proof coinage but are not true Proofs. For example, unlike Proof coins, they are not struck multiple times from the coinage dies, and therefore their striking-detail is no sharper than a regular business-strike (or circulation-issue) coin's detail. They also don't have true mirrorlike reflective fields, and unlike current Proofs they are mirrored throughout their surface and don't display cameo contrast between fields and the design area. Normally these attributes can be quite subtle; however, the differences between the Millennium Set Sacagawea dollar and the regular issue 2000-D Sacagawea are stark enough that they are readily distinguishable.

Most collectors consider the Millennium Set Sacagawea dollar to be a required element of the Sacagawea dollar series, and therefore a complete set will have two 2000-D coins: a regular Mint State example and the Millennium Set issue. Its status as a required element of any Sacagawea dollar collection has assured its enduring popularity. While the coin is often found in gem Uncirculated to superb Uncirculated condition, the best examples have very deeply reflective fields and are untoned and virtually free of contact marks or blemishes. Specialist collectors will pay substantial premiums for coins that have especially deep mirrors and are at the highest grades of preservation.

In retrospect, the most interesting aspect of this coin may be that the special finish, and therefore the desirability, of this coin was completely unexpected, and that the U.S. Mint had a special surprise for collectors who ordered the set. With 75,000 struck, it remains widely available for today's collectors, but since it's now required for set completion, demand certainly isn't going away.

	Total Certified Population	Most Commonly Certified	
		Grade	No. in Grade
NGC	36	MS-67 DMPL	17
PCGS	—	—	—
Mintage: 75,000			
Retail value in most common certified grade (MS-67 DMPL): $100			

Designed by Victor David Brenner (obverse) and Frank Gasparro (reverse). The obverse continues the design of 1909, featuring a bust of Lincoln facing right, the word LIBERTY to his left, and the date in the field in front of his coat. The legend IN GOD WE TRUST appears above his head. The reverse shows a frontal view of the Lincoln Memorial with UNITED STATES OF AMERICA and E PLURIBUS UNUM appearing above and ONE CENT below.

Weight: 2.5 grams. *Composition:* A core of 99.2% zinc and .8% copper, with a plating of pure copper. *Diameter:* 19 mm. *Edge:* Plain.

O n this aptly named variety, on the reverse of the coin the letters AM in the word AMERICA are close together, nearly touching. What makes this noteworthy is that all Lincoln cents produced from 1959 to 1991 had a comparatively broad spacing between these two letters. The design change was planned for release in 1993, and indeed all 1993 Lincoln cents, both Proof and Mint State issues, are of the Close AM variety.

The year 1992 marks a transitional year. All 1992 Proof coins are of the normal Wide AM variety, as are nearly all the currency-issue coins. But a very small number of 1992 cents from both Denver and Philadelphia are known to have the Close AM reverse. Fewer than two-dozen Denver Mint examples are reported, and only two 1992 Close AM cents from the Philadelphia Mint are known. The rare Philadelphia variety carries a catalog value in excess of $10,000.

While the payoff from finding a 1992 Close AM would be akin to winning the lottery, the odds of finding one are slim. In 1992, more than 4.6 billion cents were struck in Philadelphia, and another 4.4 billion were struck in Denver. If a single full die run were used to strike each coin, the chance of finding a Close AM may be on the order of 1 in 10,000. Based on average attrition rates, probably fewer than 60,000 survive from each Mint. To find one, you need to be deliberately looking for it.

That said, this variety isn't too hard to spot, and magnification makes the hunt a bit easier. To help with the attribution, there is a second clear difference that distinguishes the Close AM from the Wide AM variety. On a Close AM coin, the designer's initials, FG, are spaced farther away from the lower right side of the Lincoln Memorial. On the Wide AM variety, the G nearly touches the monument. It's worth confirming this diagnostic as well if attribution is ever in doubt. Of course, since most coins prior to 1992 are Wide AM and most coins dated after are Close AM, it's very easy to have coins of both reverse types for comparison.

The reason for all these minor design changes was never explicitly revealed by the Mint. They were likely aimed at improving die life to make the coin easier and more economical to produce. As numismatic author David W. Lange has noted in his *Complete Guide to Lincoln Cents*, beginning in 1992 such changes as this became a nearly annual occurrence, but most were imperceptible. The most noticeable of the changes has been this repositioning of the AM. Since all the 1993 cents, both Proof and Mint State, are of the Close AM reverse variety, many have speculated that the 1992 Close AM coins were struck as a test run before the change was implemented on full-scale production. Adding further credence to this theory, tests appear to have been conducted at both mints producing these coins, Philadelphia and Denver.

For circulating Lincoln cents, the design appears to have been an improvement, as the Close AM reverse remained in use until the final year of the Memorial reverse design in 2008. For Proof issues, the Close AM reverse was used in 1993, but in 1994 the Wide AM returned for use on all Proof issues until the end of the series. But as a boon to collectors, these rules were not applied with perfect consistency, and other Close AM and Wide AM varieties appear on the top-100 list. As some experts speculate that yet-undiscovered varieties may also exist, the hunt continues.

Pick-up point: AMERICA.

	Total Certified Population	Most Commonly Certified	
		Grade	No. in Grade
NGC	4	MS-65 RD	2
PCGS	2	MS-64 RD	2

Mintage: fraction of 9,097,578,300

Retail value in most common certified grade (MS-65 RD): $125

1982-D GEORGE WASHINGTON HALF DOLLAR COMMEMORATIVE

Designed by Elizabeth Jones. The obverse features George Washington astride a horse. The reverse depicts the eastern façade of Washington's home, Mount Vernon, with a heraldic eagle beneath.

Weight: 12.5 grams. *Composition:* 90% silver and 10% copper.
Diameter: 30.6 mm. *Edge:* Reeded.

Many were surprised in 1981 when the George Washington 250th-anniversary half dollar was announced. It had been 27 years since the last commemorative coin was struck, and collectors had all but lost hope that there would be new commemorative-coinage issues. Three factors formed the basis of inspiration for this coin, and together they overcame the long-time blockage of new commemorative programs.

First was the occasion. The year 1982 marked the 250th anniversary of George Washington's birth. While commemorative medals were being issued to recognize presidents in recent years, the milestone anniversary of the first president's birth had greater heft and was deemed more deserving of a coin. Secondly, the success of the Bicentennial coinage sold in 1975 and 1976 proved that commemorative-coinage programs could be profitably and successfully managed. Unlike later commemorative issues, proceeds for this coin would not go to a special interest or limited-purpose vehicle; rather, they would be used to pay down the national debt, a use of such general benefit that few could argue against this feature of the coin. And third, there was strong support for this coin from individuals who sought to pass a subsequent bill to make commemorative coins for the 1984 Los Angeles Olympics, which would be a greater challenge if the commemorative program had not already been restored.

The coin itself was to be struck in 90 percent silver, making it the first U.S. coin of this composition since 1964. It was also a half dollar, the denomination that accounted for all but two of the original silver commemorative coins issued between 1892 and 1954. In these ways, this coin was more similar to the early commemorative coins than the subsequent commemoratives. Other features of the program, however, suggested that this was a modern coin and a departure from the earlier issues. First, the coin was to be struck in both Proof and Uncirculated versions; this had contributed significantly to the collector sales of the Bicentennial coinage. Second, a total of 10 million coins were authorized to be struck between the two formats. This figure dwarfed any of the original commemorative-coin mintages from the earlier period, indicating that this was indeed a coin of the modern era.

The designs, created by U.S. Mint Chief Engraver Elizabeth Jones, show Washington on horseback on the obverse and Mount Vernon, his home, on the reverse. The sales cycle of the coin was not limited in duration and continued into 1985 with a modest price increase in later years. The Proofs were struck at the San Francisco Mint and Uncirculated coins at Denver, with total sales of 4,894,044 and 2,210,458, respectively. The coin and its design were so successful that it was given three awards in the inaugural Coin of the Year competition in 1984 for Most Historically Significant Coin, Most Popular Coin, and Coin of the Year.

Although they were sold individually in cellophane packs inside boxes, the Uncirculated versions did not receive special handling during production (other than multiple strikes to fully render the design). Coins were ejected from dies and allowed to tumble into bins, and thus were marred with contact marks. Later issues would be spared this rough treatment, and thus the Uncirculated 1982 George Washington half dollar is the scarcest modern commemorative at the highest grade levels.

	Total Certified Population	Most Commonly Certified	
		Grade	No. in Grade
NGC	3,644	MS-67	2,269
PCGS	2,350	MS-68	1,360
Distribution: 2,210,458			
Retail value in most common certified grade (MS-67): $75			

Designed by Elizabeth Jones. The obverse depicts a section of a Corinthian column. The obverse inscriptions read LIBERTY, 1800, FIRST CONVENING OF CONGRESS IN WASHINGTON, IN GOD WE TRUST, and 2001. The reverse features a view of the 1800 Capitol with the inscriptions UNITED STATES OF AMERICA, E PLURIBUS UNUM, and FIVE DOLLARS.

Weight: 8.359 grams. *Composition:* 90% gold and 10% silver (net weight .24187 ounces pure gold). *Diameter:* 21.6 mm. *Edge:* Reeded.

Whenever collectors first start to discover modern U.S. commemorative coins, they inevitably gravitate towards the Uncirculated Jackie Robinson $5 coin, with its impossibly low mintage of 5,174 coins. It is the most expensive coin in the set, and everyone involved in modern U.S. coins is aware of the importance of this coin. Ask which coin has the second-lowest mintage in the series, though, and the answer might not come so quickly: it's the Uncirculated version of the 2001 Capitol Visitors Center $5 coin, which has a puny mintage of just 6,761 coins. As a result, in addition to being the second-scarcest modern commemorative coin, it's also among the most expensive.

The cause of its small mintage is, of course, poor sales. It was known before the coin was issued that it could encounter some challenges. The coin commemorated the first convening of Congress in the Capitol building in 1800; this made it the fifth commemorative program in 11 years to recognize Congress either directly or through an affiliated institution. Since surcharges from the sale of this coin went to construct and maintain a new 446,000 square-foot U.S. Capitol Visitor Center, some collectors viewed this issue as Congress passing a tax on collectors for its own benefit.

The program was also large—a three-coin commemorative program with large mintage limits, making it similar in scale to the disastrously unsuccessful 1995 and 1996 Olympic coinage. There was no reason to think that the commemoration of the 6th Congress' first meeting in the Capitol building would merit a coin program with such a large scale.

Lastly, the coin designs themselves were met with little enthusiasm. Legislation only stipulated that the design be "emblematic of the first meeting of the United States Congress in the United States Capitol Building." Buildings on coins are seldom well received, but the $5 coin showed only the portion of the building that was complete in 1800: an unrecognizable, and unbalanced, square building. The Capitol building is certainly best known for its dome, which was actually the third dome to grace the building and was only completed in 1868. All three coins display the partially finished building. The $5 gold coin puts it on the reverse, while the obverse smartly shows a column, another widely recognized feature of the Capitol.

All of these features contributed to the poor sales of the coin when it was released in 2001. Despite the criticisms it received, it certainly does recognize a very worthwhile moment in U.S. history; the Capitol is, after all, among the world's greatest symbols of democracy. Fears that this bloated coinage program would mark a return to the excesses of the mid-1990s were, fortunately, unwarranted. Its fellow 2001 commemorative coin program, the American Buffalo commemorative, is among the most popular and bestselling coins in the history of modern commemoratives and marks a turn toward highly popular and successful issues, almost without exception, all the way into the next decade.

	Total Certified Population	Most Commonly Certified	
		Grade	No. in Grade
NGC	1,914	MS-70	1,054
PCGS	2,490	MS-69	2,285

Distribution: 6,761

Retail value in most common certified grade (MS-69): $1,750

1999 LINCOLN CENT, WIDE AM

Designed by Victor David Brenner (obverse) and Frank Gasparro (reverse). The obverse continues the design of 1909. The reverse shows a frontal view of the Lincoln Memorial with UNITED STATES OF AMERICA and E PLURIBUS UNUM appearing above and ONE CENT below.

Weight: 2.5 grams. *Composition:* A core of 99.2% zinc and .8% copper, with a plating of pure copper. *Diameter:* 19 mm. *Edge:* Plain.

While the precise purpose of these changes is not 100 percent clear, whether it might have been for either aesthetic reasons or to improve die life, the Mint experimented with different letter positioning on the reverse of the Lincoln cent throughout the 1990s. The most notable of these changes were adjustments to the spacing of the letters AM in AMERICA. In 1993, all coins had a "Close AM" reverse, with the letters nearly touching. This reverse was used for almost all business-strike (circulation-issue) coins until the end of the series in 2008. A reverse style with more spacing between the letters, the "Wide AM" reverse, was used for nearly all Proof issues from 1994 to 2008.

The compelling feature of these hub changes is that they were not followed with perfect consistency, and variations exist. In 2001, die-variety expert John Wexler found a circulation 2000 Lincoln cent with a Wide AM reverse, the version intended for Proof coinage. Shortly thereafter, a 1998 Wide AM Lincoln cent was also found. Both were discovered in roll quantity, and, although not common, they are available. Sometime later, the 1999 Wide AM Lincoln cent was found to fill in the gap. Today, only about 500 examples are known and they are by far the rarest of the Wide AM circulation Lincoln cents of this era.

Subtle and delicate hub variations of this type are usually not collectible because they are too minor to be noteworthy or interesting. These varieties, however, *are* noteworthy and interesting for two clear reasons. First, the difference in letter spacing is very easy to see. Reference coins for both the Wide AM and Close AM configurations can always be found from previous years' issues for comparison. Second, one hub style was used for Proof coinage, while the other was used for circulation coinage, suggesting to some that the wrong die or hub was used accidentally.

To add to the intrigue of these coins, Proof coins also exist with the Close AM reverse for the 1998-S and 1999-S issues. In other words, the business-strike-style reverse was used to make Proof coins. Enthusiasts will seek to complete the set of all reverse types for both Proof and Mint State issues. In the case of the Proof issues, the 1999-S is more common than the 1998-S, while the opposite is true for the Mint State issues.

It isn't known how many 1999 Wide AM Lincoln cents were made. Reverse dies can strike many hundreds of thousands or even a million Lincoln cents for circulation. The challenge with circulating Lincoln cent varieties is that if they are discovered well after their time of mintage, they become widely distributed and very difficult to find in quantity. While the number of known 1999 Wide AM Lincoln cents will certainly increase from today's levels, it's uncertain that a huge cache will ever be found.

Pick-up point: AMERICA.

	Total Certified Population	Most Commonly Certified	
		Grade	No. in Grade
NGC	96	MS-66 RD	29
PCGS	128	MS-65 RD	27

Mintage: fraction of 5,237,600,000

Retail value in most common certified grade (MS-66 RD): $850

Designed by John Flanagan. The obverse features the head of George Washington facing left, the word LIBERTY above his head and the date below it. The motto IN GOD WE TRUST appears in small letters in the left field. On the reverse, an eagle, with wings outspread, perches on a tight bundle of arrows. Two olive sprigs are joined beneath the eagle. The outer legends include UNITED STATES OF AMERICA above and QUARTER DOLLAR below. The motto E PLURIBUS UNUM appears in smaller letters above the eagle's head.

Weight: 6.25 grams. *Composition:* 90% silver and 10% copper. *Diameter:* 24.3 mm. *Edge:* Reeded.

The Washington quarter's design was successful from the outset. It was first produced in 1932, and its clean geometry recalls the art deco fashion of the time. To today's tastes, the design may appear overly sculptural and idealized, but it is classically well-balanced. It was also a remarkably easy design to coin, a feature perhaps more important than its aesthetics. The relief is low, and late-state die damage (a break or crack) is seldom seen on Washington quarters. It was a design that held up well to the high demands of production.

However, the low-relief design required that the Washington quarter be re-hubbed more frequently than other coinages, creating subtle variations among coins in the series. Hubs are used to create dies, and dies are then used to strike coins. When a coin is re-hubbed, a design change is made that is replicated throughout the entire coinage production. The Washington quarter was famously re-hubbed in 1934, when the relief on the obverse motto, IN GOD WE TRUST, was so low that the inscription could barely be read. A subsequent change (in two iterations) strengthened the letters. Another reverse alteration occurred in 1956.

In 1965, the reverse of the Washington quarter was re-hubbed to strengthen the detail on the reverse, most notably on the eagle's tail-feathers. This very shallow element of the coin's design was almost indiscernible on many of the Washington quarters of the early 1960s produced prior to the 1964 re-hubbing. In addition to sharpening the outline of the feathers, the Mint also added the rachis, or shaft of the feather. This feature was essentially absent from the design in previous years and makes the Reverse of 1965 Washington quarter readily distinguishable.

This new reverse hub with strengthened feather detail was intended for use on 1965 coinage. However, some of the new-style dies were impressed with D mintmarks and used to strike 1964-D quarters. The name given to this variety is "Reverse of 1965," or sometimes "Type C Reverse." While it is not known exactly how many of these coins were produced, they appear to account for only a small fraction of 1964-D Washington quarters.

This coin belongs to a class called transitional varieties, which occur when two design types, an old and a new, can be seen on a single coin. They are all very collectible, but this one is doubly special. The 1964-D quarter was the last silver quarter, while the 1965 version is the first copper-nickel-clad quarter. This transitional variety is actually the copper-nickel-clad reverse style used on a silver quarter. All 1965 quarters, even those struck in Denver, were made without mintmarks. When mintmarks resumed in 1968, they were placed on the obverse of the coin rather than the reverse, and this coin is thus also the only "Reverse of 1965"–style quarter to have a mintmark on that side.

Even though all these details make this coin interesting, there is not too much mystery about how it was produced. In 1965, the public began to pull silver coins from circulation as the Mint was striking copper-nickel-clad coins to replace them. In order to meet aggressive demand for coins, however, silver coinage was struck alongside copper-nickel-clad until 1966, but the silver coins were still dated 1964. These coins, then, could very well have been made at the same moment or even after the new reverse style came into general use. Rather than the new design being brought into use early, as some speculate, it is just as likely that these coins were produced alongside the 1965 issues or even as late as 1966.

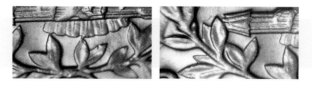

Pick-up points: Eagle's tail feathers, leaf at arrow tips.

	Total Certified Population	Most Commonly Certified	
		Grade	No. in Grade
NGC	50	MS-64	15
PCGS	17	MS-64	8

Mintage: fraction of 704,135,528

Retail value in most common certified grade (MS-64): $500

1965–1967 SPECIAL MINT SET COINAGE, ULTRA CAMEO

This entry is devoted to a particularly scarce group of highly coveted coins struck during a three-year period, from 1965 to 1967. The Coinage Act of 1965 mandated the end of circulating silver coinage in favor of copper-nickel-clad coinage. The transition was an enormous undertaking for the U.S. Mint. They were tasked with producing quantities of copper-nickel-clad coins to ultimately replace the silver coins presently in circulation. Because it was impractical—if not impossible—to completely replace all the currency at once, silver coins, too, continued to be struck until 1966. Working furiously, the Mint created an unprecedented number of coins in Philadelphia, Denver, and San Francisco.

The statistics for this period of production are staggering: before 1964, only three mintage figures of quarters exceeded 100 million, with the most coming in 1963 when the Denver Mint struck 135,288,184 quarters. In 1965, however, more than 1.8 *billion* quarters were struck! In the entire prior history of the silver quarter dollar, from 1796 to 1964, a total of 4.4 billion coins were struck for circulation. Between 1965 and 1967, more than 4.1 billion quarters were struck, so that in just three years, the U.S. Mint nearly matched the production of the previous 168.

To enable this enormous increase in production, the Mint cut back in other ways from 1965 to 1967. For one thing, they removed mintmarks from coins. Secondly, the Mint struck no Proof sets or Mint sets in these years, not wanting to devote labor and resources to that endeavor. To satisfy collectors, they issued Special Mint Sets, a hybrid of the Mint set and Proof set. There was less emphasis on packaging and production quality than for normal Proof sets, but the coins were specially struck for this purpose. Possibly as a measure to curb demand, their issue price was set at $4, nearly double the price of Proof sets or Mint sets in previous years.

The coins in these sets vary considerably in their appearance from one to another. Some of them present a rather gray satin surface with striated die polish that is unique to Special Mint Set (or SMS) coinage, particularly those coins dated 1965. Others resemble regular circulation-strike coins with few distinguishing characteristics, while others yet resemble true Proof coinage with highly reflective, mirrorlike fields and contrasting frosted devices. These are said to be early strikes from fresh dies.

Coins that display contrast between their devices (the design area of the coins) and their fields (the blank portions) are referred to as cameo, named after the carved relief jewelry with related characteristics. Coins with the strongest or sharpest level of contrast are referred to as ultra cameo or deep cameo. Although very rare, some SMS coins with this strongest level of cameo contrast are known and are valuable.

The reason that these coins are so desirable is that they resemble the highest-quality Proof coins, and SMS coinage is today sought by collectors of Proof coinage. Only a few dozen ultra cameo examples have been identified for each of the cent, nickel, dime, and quarter dollar. The Kennedy half dollar, especially the 1967 issue, is slightly more available with very deep cameo contrast, and a few hundred exist. While most SMS coins are relatively available and affordable, these high-contrast coins are the noteworthy exception.

	Total Certified Population	Most Commonly Certified	
		Grade	No. in Grade
NGC	—	—	—
PCGS	—	—	—

Mintage: fraction of 6,484,927

Retail value cannot be speculated, given the extreme rarity of this variety.

1982 LINCOLN CENT, SMALL DATE, COPPER-PLATED ZINC

Designed by Victor David Brenner (obverse) and Frank Gasparro (reverse). The obverse continues the design of 1909. The reverse shows a frontal view of the Lincoln Memorial with UNITED STATES OF AMERICA and E PLURIBUS UNUM appearing above and ONE CENT below.

Weight: 2.5 grams. *Composition:* A core of 99.2% zinc and .8% copper, with a plating of pure copper. *Diameter:* 19 mm. *Edge:* Plain.

The considerable expense of producing a mostly copper cent was recognized in the early 1970s, yet the composition of 95 percent copper and 5 percent zinc persisted until 1982. That fateful year marked the transition from a mostly copper cent to the copper-plated zinc coin that we have today (97.6 percent zinc and 2.4 percent copper). Also in 1982, a hub variation was introduced with slightly lower relief and sharper detail that made the coin easier to strike. Since the newly modified design had a smaller date, collectors named it the Small Date and the old style was called the Large Date.

All told, the change in composition and the new hub-design created seven major varieties of circulating cents in 1982:

1. Bronze 1982 Large Date
2. Bronze 1982 Small Date
3. Bronze 1982-D (all are Large Date)
4. Copper-Plated Zinc 1982 Large Date
5. Copper-Plated Zinc 1982 Small Date
6. Copper-Plated Zinc 1982-D Large Date
7. Copper-Plated Zinc 1982-D Small Date

Although the original alloy for the bronze 1982 cents no longer contained tin, and was therefore technically brass, collectors still commonly referred to its composition as bronze, the original composition of the Lincoln cent. The first Lincoln cent was released in 1909, and never before 1982 had such a variety of cents been released in a single year. Because no Mint sets were issued in 1982, many marketers issued seven-coin sets of their own. This remains one of the easiest and most economical ways to purchase all seven varieties.

Telling the seven coins apart isn't challenging. First, there are the different date styles: the Small Date is much smaller and further from the rim. Its 9 is pointed at its lower terminus and the top loop of the 8 is round rather than oval. To distinguish the metal types, it is easiest to weigh the coins. Bronze cents weigh 3.1 grams, while zinc cents weigh 2.5 grams. Some may even be able to spot bubbles underneath the surface of the copper-plating, which is another sure way to identify zinc cents.

In fact, the Mint faced a serious challenge in creating these cents with the new, zinc-heavy alloy. Air pockets underneath the plating create the appearance of a rough, blemished surface. Black spots of corrosion can also be seen on many 1982 cents. Quality control appears to have been slightly better at Denver, and the toughest coin to acquire in gem Uncirculated condition is the Philadelphia Mint copper-plated zinc 1982 Small Date variety. Although not an expensive coin per se, it carries the biggest premium of the seven different cent varieties that were minted in 1982.

In the very highest grade levels, all seven coins will pose a challenge. Through 1983, the Mint struggled with the copper-plating, and both 1982 and 1983 zinc cents suffer from production issues. The 1982 Small Date copper-plated zinc cent was the first cent produced of this composition, the first of this new hub style, and the scarcest cent of that year, all of which combine to earn it a place on the list of 100 Greatest U.S. Modern Coins.

	Total Certified Population	Most Commonly Certified	
		Grade	No. in Grade
NGC	342	MS-65 RD	191
PCGS	46	MS-67 RD	20

Mintage: fraction of 10,712,525,000

Retail value in most common certified grade (MS-65 RD): $200

1986 $1 AMERICAN SILVER EAGLE

Designed by Adolph A. Weinman (obverse) and John Mercanti (reverse). The obverse features Weinman's Liberty Walking design used on half dollars from 1916 through 1947. Weinman's initials are on the hem of the gown. The reverse design is a rendition of a heraldic eagle.

Weight: 31.101 grams. *Composition:* 99.93% silver and .07% copper (net weight 1 ounce pure silver). *Diameter:* 40.6 mm. *Edge:* Reeded.

The American silver eagle was an instant success and has become the most popular silver bullion coin in history. The first release of this coin came on November 24, 1986, when each of the 28 authorized distributors bought their full allocation of 50,000 examples, adding up to a maximum sellout of 1.4 million coins. To meet demand, the Mint announced it would produce five million coins by the end of 1986. In addition to striking coins at West Point, new production lines were added at the Denver and San Francisco mints. The total mintage of the 1986 silver eagle exceeded 5.39 million coins. Since the coin is struck without mintmark, it is not possible to distinguish coins from different mints.

The coin was introduced as a silver investment vehicle and sold at a small premium to its precious-metal content, one ounce of pure silver. It reuses the obverse design crafted by A.A. Weinman for the Liberty Walking half dollar (in use from 1916 to 1947), often called the most beautiful U.S. silver coin. The reverse shows a modern re-imagination of the heraldic eagle, designed by U.S. Mint engraver John Mercanti. It also has a symbolic one-dollar face value, even though it trades based on the value of its silver metal content.

Sales of the coin continued unabated into 1987, reaching more than 11 million coins—a record that would not be surpassed until 2008. In 1988, however, when sales declined by more than half of the previous year's totals, blame was placed on the small distribution network, and legislators advocated an open-sales system. Distributors countered that the novelty of the coin had worn off, and that current levels reflected investor interest—a claim that seems justified because sales of the coin had been steady since the first 1986 issue.

More than 200 million silver eagles have been sold to date, including a record 30 million in 2009 prompted by silver's surge in value. The price of silver more than doubled from 2007 to 2009, and increased in value five-fold from decade lows. While this reflects investor interest, the silver eagle is also among the most widely collected modern coins, and Proof coins and other special issues are avidly collected alongside the bullion issue.

The silver used to make the original silver eagles was taken from the national-defense silver stockpile managed by the Defense Logistics Agency, and sales of the coin have generated hundreds of millions of dollars for the agency. Because of the enduring popularity of the eagle, the silver stockpile was depleted in 2002. This prompted legislation that allows the Mint to purchase silver from domestic sources so as to continue production without interruption, ensuring that eagles will be produced well into the future. This 1986 bullion issue that makes the list of the 100 Greatest U.S. Modern Coins is the coin that started it all.

	Total Certified Population	Most Commonly Certified	
		Grade	No. in Grade
NGC	76,821	MS-69	75,622
PCGS	5,005	MS-69	3,692
Mintage: 5,393,005			
Retail value in most common certified grade (MS-69): $75			

Designed by Victor David Brenner (obverse) and Frank Gasparro (reverse). The obverse continues the design of 1909. The reverse shows a frontal view of the Lincoln Memorial with UNITED STATES OF AMERICA and E PLURIBUS UNUM appearing above and ONE CENT below.

Weight: 2.5 grams. *Composition:* A core of 99.2% zinc and .8% copper, with a plating of pure copper. *Diameter:* 19 mm. *Edge:* Plain.

Proof coinage is struck purposefully for presentation purposes and not for use as money in circulation. Both historically and presently, the goal of Proof coinage is to showcase a nation's coinage both to demonstrate artistry and to show off the technical capabilities of the Mint. Proof coins are made using a controlled process, with considerable attention paid to each step of their production. Specially prepared blanks receive multiple blows from a coinage die that has been treated to render the design in the best possible way. Proof coins are then sold in sets that include Proof versions of all coins struck during a given year.

Because of the careful scrutiny they receive, there are relatively few collectible die varieties of Proof coins. The few that do exist seem to have slipped through the cracks without explanation, suggesting that an error occurred at the Mint. This last point plays a major role in collectors' fascination with Proof die varieties.

This is especially true of a curious die variety found on some Proof Lincoln cents from 1998, the Proof 1998-S Close AM Lincoln cent. For one year, 1993, the reverse of all Proof Lincoln cents showed the letters AM in AMERICA nearly touching. This was part of a subtle design modification meant to improve die life (a cost-saving measure) and was put into use on both Proof and circulating coins. In 1994, the design modification was retained for circulating coins, but the Wide AM reverse, which showed the letters more widely spaced, was resumed for all Proof Lincoln cents until 1998.

The 1998-S Proof Lincoln cent can be found both ways—with either widely or closely spaced letters. Finding both is not easy. Only a few hundred Proof 1998-S Close AM Lincoln cents are known from the 2,086,507 total coins produced. The vast majority of that total is of the Wide AM variety. Some research suggests that as few as 15,000 Close AM coins, less than one percent of the total mintage, were struck in 1998.

No one knows for sure why the variety exists. One popular theory is that a hub used for creating dies for circulation coins was used; the die then received special preparation for coining Proof coins. This variety is thus sometimes referred to as having the "circulation-style reverse." The quality and appearance of the coin's finish is no different from a regular Proof, but the arrangement of the reverse letters is the same as that seen on circulating coins.

Without explanation, the variety was created again in 1999, and a 1999-S Close AM Proof Lincoln cent also exists. It's about four to five times more common than the 1998 version, though. Additionally, a typo in a widely used variety reference suggested that a 2000-S Close AM cent also exists. None have yet been reported, and the variety guide has since been corrected, but this original mis-listing is occasionally replicated and quoted.

Pick-up point: AMERICA.

	Total Certified Population	Most Commonly Certified	
		Grade	No. in Grade
NGC	12	PF-69 RDUC	9
PCGS	78	PF-69 RDDC	53

Mintage: fraction of 2,086,507

Retail value in most common certified grade (PF-69 RDDC): $100

1970-D KENNEDY HALF DOLLAR

Designed by Gilroy Roberts (obverse) and Frank Gasparro (reverse). On the obverse, the head of John F. Kennedy faces left. LIBERTY arcs across the top of the obverse; the date arcs along the bottom and IN GOD WE TRUST runs in a straight line beneath Kennedy's head. The reverse features a heraldic eagle, similar to that seen on the 1801 through 1807 and 1892 through 1915 half dollars, within a circle of 50 stars. UNITED STATES arcs around the top and HALF DOLLAR arcs along the bottom of the reverse.

Weight: 11.50 grams. *Composition:* 80% silver and 20% copper bonded to an inner core of 20.9% silver and 79.1% copper. *Diameter:* 30.6 mm. *Edge:* Reeded.

Nearly every year since 1947, the U.S. Mint has sold Mint sets—annual coin sets that include all the coins struck for circulation in a given year. From 1951 to 1981, they sold sets of some sort each year without interruption, and this became the easiest way for collectors to acquire an Uncirculated example of each coin from each mint. During these years, these annual coin sets boomed in popularity, growing from 8,654 sets sold in 1951 to two million by the late 1960s.

In 1970, for the first time, these sets contained something of a curiosity. They included the 1970-D Kennedy half dollar—a coin that was never struck for general circulation and can only be found in the 1970 Mint set. Its mintage was only the 2.15 million pieces required for the net sales of 1970 Mint sets. To find another half dollar with a similarly low mintage, one must go all the way back to the 1938-D Liberty Walking half dollar, a classic rarity.

In 1964, the first Kennedy half dollar was introduced with a composition of 90 percent silver. An incredible 273 million examples were struck in Philadelphia, while the Denver Mint struck another 156 million. The Coinage Act of 1965, which suspended the striking of silver coins for circulation, included a special provision for the half dollar, then the largest circulating coin. The act stipulated that the half dollar was to be struck in a silver-clad composition that included 40 percent silver through 1970, and then silver was to be phased out entirely. To meet demand from those who desired silver, half dollars were made in considerable numbers, reaching a peak of 295 million in 1967. The Mint made another 247 million half dollars in 1968, and struck nearly 130 million half dollars for circulation in 1969. But the very next year, in 1970, not a single half dollar was struck for circulation.

This puts the rarity of the 1970-D half dollar into context. Such a low mintage (only two million struck) would not be seen again until 2006, long after half dollars ceased to have wide use in circulation. By 1970, the production boom had created enough coins to meet demand, and more Kennedy half dollars were not needed for circulation. This is a situation that is being repeated today. Now, Kennedy half dollars are struck almost exclusively for collectors. Sales of Mint sets, rolls, and bags from the Mint directly to collectors account for the entire current production of half dollars. It's thought that present demand for coins in circulation can still be met using a stockpile of coins struck before 2001, as their current use is mostly confined to casino payouts.

Because of its low mintage, the 1970-D is the most valuable Kennedy half dollar in average Uncirculated grades and the key date in the series. Many Kennedys of this era are challenging coins in the very highest grades because their production quality was rather low, but examples from all levels are known from Mint sets and from the large quantity of coins struck for circulation. Because of its low original mintage, the 1970-D variety's place among the most important business-strike Kennedy half dollars is unlikely to be challenged.

	Total Certified Population	Most Commonly Certified	
		Grade	No. in Grade
NGC	1,044	MS-64	442
PCGS	2,158	MS-65	934

Mintage: 2,150,000

Retail value in most common certified grade (MS-65): $100

Designed by Augustus Saint-Gaudens (obverse) and Miley Busiek (reverse). The obverse features a modified rendition of the Augustus Saint-Gaudens design used on U.S. $20 gold pieces from 1907 until 1933. The reverse displays a "family of eagles" motif.

Weight: 33.931 grams. *Composition:* 91.67% gold, 3% silver, and 5.33% copper (net weight 1 ounce pure gold). *Diameter:* 32.7 mm. *Edge:* Reeded.

Collector demand for Proof gold eagles always contracts when gold prices decline. Unlike investors, who see dips in prices as buying opportunities, collectors become fickle when prices fall. While this may seem counterintuitive, collectors are slow to return for more when they buy coins from the Mint only to see them trading for discounts in the aftermarket. Collectors of Proof gold eagles experienced this frustration as the price of gold steadily declined from the mid-1990s through 2001.

In 1998, the Mint announced that it would lower the issue price of the one-ounce gold eagle $50 Proof coin from $589 to $570, a rollback that brought its price to the same level it had been at in 1990. "We looked at the substantial fall in gold prices in recent months and concluded that we needed to share these lower costs with our customers," Mint Director Philip N. Diehl said in a U.S. Mint press release announcing the decrease.

In order to further spur sales, the maximum mintage was also lowered from 45,000 to 35,000 examples, a measure that typically appeals to collectors. Buyers responded modestly to lower prices and mintage limits, buoying sales. One major factor is worth noting: in 1990, gold teetered around $400 per ounce, while in 1998, it had slid to the $300-per-ounce mark. Had the Proof eagle's prices been adjusted accordingly, much more aggressive sales increases certainly would have been seen.

In the following years—1999, 2000 and 2001—prices remained unchanged and mintage maximums were only slightly increased, up to 40,000 in 1999 and 41,000 in 2000 and 2001. With European central banks selling off gold, however, the metal's value declined further still, bouncing around the $260-per-ounce mark. The Mint did not respond to these new levels, and kept its prices steady.

During this same time, wholesale trading of the one-ounce Proof gold eagles continued at levels of roughly $150 to $200 above the per-ounce price of gold, but this was still $100 to $150 lower than the U.S. Mint issue price. Fed-up collectors backed away, and only 24,555 of the 2001-W gold eagle $50 Proof were sold, the lowest in the coin's history. As the value of gold increased in 2002 and in each subsequent year, so did the total number of units sold, leaving the 2001 issue as the lowest-mintage one-ounce gold eagle $50 Proof in the series. Since collectors of one-ounce Proof gold eagles commonly seek to build the whole series by date, the 2001-W is emerging as a key date. To avoid years of stagnant prices leading to a decline in sales, the U.S. Mint ultimately revised its pricing policy; starting in 2009, the Mint began re-pricing coins weekly to accord with price movements in precious metals.

	Total Certified Population	Most Commonly Certified	
		Grade	No. in Grade
NGC	1,278	PF-69 UC	862
PCGS	1,312	PF-69 DC	1,213

Mintage: 24,555

Retail value in most common certified grade (PF-69): $2,200

1990-S DOUBLED-DIE OBVERSE WASHINGTON QUARTER, PROOF

Designed by John Flanagan. The obverse features the head of George Washington facing left, the word LIBERTY above his head and the date below. The motto IN GOD WE TRUST appears in small letters in the left field. On the reverse, an eagle with wings outspread perches on a tight bundle of arrows. Two olive sprigs are joined beneath the eagle. The outer legends include UNITED STATES OF AMERICA above and QUARTER DOLLAR below. The motto E PLURIBUS UNUM appears in smaller letters above the eagle's head.

Weight: 5.67 grams. *Composition:* Outer layers of 75% copper and 25% nickel bonded to a core of pure copper. *Diameter:* 24.3 mm. *Edge:* Reeded.

This coin is almost too rare to be included among the 100 Greatest U.S. Modern Coins. Because fewer than 20 examples have been identified since it was first discovered nearly two decades ago, this coin has failed to create the publicity that has been generated by a number of its counterparts on this list. It is unquestionably one of the best doubled dies in the Washington quarter series.

One thing that makes this coin so interesting for specialists is its attribution diagnostics. *Diagnostics* are the specific details of a coin that distinguish it. Doubled dies are created when a working die receives two impressions of the coin's design as the die is created. Usually, this occurs when the hub or die has rotated. Close to the pivot point of the rotation, doubling will be minor. It will widen farther away from the pivot. The exact features of the doubling will be identical on all the coins struck by the doubled die.

The doubling is most-visible in two areas of this particular coin. First, it can be seen on the date, where a second impression sits northeast of the first date. Second, doubling can be seen most prominently on the mintmark, which shows two S's, one slightly above and to the right of the other one that sits underneath it. It is just the luck of the way that this doubled die was created that

imparted this trait, the diagnostic feature that makes this coin so exciting.

Doubling on the mintmark wasn't seen on a doubled die before this coin. Until 1985, mintmarks were added to Proof dies after they were hubbed in a separate process. Starting in 1968, a small mintmark punch would add the S mintmark for San Francisco, where all Proof versions of circulating coinage were made. If the mintmark was doubled, that doubling was confined to the mintmark—a variety called a *repunched mintmark.* By 1990, however, since the mintmark was now imparted in the same process as the rest of the coin's design, a doubled mintmark meant something else—a true doubled die. Not only is the diagnostic exciting, but the amount of separation is significant. The doubling is readily visible with the naked eye, but, like with most die varieties, the coin is best observed under magnification to really appreciate its drama.

The other shocking aspect of the coin is that so few have been found. It was first discovered by New Hampshire coin dealer Jim Carr not long after the Proof set's release. The 1990 Proof set and 1990 Prestige Proof set are home to three great varieties, including the 1990 No S Lincoln cent (number 13 on this list), this doubled die, and a doubled-die Jefferson nickel (see number 60). Because of all the wonderful coins that can be found in this set, 1990 Proof sets are probably examined more closely than any other date of modern Proof set. It's estimated that there are 2,000 to 2,500 of these coins spread among the 3.2 million Proof and Prestige Proof sets issued in 1990. Even though these quarters are widely distributed, it's still hard to explain why so few have been found. Some have begun to speculate that the mistake was discovered at the Mint prior to release and many of the coins were destroyed. If this is true, the estimated mintage number will need to be revised downward.

Pick-up points: Date, mintmark.

	Total Certified Population	Most Commonly Certified	
		Grade	No. in Grade
NGC	3	PF-69 UC	3
PCGS	7	PF-69 DC	3

Mintage: fraction of 3,299,559

Retail value unknown due to rarity; most common grade, PF-69 DC.

Designed by William Krawczewicz (obverse) and Malcolm Farley (reverse). The obverse design features a male swimmer with the inscriptions LIBERTY and IN GOD WE TRUST, along with the date 1996. The reverse features symbols of the Olympic Games, including a torch, rings, a Greek column, and the number 100, representing the 100th anniversary of the modern Olympic Games. The inscriptions around the edge read UNITED STATES OF AMERICA, E PLURIBUS UNUM, and ATLANTA 1996.

Weight: 11.34 grams. *Composition:* 75% copper and 25% nickel bonded to an inner core of pure copper. *Diameter:* 30.6 mm. *Edge:* Reeded.

A number of modern commemoratives appear on this list of the 100 Greatest U.S. Modern Coins, and for the most part they fall into two categories: First are coins that are thematically relevant, so that there is always a strong base of demand. Second are coins that proved unpopular at the time of issue and, as a result, few examples were coined. Their low mintage makes them desirable to collectors—those coins that originally proved unpopular become the most coveted. The Uncirculated 1996-S Olympic Swimming half dollar is among the most significant of the coins that fall into the latter category, because it heralded wide-sweeping changes in the commemorative-coinage program.

As the Olympic Games were being held in Atlanta, there was reason to think that the commemoratives would be popular. For the 1996 Olympics commemorative half dollars, a maximum mintage of three million coins was authorized by Congress for the Proof and Uncirculated versions combined. Being one of the most popular sports at the Games and having the most events, swimming was a logical sport to choose for a commemorative. The United States is also dominant in Olympic swimming, having won a total of 489 medals in competition over the years, followed by Australia in second place with 168. The coin design itself was also pleasing and modern.

The slow sales of the Swimming half dollar were recognized immediately. The coin design and theme were not to blame. The cause was the sheer number of commemorative coins that were issued in the mid-1990s. The 1995 and 1996 Atlanta Olympic Games commemorative-coinage program consisted of 16 different coins (or 32 if both Proof and Uncirculated versions are counted). Furthermore, during those same two years, there was a three-coin Civil War Battlefields commemorative program, a Special Olympics dollar, a National Community Service dollar, and the two-coin Smithsonian commemorative program. Counting Proof and Uncirculated versions, this is 46 total commemorative coins in just two years. Adding to the list, the Olympics had already been the theme for commemorative coins in 1983, 1984, 1988, and 1992, accounting for 23 additional Olympic coins over the span of 10 years.

On August 1, 1997, sales were progressing so slowly that the U.S. Mint issued a press release. Of the three million coins authorized, it said, only 49,571 Swimming half dollars had sold. "The consequences of the low demand for 1995-96 Olympic Coins is that collectors still have the opportunity to purchase coins that will have among the lowest mintages of all the modern commemoratives," said Mint Director Philip N. Diehl. "Some mintages are remarkably low, especially among the uncirculated coins, and many of these were sold overseas in 32-coin sets that are unlikely to be broken up. We want our collectors to be aware of this unique opportunity while the Olympic coins are still available from the Mint."

This was a unique opportunity for collectors, but poor sales meant that the U.S. Mint was losing money. The Mint reported a $3.2 million loss for the Olympics program as of March 31, 1996, according to a U.S. Government Accountability Office report titled "Commemorative Coins Could Be More Profitable," published in 1996. The report also outlined a series of recommendations that included limiting the number of commemorative programs and limiting their mintages. For the most part, the recommendations were instituted and have contributed to the resurgence in popularity of modern commemoratives over the past decade. The low mintage of the Swimming half dollar makes it by far the most valuable of all the commemorative half dollars, and as an agent of change in the U.S. Mint commemorative program it has an important place in the annals of numismatics.

	Total Certified Population	Most Commonly Certified	
		Grade	No. in Grade
NGC	478	MS-69	375
PCGS	667	MS-69	593

Distribution: 49,533

Retail value in most common certified grade (MS-69): $175

(2007) GEORGE WASHINGTON DOLLAR, MISSING EDGE LETTERING

Designed by Joseph Menna (obverse) and Don Everhart (reverse). The obverse features a portrait of George Washington with the inscriptions GEORGE WASHINGTON, 1st PRESIDENT, and the years of his administration, 1789-1797. The reverse features a rendition of the Statue of Liberty with the inscriptions UNITED STATES OF AMERICA and $1. The date, mintmark, and mottos IN GOD WE TRUST and E PLURIBUS UNUM are missing from the edge.

Weight: 8.1 grams. *Composition:* Outer layers of 77% copper, 12% zinc, 7% manganese, and 4% nickel over a core of pure copper. *Diameter:* 26.5 mm. *Edge:* Lettered.

Each modern coin now includes the motto IN GOD WE TRUST, the word LIBERTY, the phrase E PLURIBUS UNUM, the date, and the mintmark in its design. For the new series of Presidential dollar coins, the name of the president, the number denoting the order in which each served, and the years in office were also to appear on the coin. This was so much text that, quite naturally, there was concern about how to still balance an attractive design.

In order to leave as much room as possible for a large portrait while nevertheless rendering a great design, a solution was proposed in the Presidential $1 Coin Act of 2005: "In order to revitalize the design of United States coinage and return circulating coinage to its position as not only a necessary means of exchange in commerce, but also as an object of aesthetic beauty in its own right, it is appropriate to move many of the mottos and emblems, the inscription of the year, and the so-called 'mint marks' that currently appear on the 2 faces of each circulating coin to the edge of the coin, which would allow larger and more dramatic artwork on the coins."

Opening up the design in this way presented a great opportunity, to be sure, but no circulating coin in the United States had had an edge inscription in more than 170 years! The U.S. Mint simply did not possess the equipment or the experience to repeat this process hundreds of millions of times. They scrambled to find a solution, buying new minting equipment and installing it at the mints in Philadelphia and Denver, where coins for circulation were to be struck. Certainly, the single most-compelling characteristic of the newly issued Presidential dollar coins was their edge lettering.

Collectors around the country clamored to get their first look at these coins and their unique incuse, inscribed edge. But only days after the first George Washington dollar coins were released, coins were found with plain edges, having missed the edge-lettering process entirely: the date, mintmark, and other legends were all absent. Names sprung up for these errors, including the Plain Edge or, more colloquially, the Smooth Edge Washington dollar. But because this coin lacked the motto IN GOD WE TRUST, it soon garnered a new nickname—the "Godless dollar." That name, along with the sensation of this new error coin, caught the attention of the national media.

In response, only three weeks after the coin was first released, the U.S. Mint issued a statement indicating that they had struck more than 300 million Washington dollar coins and, due to the implementation of this new complex, high-volume system, the edge lettering had been missed on an unspecified number of coins. They stated that this error occurred at the Philadelphia Mint.

Today, experts suggest that more than 200,000 George Washington dollar coins were struck without edge lettering. Their high mintage makes them easily obtainable, and many collectors include an example as part of their regular collection. Altered Washington dollars sanded down to simulate the missing inscription are abundant, and third-party authentication is recommended.

Standard edge lettering (left) and blank edges (right).

	Total Certified Population	Most Commonly Certified	
		Grade	No. in Grade
NGC	40,817	MS-65	24,897
PCGS	20,229	MS-65	10,699

Mintage: fraction of 176,680,000

Retail value in most common certified grade (MS-65): $200

Designed by John R. Sinnock. On the obverse, the head of Franklin Roosevelt faces left. LIBERTY appears in large letters along the left rim; IN GOD WE TRUST appears in small letters at the lower left, and the date appears at the bottom right. The reverse features a lit torch flanked by sprigs of olive and oak. UNITED STATES OF AMERICA arcs above, ONE DIME arcs below, and the motto E PLURIBUS UNUM runs in a straight line through the bottoms of the sprigs and torch.

Weight: 2.27 grams. *Composition:* A pure copper core sandwiched between outer layers of 75% copper and 25% nickel. *Diameter:* 17.9 mm. *Edge:* Reeded.

The Proof 1970 No S dime is said to be the most common of all the No S Proof coins, although this by no means makes it common: far fewer than 500 examples are known. Since 1968, all Proof versions of circulating coinage have been struck at San Francisco and included an S mintmark. In at least five instances, the S mintmark was mistakenly omitted from the dies, creating these highly desirable varieties.

First discovered in an original Proof set in early 1971, the 1970 No S Roosevelt dime was officially confirmed by the Mint. They also acknowledged that they had made 2,200 examples, which were then packaged among the more than 3.2 million Proof sets for that year. In one sense, the small likelihood of finding one of these coins makes it surprising that so many have been found. They are easy to identify, though, and their value makes searching them out worthwhile.

These coins are often in very good, attractive condition, and examples will frequently show mild cameo contrast. Professional authentication is recommended to avoid spurious coins made from business-strike 1970 dimes that have been altered to look like Proofs. Proof coins are struck twice from specially prepared dies and have crisp detail and sharp, squared rims. Fortunately, if ever in doubt about a coin's authenticity, it's possible to acquire a regular S mintmark Proof example for comparison, as these are readily available.

The first No S dime was made in 1968 (see number three), the first year the Proof dimes included the S mintmark. That first coin is incredibly scarce, with just a few dozen known, compared with a few hundred for this coin. But if this is the most common No S dime, there is still some debate over which is the rarest. In 1978, two Proof 1975 No S dimes were discovered and confirmed by prominent numismatists.

Since that time, no other discoveries have been made of the 1975 variety and no example has ever been certified by a major grading service. This variety is now starting to be dropped from published resources and reverting to unconfirmed status—many specialists now doubt its existence entirely. If it does exist, the 1975 No S dime is one of the great rarities of the 20th century and will assume a vaunted position on the list of 100 Greatest U.S. Modern Coins—likely the number one spot. But until it's confirmed, it remains off the list.

	Total Certified Population	Most Commonly Certified	
		Grade	No. in Grade
NGC	4,282	MS-65	1,652
PCGS	2,773	MS-64	1,190

Mintage: fraction of 2,632,810

Retail value in most common certified grade (PF-68): $1,500

1995 DOUBLED-DIE OBVERSE LINCOLN CENT

Designed by Victor David Brenner (obverse) and Frank Gasparro (reverse). The obverse continues the design of 1909. The reverse shows a frontal view of the Lincoln Memorial with UNITED STATES OF AMERICA and E PLURIBUS UNUM appearing above and ONE CENT below.

Weight: 3.11 grams. *Composition:* 95% copper and 5% tin and zinc. *Diameter:* 19 mm. *Edge:* Plain.

In late February 1995, Felix Dausilio of Bridgeport, Connecticut, a 47-year-old school custodian who had been collecting coins for only three years, made a very important discovery. Examining coins from just two rolls of Lincoln cents, he spotted an example with doubled lettering. Although he had not been collecting for very long, he knew exactly what he had found: the first 1995 Doubled-Die Obverse Lincoln cent.

The first weekend in March 1995, the coin was displayed at a major coin convention in Atlanta, Georgia, and word spread throughout the numismatic press. Because the coin's discovery came 40 years after the most visually dramatic Lincoln cent doubled die, the 1955 variety, numerous comparisons were made, further helping to cement the status of the coin among collectors. And then, the national media caught wind of the story, and a number of articles appeared throughout local and national newspapers, including, famously, a front page mention in *USA Today*. The Associated Press ran a wire story and Dausilio appeared on a Hartford, Connecticut, television station. The nation was captivated by a Lincoln cent that could be found in pocket change and carried a collector value of more than a hundred dollars.

The coin was created, like all doubled dies, when the hub used to create its die rotated between impressions. All examples struck from this obverse die show identical doubling on the design elements. The 1995 Doubled-Die Obverse Lincoln cent shows a clearly doubled and nicely separated impression of the word LIBERTY and slightly less prominent doubling on the motto, IN GOD WE TRUST. From all accounts, it seems likely that a full production run of cents was struck from this die, with typical die life exceeding 600,000 coins. In 1995, the media attention created a frenzy, and collectors began furiously searching for 1995 Doubled-Die Obverse Lincoln cent coins. Surprisingly, they were found in significant numbers. Dealers and collectors probably rounded up more than 50,000 of them from original rolls.

In a sense, it is fortunate that so many examples of these cents have been preserved, making it a popular and findable variety. Sometimes, exciting discoveries prove too elusive to become collectible. In this instance, high-grade pieces, even MS-68 Red examples, can readily be found, allowing this major variety to become a requirement for a complete set. Virtually all serious collectors of Lincoln Memorial cents will include a 1995 Doubled-Die Obverse in their collection, assuring its long-term desirability.

This coin also continues to garner publicity as one of the most interesting coins that can be found in circulating coinage, although with one billion cents produced each year, the statistical likelihood of finding one in your pocket change is still remote. Having interesting varieties in circulation is one of the essential recruitment tools of numismatics, and this coin helps to meet that need. While there are certainly more valuable error coins in circulation, this coin got large amounts of publicity and remains well regarded.

Pick-up point: LIBERTY.

	Total Certified Population	Most Commonly Certified	
		Grade	No. in Grade
NGC	16,794	PF-67 RD	9,164
PCGS	11,171	PF-66 RD	4,357
Mintage: fraction of 6,411,440,000			
Retail value in most common certified grade (PF-67 RD): $150			

Designed by Alfred Maletsky (obverse) and James T. Ferrell (reverse). The obverse features a bust of James Smithson. The inscriptions include FOR THE INCREASE AND DIFFUSION OF KNOWLEDGE, IN GOD WE TRUST, the dual date 1846–1996, JAMES SMITHSON, and LIBERTY. The reverse features the Smithsonian sunburst logo with SMITHSONIAN beneath. The inscriptions include UNITED STATES OF AMERICA, E PLURIBUS UNUM, and the denomination FIVE DOLLARS.

Weight: 8.359 grams. *Composition:* 90% gold and 10% copper (net weight .2418 ounces pure gold). *Diameter:* 21.6 mm. *Edge:* Reeded.

In 1995 and 1996, the number of commemorative-coinage issues swelled to reach unprecedented numbers. Counting Mint State and Proof issues, a combined total of 46 different coins were issued in those two years. The 1996 Atlanta Olympics commemorative-coinage program, consisting of 32 coins, overshadowed the other, concurrent issues. There were so many coins to buy in the mid-1990s that collectors were overwhelmed, and the last several coins didn't sell particularly well. The 1996 Smithsonian $5 gold coin, released in August 1996, was among the biggest duds of all. It is precisely because this coin didn't sell well at the time that it's so desirable today.

Although a combined 100,000 coins could be struck under congressional authorization in Proof and Mint State formats, fewer than 30,000 sold in total. The Uncirculated-finish coin, issued at a slightly higher price, sold a mere 9,068 pieces, making it the fourth-rarest modern commemorative issue.

The Smithsonian $5 coin has a relatively straightforward design, jointly credited to U.S. Mint sculptor-engravers Alfred Maletsky (who designed the obverse) and James T. Ferrell (who designed the reverse). The obverse shows a bust of James Smithson with the inscription, FOR THE INCREASE AND DIFFUSION OF KNOWLEDGE. Hardly a household name in the United States, Smithson was an Englishman who bequeathed his large fortune to the United States in 1829 in order to form a museum institution in his name. The fascinating mystery is that no one knows why he did so. Smithson never traveled to the United States, nor is there evidence that he corresponded with anyone in the country. His considerable generosity, albeit mysterious, is unquestionably worthy of his portrayal on a commemorative coin. However, as a little-known figure and a foreigner, a coin featuring his likeness was not destined to be a best-seller.

In the commemorative tradition of celebrating sesquicentennials, the 1996 issue of this coin marked the 150th anniversary of the Smithsonian Institution, as 1846 was the year President James K. Polk finally signed the long-debated act of Congress establishing the Smithsonian. Today, the Smithsonian is the world's largest museum complex and the national museum of the United States. Its National Numismatic Collection is worthy of being the country's coin collection, as it is among the most important and most valuable coin collections housed in public hands. Included among the museum's countless rarities are all three classes of the 1804 dollar, two 1933 $20 gold pieces, a 1913 Liberty Head nickel, and the unique 1849 $20 coin, considered the most valuable coin in existence.

The Smithsonian $5 gold commemorative coin, always a worthy issue, is only now starting to garner more respect. It is among the more sought-after issues in the series but still doesn't trade at price levels in line with its overall scarcity. Many who avidly follow this series describe it as a "sleeper" issue. Whenever it finally wakes up, it will become a hard coin to find.

	Total Certified Population	Most Commonly Certified	
		Grade	No. in Grade
NGC	715	MS-69	388
PCGS	798	MS-69	718

Distribution: 9,068

Retail value in most common certified grade (MS-69): $1,250

2007-P JOHN ADAMS DOLLAR, DOUBLED EDGE LETTERING

Designed by Joel Iskowitz (obverse) and Don Everhart (reverse). The obverse features a portrait of John Adams with the inscriptions JOHN ADAMS, 2nd PRESIDENT, and the dates 1797–1801. The reverse features a rendition of the Statue of Liberty with the inscriptions UNITED STATES OF AMERICA and $1. The date, mintmark, and mottos IN GOD WE TRUST and E PLURIBUS UNUM are incused on the edge.

Weight: 8.1 grams. *Composition:* Outer layers of 77% copper, 12% zinc, 7% manganese, and 4% nickel over a core of pure copper. *Diameter:* 26.5 mm. *Edge:* Lettered.

During striking of the second coin in the Presidential dollar coin series, the John Adams dollar, the Philadelphia Mint showed that it was determined not to make the same mistake twice. While producing the first coin of the series, the Mint had inadvertently released hundreds of thousands of George Washington dollars before they had passed through the edge-lettering machine (see number 53). On the edge of the Presidential dollars were supposed to be the date, the mintmark, and required coinage inscriptions IN GOD WE TRUST and E PLURIBUS UNUM.

No one really seemed to care, quite frankly, that the date and mintmark were missing from the coin. It did, however, strike a chord with many that the motto IN GOD WE TRUST had been left off. These George Washington dollars Missing Edge-Lettering quickly earned the moniker "Godless dollars." The U.S. Mint must have been overwhelmed with media requests, as well as letters from the public, because they immediately issued a statement written in response to the public outcry. It read, in part, "The United States Mint understands the importance of the inscriptions. . . . We take this matter seriously." They further stated, "As we adjust this new process, we intend to eliminate any such defects."

The challenge was that the lettering was applied by an edge-lettering machine in a secondary process after the coins were initially struck, so the Philadelphia Mint instituted a new control process to assure that the edge-lettering step would not be missed. They were successful, and the John Adams Missing Edge Lettering dollar is, by any comparative measure, a scarce error coin. Subsequent issues of the Presidential dollar coins without edge lettering are scarcer still. But the new control methods were soon found to be overzealous, as a new type of error coin would indicate.

A significant number of 2007-P John Adams dollars show doubled edge lettering! This means that they were passed through the edge-lettering machine twice, which then reapplied the full edge inscription. Indeed, the controls were tight enough that coins were far more likely to pass through the machine twice than to miss the process entirely. According to some estimates, more than 50,000 Doubled Edge Lettering John Adams dollars were made in Philadelphia, while only 10,000 Missing Edge Lettering coins were made. Examples of the John Adams dollar from the Denver Mint are very scarce and only a few hundred are thought to exist.

Because the orientation of the edge lettering is random, the second inscription can either be in the same direction as or opposite to the first. When the inscriptions both travel in the same direction, they are said to be *Overlapped*. When they are opposite, that is, when one is upside down when compared to the other, they are said to be *Inverted*. These exist in equal proportion, as would be expected; however, the most readable inscriptions are those that show a close overlapping of the two legends, which then read IINN GGOODD WWEE TTRRUUSSTT.

	Total Certified Population	Most Commonly Certified	
		Grade	No. in Grade
NGC	11,176	MS-64	6,167
PCGS	3,369	MS-64	2,282

Mintage: fraction of 112,420,000

Retail value in most common certified grade (MS-64): $200

Designed by Frank Gasparro. A bust of Susan B. Anthony faces right within an angular border. LIBERTY appears above her head and the date is below, while 13 stars are arranged on the left and right sides. IN GOD WE TRUST appears in small letters at the lower right. The reverse is a miniature version of the design on the regular Eisenhower dollar, also within an angular border.

Weight: 8.1 grams. *Composition:* Outer layers of 75% copper and 25% nickel bonded to an inner core of pure copper. *Diameter:* 26.5 mm. *Edge:* Reeded.

Until 1999, there were only three years of Proof issues of the Susan B. Anthony dollar: 1979, 1980, and 1981. With such a scant number of issues, it is easy to see why collectors sought out varieties to collect, expanding opportunities and interest in the series.

Fortunately, great mintmark varieties do exist! When first issued, the 1979-S Proof Susan B. Anthony contained an S mintmark that was little more than a blob, with the upper and lower portions mashed into a thick, ill-defined base. This coin is numismatically named Type 1 since it was the first version issued, and it also bears the more descriptive name Filled S. Later that year, a better-defined mintmark punch was used instead, the Type 2 or Clear S variety. Its use persisted through all of 1980 and into 1981.

In 1981, a further refinement of the mintmark was attempted and a clearer-yet version was created. Since this happened well into the year, the original is called the Type 1 or, popularly, the Filled S version—even though it had the exact opposite name in 1979! The new version, showing wider loops and bulbous terminations

at both ends of the S, is called the Type 2 or Clear S variety. One should note that the major certification services use the Type 1 and Type 2 naming schema, while most published resources refer to Filled-S and Clear S.

Although clarity is a relative measure, there are ways to tell the two mintmarks apart without the other type present for comparison. One conclusive way to tell the marks apart is that the high points of the Type 1 S are rounded like an arch when viewed in cross-section, while the top of the Type 2 S is flattened, and thus its cross-section will resemble a mesa or step. Also, if you see thickened bulbs at the ends of the S and a circular shape to the top loop, you have a Type 2 coin. The Type 1 mintmark has smaller, rounded serifs, and the loop at the top of the S pinches together, making it appear elliptical in shape. On the Type 1 variety, the ends of the S will often, but not always, touch the center portion of the S, while the ends of the S on a Type 2 are most often, but not always, detached. One should use a magnifier to examine these fine details.

Although more than four million Proof Susan B. Anthony dollars were produced in 1981, less than 10 percent are the Clear S or Type 2, making the estimated mintage approximately 350,000. This is a low mintage for any widely collected variety, and means that Type 2 examples trade for five times (or more) the value of a Type 1. An exciting aspect of these coins is that they can be found in 1981 Proof sets, so it's possible to be rewarded with a valuable find just by looking through these sets.

Also of note, when production of the coin resumed in 1999, it seems there was no need to revisit the mintmark issues of the past. The coin was struck in Philadelphia and bears the P mintmark.

Filled S (Type 1) mintmark (left) and Clear S (Type 2) mintmark (right).

	Total Certified Population	Most Commonly Certified	
		Grade	No. in Grade
NGC	1,220	PF-69 UC	827
PCGS	3,222	PF-69 DC	1,904

Mintage: fraction of 4,063,083

Retail value in most common certified grade (PF-69): $285

1994-P $1 AMERICAN SILVER EAGLE, PROOF

Designed by Adolph A. Weinman (obverse) and John Mercanti (reverse). The obverse features Weinman's Liberty Walking design used on half dollars from 1916 through 1947. Weinman's initials are on the hem of the gown. The reverse design is a rendition of a heraldic eagle.

Weight: 31.101 grams. *Composition:* 99.93% silver and .07% copper (net weight 1 ounce pure silver). *Diameter:* 40.6 mm. *Edge:* Reeded.

Along with the introduction of bullion coinage in the United States in 1986, Proof versions sold directly by the Mint to collectors were also introduced. The designs of the silver eagle and gold eagle Proof coins were the same as for the bullion versions intended for investors, although they did include the mintmark, which was omitted from the bullion issues. Proofs were also specially manufactured: they were struck twice on polished blanks from dies that were prepared to impart a mirrored field as well as the frosted devices that lend the silver eagle Proof a rich, cameo-like appearance.

It's clear that collectors were hungry for a one-ounce U.S. silver coin. Before the silver eagle, collectors of modern issues had to buy foreign coins if they wanted silver. This gap in U.S.-minted coinage was a contributing factor to the issuance of the silver eagle.

The design of the silver eagle was also a strong draw to collectors, as it reused the Liberty Walking design created by A.A. Weinman for the half dollar that circulated from 1916 to 1947. The Liberty Walking half dollar has often been called the most beautiful U.S. silver coin ever produced. For all these reasons, in addition to the fact that this was the first silver dollar to be produced in nearly a decade, sales of the 1994-P American silver eagle Proof were strong right out of the gate.

In 1986, an as-yet-unsurpassed 1.4 million Proof silver eagles were sold. In 1987, another 900,000 were sold. Thereafter, sales began to cool. After peaking at more than $10 an ounce in 1987, silver prices declined. Silver traded between $6 and $7 an ounce throughout much of the late 1980s, but would fall below $4 an ounce in the early 1990s, souring collectors on buying coins from the Mint that were trading in the secondary market for less than the $23 issue price.

Sales of the Proof silver eagle hit a new low in 1994, reaching only 372,168 coins—the lowest figure in the series up to that point. In response to stunted sales, the Mint made several changes in 1995. First, they lengthened the sales period for the Proof silver eagle from just two months to extend throughout much of the year. Second, they issued a special 10th-anniversary coin, the Proof 1995-W silver eagle (number four on the list of 100 Greatest U.S. Modern Coins!). Increased marketing efforts boosted silver eagle sales 10 to 20 percent in subsequent years.

Silver prices flat-lined until the early 2000s, when they began a steadily aggressive upward move. Sales of the American silver eagle Proof began to increase, and by 2001 it was doubling its 1994 low each year. The series became increasingly popular with collectors, who seek to assemble complete sets by date. The result is that the 1994 issue has emerged as a key date, often more difficult to locate than the 2006-W Reverse Proof issue, and therefore it can also be more expensive.

	Total Certified Population	Most Commonly Certified	
		Grade	No. in Grade
NGC	8,827	PF-69 UC	8,327
PCGS	3,946	PF-69 DC	3,326
Mintage: 372,168			
Retail value in most common certified grade (PF-69): $200			

Designed by Felix Schlag. The obverse features a bust of Thomas Jefferson facing left. IN GOD WE TRUST appears inside the left edge, and LIBERTY and the date appear inside the right edge. On the reverse, Jefferson's home, Monticello, appears as the central device, while E PLURIBUS UNUM arcs above. The word MONTICELLO captions the building, and the words FIVE CENTS and the legend UNITED STATES OF AMERICA appear below.

Weight: 5.00 grams. *Composition:* 75% copper and 25% nickel. *Diameter:* 21.2 mm. *Edge:* Plain.

If ever there were a Proof set that has been a boon to collectors of modern U.S. coins, it is the 1990 Proof set. Three very significant varieties can be found in it, including the 1990 No S Lincoln cent (see coin number 13), the 1990-S Doubled-Die Obverse quarter (see coin number 51), and this coin.

Like other doubled-die coins, its genesis can be traced to a blunder that occurred when the die was made. It received a duplicate, and misplaced, impression from the hub that imparted the design. All the coins struck from this doubled die show doubling in the same exact way, and these distinct diagnostic features are used to identify the variety. This example exhibits moderate doubling on the motto, IN GOD WE TRUST. Stronger doubling is evident on the designer's initials, showing nearly complete separa-

tion between the two sets. Light doubling is also visible on the profile of Jefferson, most readily of his top eyelid. Examination with a loupe is recommended to see these pick-up points properly so as to confirm attribution.

Of course, Proof coins are made with great care and attention and receive a number of inspections at the mint. As a result, moderate doubled dies of this type are uncommon, and this is unquestionably the best Proof doubled-die Jefferson nickel of the modern coinage time period, if not the entire series. Each obverse die is used to strike only 2,500 nickels, and sometimes far fewer than that, to keep the quality high. That figure is the maximum estimated mintage of this coin, but fewer than 50 are known in total. Considering that 1990 Proof sets are carefully examined for varieties by specialists, it's very surprising that so few are known.

This coin was reported to the numismatic community in 1999, a late date for such a grand discovery. It was first identified in 1997 by collector Charles Clark III. He shared the discovery with just a small network of friends in hopes that more coins could be found to confirm and validate the discovery. It's not unusual for new varieties to be initially kept quiet by their discoverer in the hope that more examples will be found that can be sold in the wake of the first reporting. After two years of searching for, but failing to find, a second example, Clark had the coin authenticated at a Texas Numismatic Association convention in 1999. He then reported the confirmed discovery to CONECA, an organization that records varieties and promotes them within the hobby.

Even after more than a decade since first being reported, 1990-S Doubled-Die Obverse Jefferson nickels are very scarce. When they are found, as with virtually all 1990 Proof coinage, they exhibit very strong cameo contrast and are in the highest states of preservation. Certainly, more examples are out there to be found in Proof sets and Prestige sets. The hunt for this variety remains well-underway.

	Total Certified Population	Most Commonly Certified	
		Grade	No. in Grade
NGC	19	PF-69 UC	16
PCGS	—	—	—
Mintage: 3,299,559			
Retail value in most common certified grade (PF-69 UC): $1,000			

1984 DOUBLED-DIE OBVERSE LINCOLN CENT

Designed by Victor David Brenner (obverse) and Frank Gasparro (reverse). The obverse continues the design of 1909. The reverse shows a frontal view of the Lincoln Memorial with UNITED STATES OF AMERICA and E PLURIBUS UNUM appearing above and ONE CENT below.

Weight: 2.5 grams. *Composition:* A core of 99.2% zinc and .8% copper, with a plating of pure copper. *Diameter:* 19 mm. *Edge:* Plain.

The 1984 Doubled-Die Obverse Lincoln cent has a nickname that is also the key to its attribution—sometimes it's called the "Doubled Ear Lincoln cent." Rather unusually, the doubling of this coin appears almost exclusively on the bust of Lincoln, instead of on the lettering that surrounds him. It is so dramatic that the doubling creates a fully duplicated and well-spaced earlobe beneath Lincoln's full ear. Doubling can also be seen on Lincoln's beard, giving him a full double chin and a rather portly appearance. Variety expert Ken Potter notes that the widest doubling is seen on Lincoln's bowtie, although this feature usually gets less mention.

The discovery of this coin mirrored that of the 1983 Doubled-Die Reverse cent (see number 31), with both being found in large caches. Because these two coins appeared in consecutive years, it seems natural to compare them. Since the variety's discovery in 1984, experts have speculated that the 1984 Doubled-Die Obverse is more common than the previous year's Doubled-Die Reverse. A large find by a single coin dealer, believed to number 2,000 pieces, contributed to this thinking. Over time, certification reports have yielded additional insights, and it now appears that the two coins are of comparable rarity, with about 4,000 examples of each known to collectors.

Compared to its 1983 counterpart, the 1984 Doubled-Die Obverse does not exhibit severe planchet flaws nearly as frequently. Many of the problems that the Mint experienced beginning in 1982 in creating Lincoln cents from a copper-layered zinc-core planchet were resolved by 1984, and therefore spotting and corrosion are less severe on this issue. As a result, higher-condition examples are much more plentiful, and the average grade of this cent is a full grade point higher than for the 1983 variety. Hence, at any given grade level, the 1984 issue trades for much less than the 1983, although overall interest level and availability are again similar. Both coins are considered requirements of a complete set of Lincoln Memorial cents.

It is also very important to note that there are other collectible doubled-die obverses for this date, although the doubled-ear variety described here is by far the most valuable of them. One of the major pitfalls of variety collecting is that less-frequently collected varieties have significantly lower values, and, at one point or another, most variety collectors mistakenly purchase a coin that they believe is more desirable (and therefore more valuable) than it actually is. When purchasing this coin, especially when the example has not been attributed by a major grading service, make sure that the coin is indeed the doubled-ear example described here.

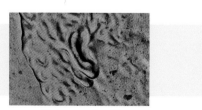

Pick-up point: Ear.

	Total Certified Population	Most Commonly Certified	
		Grade	No. in Grade
NGC	342	MS-67 RD	119
PCGS	1,053	MS-66 RD	414

Mintage: fraction of 8,151,079,000

Retail value in most common certified grade (MS-66 RD): $350

Designed by Frank Gasparro. The head of Dwight Eisenhower faces left on the obverse. LIBERTY arcs around the top of the obverse, and the date appears below the head. IN GOD WE TRUST appears at the lower left. On the reverse, an eagle with an olive branch in its talons alights upon the surface of the moon; a tiny Earth can be seen in the background. Thirteen small stars surround the eagle, and UNITED STATES OF AMERICA and E PLURIBUS UNUM appear above the eagle; ONE DOLLAR appears below.

Weight: 22.68 grams. *Composition:* Outer layers of 75% copper and 25% nickel bonded to an inner core of pure copper. *Diameter:* 38.1 mm. *Edge:* Reeded.

The time was right for a new dollar coin. Despite a brief flirtation with a new silver dollar in 1964, no dollar-denominated coin had been issued in the United States since 1935. After President Dwight Eisenhower passed away in 1969, a new bill was introduced to honor him on a circulating coin as had been done for both presidents Franklin Roosevelt and John F. Kennedy. The authorizing legislation, attached to the Bank Holding Company Act, was signed into law on December 31, 1970, and called for a copper-nickel-clad circulating dollar.

The obverse design, created by Mint Chief Engraver Frank Gasparro, shows a bare-headed profile of the president. The reverse shows the bald eagle landing on the moon, with the earth visible in the sky, adopted from the Apollo 11 logo. This homage to the recent moon landing was an indication that this coin was meant to be forward-looking, a coin for the future. The reality, however, was quite different. It never gained use outside of Nevada casinos, and, aside from early speculator interest, it never gained a foothold with collectors until recently.

This first circulation issue of the Eisenhower dollar makes the top-100 list because it is so elusive in higher grades. An astute collector seeking a gem Mint State (MS-65) example faces a bit of a hunt, despite the large mintage—47.8 million of these coins were struck in Philadelphia.

Eisenhower dollars from 1971 were almost always inadequately struck, and they display considerable *planchet abrasion*. Planchet abrasion is a general term used to describe the marks or roughness present on planchets—coin blanks—before they are struck that still remain visible on the coin even after striking. Fortunately, when a coin is struck, its surface metal is pushed into the design of the die and the planchet abrasion disappears—unless, of course, the coin is not fully struck. On Eisenhower dollars, this is seen in small pit-like marks, roughness, or extensive hairlines in an area of the coin that has not been fully struck.

There are a number of reasons why a coin wouldn't be fully struck. For one, it can be struck using insufficient pressure; striking pressure was certainly a relevant consideration for Eisenhower dollars because they were made from copper-nickel (a hard alloy) and were the largest coin struck in this composition, which means enormous pressure was required to strike them properly. Another reason a coin might not be well-struck is that it could be struck from dies that had been used for a very long time, and their fine details had begun to erode. We know from Mint records that each Eisenhower dollar die struck more than 200,000 coins for circulation. By contrast, Proof dies of the same era were used to strike a mere 2,000 coins!

For these reasons, the 1971-P is highly sought-after in high grades. Nice examples in gem Uncirculated condition (MS-65) can sell for a couple hundred dollars, while other dates in the series in comparable condition can be had for $20. While several hundred examples have been graded at this level by the major grading services, fewer than a hundred examples have been graded MS-66 by NGC and PCGS combined, and none have ever been graded MS-67.

	Total Certified Population	Most Commonly Certified	
		Grade	No. in Grade
NGC	1,123	MS-65	563
PCGS	2,620	MS-64	1,335

Mintage: 47,799,000

Retail value in most common certified grade (MS-64): $75

2008-W $50 AMERICAN GOLD BUFFALO, PROOF

Designed by James Earle Fraser. The obverse and reverse designs are based on the original 1913 Buffalo nickel, with modified inscriptions on the reverse. The obverse features a portrait of a Native American facing right with the inscription LIBERTY and the date 2008. The reverse features the figure of a bison standing and facing left. The inscription reads UNITED STATES OF AMERICA, E PLURIBUS UNUM, IN GOD WE TRUST, $50, and 1 OZ. .9999 FINE GOLD.

Weight: 31.1035 grams. *Composition:* 24-karat (.9999 fine) gold. *Diameter:* 32.7 mm. *Edge:* Reeded.

In 2006, the U.S. Mint released the American gold buffalo—the first 24-karat, or .9999 fine, U.S. gold bullion coin. This coin was greatly anticipated after the less-fine American gold eagle was first released in 1986. Several other countries had since entered the gold bullion marketplace; most notably, the Royal Canadian Mint began its gold Maple Leaf program in 1988 and the Austrian Mint released its Philharmonic gold bullion coin in 1989. Both of these issues were .9999 fine, while the American gold eagle was only .9167 fine, or 22-karat.

Investors throughout the world preferred purer bullion products, which put the original American gold eagle at a disadvantage as an investment product. This was partially offset by the desirability of a U.S.-guaranteed coin and U.S. Mint product. In 1990, 1992, 1995, and 1996, the Austrian one-ounce gold coin outsold the American gold eagle. In response to the success of purer gold coins in other countries, the first American effort to introduce a pure gold coin was made in 1996, when a bill to authorize this coin passed in the House of Representatives but was not made into law. This was rectified by the Presidential Coin Act of 2005, which included authorization for a coin of 99.99 percent pure gold. The designs were to be those created by James Earle Fraser for the 1913 Type 1 Buffalo nickel. This original design shows a bison on a hill on the reverse and an Indian chief on the obverse.

The coin was issued in one-ounce format as a $50 denomination and was an instant success. The 2006 buffalo issue outsold the one-ounce 2006 American gold eagle by more than 100,000 units. Legislation also allowed for Proof versions to be struck for collectors; the mintage limit was to be prescribed by the secretary of the Treasury in the amount deemed necessary. An astonishing 246,267 were sold, compared with only 37,096 one-ounce American gold eagles. In fact, the only Proof gold eagle with a higher mintage was the first year of issue, the 1986 version, when it was the only Proof gold coin sold by the Mint (along with a single gold commemorative issued that year). Sales for the Proof gold buffalo were strong in 2007, with about 60,000 units sold, but dropped off to only 15,426 units in 2008.

This mintage was surprisingly small and is, by far, the lowest for any Proof one-ounce U.S. gold bullion coin. It is little more than half the lowest figure for any Proof gold eagle. Among Proof bullion coins, the 2008 buffalo's low mintage makes this coin an obvious standout.

The low mintage figure is related to U.S. Mint supply channels for the raw materials. With world financial markets experiencing unprecedented volatility, demand for gold spiked in 2008. The Mint had difficulty securing sufficient pure-gold blanks to strike the coins, and had less time to produce them. Consider that in 2007, the Mint produced 140,016 one-ounce American gold eagles. In 2008, they would sell 710,000, a five-fold increase. With so few planchets available and little time to produce the coins, the Mint waited until late in the year and released a mere 15,426 pieces before declaring a sellout. Overwhelmed with similar issues, there were no Proofs produced in 2009 for the buffalo coins.

	Total Certified Population	Most Commonly Certified	
		Grade	No. in Grade
NGC	3,525	PF-70 UC	2,549
PCGS	1,212	PF-69 DC	618
Mintage: 18,863			
Retail value in most common certified grade (PF-70 UC): $3,750			

Designed by Adolph A. Weinman (obverse) and John Mercanti (reverse). The obverse features Weinman's Liberty Walking design used on half dollars from 1916 through 1947. Weinman's initials are on the hem of the gown. The reverse design is a rendition of a heraldic eagle.

Weight: 31.101 grams. *Composition:* 99.93% silver and .07% copper (net weight 1 ounce pure silver). *Diameter:* 40.6 mm. *Edge:* Reeded.

Since the start of the American Eagle Bullion program, coins were issued in two formats: For the most part, they were sold by the Mint to officially authorized distributors as bullion coins and priced at only a small premium to their intrinsic metal value. Also, American eagles were available as Proof coins, sold by the Mint directly to collectors. The Proof versions, with special finish and packaging, sold at a premium to their metal value. In 2006, the U.S. Mint took the unprecedented step of producing Uncirculated American eagle coins, a new version of the eagle for sale directly to collectors and priced in between the bullion and the Proof coins.

Although the finish of the Uncirculated coin is essentially indistinguishable from the bullion issue's, there are two notable differences. First, and most importantly, the Uncirculated coins featured a W mintmark, indicating their origin at the West Point Mint. The second difference was identified in a curious statement from the U.S. Mint: the coins were said to be struck on specially burnished blanks. With little additional information, collectors speculated wildly about what this could mean, and the

2006-W Uncirculated eagles became popularly known as "burnished coins."

All coin blanks are burnished prior to striking. The process of burnishing blanks normally involves tumbling or spinning a number of blanks with stainless steel balls or other media. It's a rough treatment that brightens the coin blanks while removing scaling and other surface irregularities. Chemicals, lubricants, and anti-tarnishing agents are often added during this step. The exact process for burnishing coin blanks has not been revealed by the Mint, so it is unknown what exactly makes the burnishing process for the 2006-W Uncirculated eagles special. The planchets (or coin blanks) for the bullion-issue silver eagles are thought to be purchased fully ready for coining, and thus no burnishing is performed at the West Point Mint prior to striking these coins.

When the Uncirculated eagles came out in 2006, there was a plethora of new eagle products in celebration of the 20th anniversary of the silver eagle. Accordingly, the 2006-W Uncirculated silver eagle was available for purchase from the Mint in one of three different ways. It was included in the Three-Piece Silver Eagle 20th-Anniversary Set and the Two-Piece Gold and Silver Eagle 20th-Anniversary Set. These two product options went on sale on August 30, 2006. Later in the year, on September 28, the coin was sold by itself for $19.95, priced in between the Proof and bullion coins.

The coin market was hungry for the new Uncirculated eagle with the W mintmark, and it felt like there were never enough. Individual pieces traded for more than $50 even as they were still being sold by the Mint for $20. Order-fulfillment on these coins became so backed up that they continued to ship into 2007. The prices kept on increasing after all of the coins were shipped, and the coins have since sustained their value.

Although this coin is sought-after as the first mintmarked Uncirculated-finish silver eagle, part of the justification for the price premium comes from the variety's low mintage: a total of only 466,573. Only 198,553 were sold as single coins and the balance were sold as part of the anniversary sets. Assuming that a great number of these sets remain intact, it is suspected that few individual coins are still available.

	Total Certified Population	Most Commonly Certified	
		Grade	No. in Grade
NGC	94,516	MS-69	79,284
PCGS	8,308	MS-69	7,590
Mintage: 468,020			
Retail value in most common certified grade (MS-69): $125			

1976 WASHINGTON QUARTER

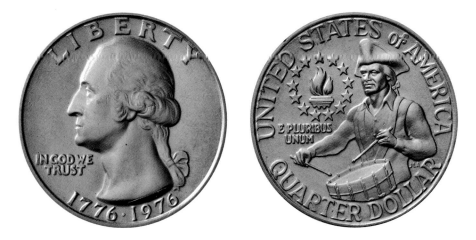

Designed by John Flanagan (obverse) and Jack Ahr (reverse). The obverse features the normal design for the Washington quarter, except that the date now reads 1776-1976. On the reverse, a colonial drummer faces left. A torch of freedom, surrounded by 13 stars, appears in the field before the drummer. The outer legends include UNITED STATES OF AMERICA above and QUARTER DOLLAR below. The motto E PLURIBUS UNUM appears in small letters below the torch.

Weight: 5.67 grams. *Composition:* Outer layers of 75% copper and 25% nickel bonded to a core of pure copper. *Diameter:* 24.3 mm. *Edge:* Reeded.

W hile not a rare coin in any of its forms, the Bicentennial quarter is squarely among the most important of all modern U.S. coinage issues. As a coin, it established the framework for future commemorative-coinage issues, and, as the first thematic circulating coin of its type, it also paved the way for the statehood quarters and America the Beautiful quarters.

Near the end of 1973, an open contest was announced to select designs for the Bicentennial coinage to be issued in celebration of the 200th anniversary of U.S. independence. This announcement came after a long year of debate. Everyone, it seemed, was in agreement that the event was worthy of recognition, but many thought that a commemorative coin went against the primary purpose of the country's coinage program: to produce coins that would be used readily in commerce. Based on that goal, no U.S. commemorative coin had been issued since 1954, and in recent years, from 1965 to 1967, coins had not had mintmarks so as to discourage hoarding. Now, it was proposed that coins would have a special design, making them sure candidates for hoarding.

Initially, proponents of Bicentennial coinage sought to have all coins from the cent to the dollar redesigned. This proposal met strong resistance, and focus shifted to a redesign of only the half dollar and the dollar. Since these two denominations were less-used in commerce, plans proceeded with little resistance. As debate came into full swing, U.S. Mint director Mary Brooks and John Jay Pittman, director of the American Numismatic Association, pressed to have the quarter included in the redesign as well. With the numismatic press supporting them, they argued that Americans should have a coin in their pocket that represented the ideals of the country and told its story. Some, too, must have sensed the obvious omission if the quarter were not included—Washington, after all, was a great Revolutionary War general, but the Bicentennial coins being redesigned, the Kennedy half dollar and Eisenhower dollar, both featured 20th-century figures.

When the design was announced, a plan was laid out that would be replicated by many future programs. Competitions are now regularly held to find and select new designs. The winner for the Bicentennial design was Jack L. Ahr's reverse design of a colonial drummer and a torch surrounded by 13 stars. The obverse of the coins bore the dual date 1776–1976. To prevent hoarding and any potential interruption in commerce, a large number of coins were struck in advance of their 1975 release. Coins were released in both 1975 and 1976, with a special legislative allowance granted so that postdated coins could circulate.

There are, in fact, five different Bicentennial quarters. More than 1.6 billion pieces were struck at both the Philadelphia and Denver Mints for circulation in the standard copper-nickel-clad composition, while regular copper-nickel Proof coins struck at San Francisco were included in the 1975 and 1976 Proof sets. Silver-clad examples were also struck at San Francisco in both Proof and Uncirculated formats that were each sold to collectors in three-coin sets alongside silver examples of the Bicentennial half dollar and dollar.

All five different quarters are widely available today, with the Proof silver-clad version being the most valuable. Very high grade examples of the circulating coins can also be surprisingly elusive.

	Total Certified Population	Most Commonly Certified	
		Grade	No. in Grade
NGC	282	MS-66	132
PCGS	583	MS-66	225
Mintage: 1,691,961,954			
Retail value in most common certified grade (MS-66): $75			

Designed by Calvin Massey (obverse) and Thomas D. Rogers (reverse). The obverse features an athlete performing the Fosbury Flop maneuver. The inscriptions include LIBERTY, IN GOD WE TRUST, 1996, and the U.S. Olympic logo. The reverse portrays the Atlanta Committee for the Olympic Games logo with torch and flame. The inscriptions read UNITED STATES OF AMERICA, ONE DOLLAR, E PLURIBUS UNUM, ATLANTA 1996, and CENTENNIAL OLYMPIC GAMES.

Weight: 26.73 grams. *Composition:* 90% silver and 10% copper (net weight .77344 ounces pure silver). *Diameter:* 38.1 mm. *Edge:* Reeded.

The high jump has been contested at every modern summer Olympic Games. Most of the coins from the 1996 Olympic commemorative series depicted sports, such as swimming or cycling, that covered several disciplines or accounted for a number of contested events. Just 82 medals have been awarded to men and 58 to women for high jump in all modern Olympic Games since the first in 1896. There are other jumping events held at the Games, including the long jump, the triple jump, and the pole vault, all of which have also been contested at every Olympics.

One reason that this sport may have been chosen for a commemorative was the wonderful design created by artist Calvin Massey for the coin. Seventy years old at the time his design was selected, Massey had created hundreds of medallic designs, including some he made while working as a staff member of the Franklin Mint. He was well known for his portrayal of African-American women in bas-relief and painting.

The coin's obverse shows an African-American female athlete in mid-execution of the "Fosbury Flop," a high-jumping technique popularized by Dick Fosbury in the 1968 Olympics. The wonderful aspect of the composition is that, while jumping, the athlete arches her back as her legs dangle on the opposite side of the bar, her body forming an arch that matches the roundness of the coin. The word LIBERTY is spelled out above her, matching her shape, while USA and the Olympic rings are below.

The masterful design, alas, could not rescue the coin from suffering the same fate as the other 1996 Olympic commemoratives. Far too many coins were issued, and collector apathy took over. To spur sales, Congress lowered the authorized mintage from 1,000,000 coins to 500,000, but this had little effect.

As with virtually all commemorative issues, the Proof version struck at the San Francisco Mint proved much more popular than the Uncirculated variety. The Proof version totaled 124,502 sales, while the Denver Mint's Uncirculated version only sold 15,697, the second-lowest mintage of any silver commemorative dollar. Today, its low mintage and popular design combine to make the 1996-D Olympic High Jump dollar the most valuable of all the Uncirculated dollars in the series.

	Total Certified Population	Most Commonly Certified	
		Grade	No. in Grade
NGC	421	MS-69	341
PCGS	713	MS-69	647

Distribution: 15,697

Retail value in most common certified grade (MS-69): $500

1996 $1 AMERICAN SILVER EAGLE

Designed by Adolph A. Weinman (obverse) and John Mercanti (reverse). The obverse features Weinman's Liberty Walking design used on half dollars from 1916 through 1947. Weinman's initials are on the hem of the gown. The reverse design is a rendition of a heraldic eagle.

Weight: 31.101 grams. *Composition:* 99.93% silver and .07% copper (net weight 1 ounce pure silver). *Diameter:* 40.6 mm. *Edge:* Reeded.

Without question, the most common way to collect any given type of modern coin is to complete the series. That means buying every different issue of the coin that is available. When collecting by series, the date of the lowest mintage normally emerges as the *key date*—the toughest example to acquire and also the most expensive. For the first 20 years of the silver eagle, the 1996 issue was the key. Although its status has since been eclipsed by coins issued in 2006 and after, it still remains among the most desirable issues even today.

As we see repeatedly in this book, during the mid-to-late-1990s, demand dwindled for a number of U.S. Mint products. That

is certainly true of the silver eagle, which had depressed mintage figures from 1994 to 1998. These coins are struck to order, and in 1996, only 3,603,386 were made to satisfy the diminished demand. This figure is about 600,000 fewer coins than were struck for any other date, and well less than half of the number that would be struck for most bullion issues in the decade-long period from 1999 to the present, when mintage figures have approached 10 million coins every year.

While the fluctuation might not seem extreme, it was noticeable, and the relative scarcity of 1996 issues was recognized almost immediately. One prominent trader of the period recalled a conversation in which he stated, "We just knew they were going to be worth a premium. You just never saw them." He was aware that some dealers had personally stashed a few monster boxes of 1996 eagles, knowing that they would be worth a premium one day. By the late 1990s, dealers were paying a few extra dollars per coin for 1996 silver eagles irrespective of grade. Today, it is not unusual for dealers to pay two to four times the prevailing rate for silver eagles for coins dated 1996!

Buying 1996 silver eagles does come with some hazards. Like other issues from the mid-to-late-1990s, they are prone to spotting, and even coins in unopened boxes can develop a speckled, milky-white haze, frequently called "milk spotting." The spotting is irreversible and will usually prevent a coin from grading any higher than MS-68 at the major certification services. Concern regarding spotting dissuades dealers from bidding too aggressively on these issues and keeps their price in check, despite their scarcity. This creates an opportunity for collectors who can take the extra time to search out a pristine example.

	Total Certified Population	Most Commonly Certified	
		Grade	No. in Grade
NGC	70,786	MS-69	68,683
PCGS	7,047	MS-69	3,488

Mintage: 3,603,386

Retail value in most common certified grade (MS-69): $150

Designed by Thomas D. Rogers (obverse) and William C. Cousins (reverse). The obverse was adapted from a 1905 medal designed by Augustus Saint-Gaudens. The inscriptions include LIBERTY, IN GOD WE TRUST, NATIONAL COMMUNITY SERVICE, and the date 1996. The reverse design features the words SERVICE FOR AMERICA with a laurel wreath around them. Below is the motto E PLURIBUS UNUM, while around the wreath are the additional inscriptions UNITED STATES OF AMERICA and ONE DOLLAR.

Weight: 26.73 grams. *Composition:* 90% silver and 10% copper (net weight .77344 ounces pure silver). *Diameter:* 38.1 mm. *Edge:* Reeded.

The lowest-mintage commemorative coinages come from the years 1995 through 1997. The reason is simple: the Mint sold 28 distinct commemorative coins as part of nine different coinage programs during that three-year period. Considering that each coin is issued in both Proof and Mint State formats, it's a total of 56 coins—way too many coins for collectors to consume.

It was a clear case of history repeating itself. Sixty years earlier, in 1936, a total of 32 coins were released as part of 20 different commemorative programs. Then, too, it led to apathy toward the program and, ultimately, a 28-year hiatus from commemorative-coinage production between 1954 and 1982.

The problems created by this coinage glut were well-recognized. Philip N. Diehl, then the deputy director of the Mint, issued this warning to lawmakers when reporting to the Senate Banking Committee in May 1994: "As demonstrated by an overall, steep decline in Mint commemorative sales over the last seven years, there is growing collector resistance to a glutted coin market, where Mint products seldom hold their initial value." Diehl elaborated that collectors at the time were buying between three and four million coins from the Mint each year. He was sure that coinage programs would continue their decline if Congress continued to authorize new commemorative issues. As he spoke to the committee, more than eight million coins had already been authorized for sale in 1996.

Ironically, the National Community Service commemorative dollar was introduced to Congress for authorization in May 1994—the very same month as when Diehl made his report. A maximum of 500,000 could be struck in Proof and Mint State formats, with a $10 surcharge on each coin. The surcharge would benefit the National Community Service Trust for the purpose of funding community-service programs and education at American universities. The coin's design is an allegorical representation of service: Liberty holding a lamp of knowledge. The reverse contains the motto SERVICE FOR AMERICA within a laurel wreath.

The design was deliberately and heavily inspired by a medal created by Augustus Saint-Gaudens in 1905 for the Women's Auxiliary of the Massachusetts Civil Service Reform Association. As Saint-Gaudens is a well-regarded and collectible designer of U.S. coinage (he also designed the $20 gold piece that collectors identify by his name), the Mint has used his designs to stimulate collector interest in new issues on several occasions. Saint-Gaudens's $20 gold piece also served as the model for the gold eagle and the 2009 Ultra High Relief double eagle.

The Community Service commemorative dollar is an especially significant collectible for anyone interested in the role that Saint-Gaudens played in U.S. coin design. Even so, the Saint-Gaudens-influenced design wasn't enough to save the coin. Diehl's warnings proved well-founded, and due to the glut of new issues this coin did not sell well. A total of 125,043 out of the authorized 500,000 were sold, and of those only 23,500 were of the Uncirculated format, among the lowest of all modern commemorative silver dollars. Both its low mintage and an interesting design contribute to its appeal today, making it among the most valuable of all commemorative dollars.

	Total Certified Population	Most Commonly Certified	
		Grade	No. in Grade
NGC	643	MS-69	465
PCGS	904	MS-69	824
Distribution: 23,500			
Retail value in most common certified grade (MS-69): $275			

1997-P LAW ENFORCEMENT OFFICERS MEMORIAL DOLLAR COMMEMORATIVE

Designed by Alfred Maletsky. The obverse depicts two U.S. Park Police officers making a rubbing of a fellow officer's name, based on a photo by Larry Ruggieri. The inscriptions include NATIONAL LAW ENFORCEMENT OFFICERS MEMORIAL, IN GOD WE TRUST, LIBERTY, and the date 1997. The reverse of the coin features a shield with a rose across it, evocative of the sacrifices made by the officers. Inscriptions include UNITED STATES OF AMERICA, TO SERVE AND PROTECT, E PLURIBUS UNUM, and ONE DOLLAR.

Weight: 26.73 grams. *Composition:* 90% silver and 10% copper (net weight .77344 ounces pure silver). *Diameter:* 38.1 mm. *Edge:* Reeded.

In an unusual stroke, the same legislation that authorized the 1997 National Law Enforcement Officers Memorial coin established the National Law Enforcement Officers Memorial Maintenance Fund. The fund was created to cover the costs of maintaining the memorial in Washington, D.C., and to provide educational scholarships to family members of officers killed in the line of duty. The 500,000 coins, authorized at the same time, were each to be sold with a $10 surcharge, thereby contributing $5 million to the newly established fund. Sadly, these well-laid plans were not realized, as, like all the other commemorative issues of 1997, the coin did not sell well. Only 139,003 were sold, yielding less than $1.4 million for the fund.

Proof examples comprised the majority of the gross sales, and only 28,575 Uncirculated pieces were sold, putting this coin among the lowest-minted commemorative dollars in the series. In combination with the low mintage, its evocative theme makes the 1997-P

Law Enforcement Officers Memorial Uncirculated dollar one of the most coveted coins in the series and, therefore, one of the most valuable.

Designed by U.S. Mint sculptor-engraver Alfred Maletsky, the coin's obverse is based on a photograph by Larry Ruggieri showing two police officers making a rubbing of a name off of the National Law Enforcement Memorial wall. The reverse shows the memorial's emblem, a shield and a solitary rose, above the phrase TO SERVE AND PROTECT.

This coin does not commemorate a specific date or event, and it certainly would have performed better had it been issued at a different time. In the late 1990s, collectors were fed up with the glut of commemorative coins, all of which traded for less than their issue price soon after the Mint's sales period ended. As a result, the coin's sales suffered. The Proof coin was sold paired with an enamel pin and patch in the Insignia Set, and the Mint offered the Uncirculated coin attached by a bezel to a sterling-silver money clip. These programs contributed enough for the U.S. Mint to deem the coin a success. As stated in the 1998 Mint report, "The National Law Enforcement Memorial silver dollar ended with Proof and Uncirculated (gross) sales of $4,898,000, a good showing given recent commemorative coin trends. Strong management closed this program with a profit."

In later years, greater restraint was exercised in approving new commemorative issues for mintage, which increased the success of the U.S. commemorative-coinage program. The Law Enforcement Memorial theme brought new collectors to the hobby and expanded demand—as is often the case on low-mintage commemorative issues. Numismatic author David L. Ganz comments that the Law Enforcement Officers Memorial dollar is evidence that Congress has the ultimate say regarding which coins are made: this coin was the fifth in the modern commemorative program to fund a national memorial. Previous issues included the Vietnam Veterans Memorial, the Women in Military Service Memorial at Arlington National Cemetery, the Battle of Normandy Foundation Memorial Wall in France, and the Korean War Memorial on the National Mall, and more would follow.

	Total Certified Population	Most Commonly Certified	
		Grade	No. in Grade
NGC	554	MS-69	374
PCGS	785	MS-69	677
Distribution: 28,575			
Retail value in most common certified grade (MS-69): $275			

2000-P SACAGAWEA DOLLAR, "GOODACRE PRESENTATION" VARIETY

Designed by Glenna Goodacre (obverse) and Thomas D. Rogers (reverse). The front of the coin features the Indian guide Sacagawea and her infant son. LIBERTY appears above her head; IN GOD WE TRUST appears on the left, and the date appears on the right side. The reverse features an eagle in flight surrounded by 13 stars. UNITED STATES OF AMERICA arcs around the upper reverse, while ONE DOLLAR arcs around the bottom. E PLURIBUS UNUM appears in small letters in the left field.

Weight: 8.1 grams. *Composition:* Outer layers of 77% copper, 12% zinc, 7% manganese, and 4% nickel over a pure copper core. *Diameter:* 26.5 mm. *Edge:* Plain.

Artist Glenna Goodacre designed the obverse of the Sacagawea dollar. She accepted her $5,000 commission for her work for the Mint in the form of "sacks of golden dollars," according to a press release for the April 5, 2000, event held at her New Mexico studio. Rather than giving her standard circulation-issue coins, however, she was given specially prepared presentation coins.

Not long after the presentation, Goodacre submitted a large group of her coins to a certification service for grading and encapsulation. At that time, the full details of the coins' special attributes were revealed to the numismatic community. First, these coins had been burnished by the Mint after they were struck, evident from their high-gloss sheen, and they were treated with an anti-tarnishing agent. The coins were largely high grade and had few contact marks, suggesting that they had received extra-attentive handling after striking. The Goodacre presentation coins were well-struck, which led to some speculation that higher striking pressure was used. Of the 5,000 coins, slightly more than a hundred appeared to have not been burnished. Examination of these unburnished coins revealed that the Goodacre presentation coins had been struck on polished or Proof blanks from specially finished dies, information that could not have been readily discerned from the burnished coins themselves.

Of the 5,000 coins that she was presented, Goodacre retained 2,000. The other 3,000 she sold for $200 each. In the secondary market since then, their value has continued to grow. These coins are visually distinctive. Unlike so many other modern rarities, their full story and origin is also very well-known. The direct association with the coin's designer also contributes to collector demand.

Goodacre's design shows Sacagawea, the Shoshone woman who served as guide and interpreter on the Lewis and Clark Expedition, carrying her baby, Jean Baptiste, who was born during the journey. Since no contemporary image of Sacagawea exists, the portrait is really the likeness of a Shoshone woman named Randy'L He-dow Teton, who sat for Goodacre. The coin is distinctly American, and the design was well-received.

Goodacre was also fortunate to receive payment in coin form the way that she did. With less forethought, a designer might have simply requested payment by check! The designer of the reverse, Thomas Rogers, was not eligible to receive a similar commission because he was a U.S. Mint employee. The total value of the $5,000 in coins paid to Goodacre in 2000 exceeds $2 million in today's market, a handsome commission by any measure.

It is best to buy examples that have been certified. Since all of the Goodacre presentation dollars were originally sold in third-party certification holders, it's logical to question the provenance of any example that was removed from its holder. Also, deceptively altered coins can appear to be burnished in a similar way, and thus it's important to have a properly authenticated coin.

	Total Certified Population	Most Commonly Certified	
		Grade	No. in Grade
NGC	—	—	—
PCGS	2,639	SP-67	1,385

Mintage: 5,000

Retail value in most common certified grade (SP-67): $1,250

1977-D EISENHOWER DOLLAR, STRUCK IN SILVER-CLAD COMPOSITION

Designed by Frank Gasparro. The head of Dwight Eisenhower faces left on the obverse. LIBERTY arcs around the top of the obverse, and the date appears below the head. IN GOD WE TRUST appears at the lower left. On the reverse, an eagle with an olive branch in its talons alights upon the surface of the moon. A tiny earth can be seen in the background, and 13 small stars surround the eagle. UNITED STATES OF AMERICA and E PLURIBUS UNUM appear above the eagle; ONE DOLLAR appears below.

Weight: 24.59 grams. *Composition:* Outer layers of 80% silver and 20% copper bonded to an inner core of .209 silver. *Diameter:* 38.1 mm. *Edge:* Reeded.

On the roster of the 100 Greatest U.S. Modern Coins are a number of die varieties and a couple of errors. It's important to know the difference between these two types of coins. A *die variety* is created when something unusual or distinctive happens to a die that is used to strike coins. The coins it makes can be differentiated from other coins by this distinctive feature they all share, and they are thus collectible. For example, if the die contained two misaligned impressions of the coin's image, all the coins that it struck would be a doubled-die variety.

An *error coin*, by contrast, is produced when something unusual occurs during the process of striking an individual coin, whether mechanical or otherwise. If a coin is struck twice by a die, it is a double-struck error, and only that single coin is affected. It is a coin that was somehow produced improperly, the result of a mistake in its manufacture. This type of error—affecting individual coins rather than an entire group produced from the same die—is what happened to this coin, the 1977-D Eisenhower dollar struck in silver-clad composition. In this case, the wrong type of planchet (or coin blank) was fed into a coin press, and thus a silver coin was produced when the Mint intended to make coins of copper-nickel.

The bill that authorized the Eisenhower dollar specified that for circulation purposes the dollar was to be struck in copper-nickel-clad, the same composition as the circulating dime, quarter, and half dollar. It also allowed for silver-clad versions (40 percent silver in composition) to be produced for sale to collectors. Uncirculated versions of the silver coin were struck at San Francisco and sold for $3 each.

The Denver Mint was given the dual responsibilities of preparing planchets for San Francisco's production of silver coins as well as making copper-nickel-clad planchets for its own coins. Although Denver itself was meant to strike only the copper-nickel coins, silver blanks became inadvertently mixed with the copper-nickel blanks and were accidentally used to strike coins in Denver. Silver Denver Mint Eisenhower dollars are coins that were never meant to be.

Interestingly, this error has occurred on a number of occasions. Silver Denver Mint Eisenhower dollars are known for the 1974-D, 1976-D, and 1977-D issues, with the 1977-D being the rarest of these error coins: only an estimated few dozen are known. The reason for its scarcity is obvious. Production of silver Eisenhower dollars began in 1971 and ceased in 1976 with the Bicentennial issue. No silver dollars were intended to be produced in 1977 at all (and certainly not in Denver). These coin blanks must have been left over from the previous year's production, and only a handful remained to find their way to the coinage press.

	Total Certified Population	Most Commonly Certified	
		Grade	No. in Grade
NGC	—	—	—
PCGS	—	—	—
Mintage: unknown			
Retail value cannot be speculated, given the extreme rarity of this variety.			

1981-S LINCOLN CENT, CLEAR S (TYPE 2), PROOF

Designed by Victor David Brenner (obverse) and Frank Gasparro (reverse). The obverse continues the design of 1909. The reverse shows a frontal view of the Lincoln Memorial with UNITED STATES OF AMERICA and E PLURIBUS UNUM appearing above and ONE CENT below.

Weight: 3.11 grams. *Composition:* 95% copper and 5% tin and zinc. *Diameter:* 19 mm. *Edge:* Plain.

Identified by their S mintmark, cents from the San Francisco Mint have always been popularly collected. For early dates, knowing the shape and position of mintmarks is a useful tool for authenticators, allowing them to discern fakes from genuine examples. For later-date coins, mintmarks are looked at enthusiastically by variety hunters who search for repunched or otherwise unusual mintmarks. Styles and changes of mintmarks over the years are also well-studied. For example, we know that six different S-mintmark styles were used on Memorial cents between 1959 and the end of the series in 2008. Of all the mintmark styles, there is just one that was only used for a single year, and only for part of that year at that: the Clear S, or Type 2, mintmark used on the Proof 1981-S Lincoln cent.

By 1979, the punch that imprinted the S mintmark onto dies had filled, becoming an amorphous blob. It was replaced by a clearer, sans serif version, which was used to make Proof coinage for part of 1979, all of 1980, and on into 1981. By 1981, however, it was clear that this punch, too, was wearing and beginning to fill. A new punch, a modest refinement over the previous version, was used to create dies for Proof 1981-S cents for the remainder of the year. This mintmark is referred to as the Clear S or Type 2 mintmark, while the earlier version is called either the Filled S or Type 1.

Distinguishing the two types requires a touch of familiarity with the characteristics of both mintmarks. The easiest way to tell them apart is to look at the letter-top of the upper portion of the mark. On the Filled S (Type 1) variety, the letter-top is curved. On the Clear S (Type 2), the top of the letter is a flattened shelf and terminates in a rounded bulb. Magnification is helpful in making this determination. For the Clear S version, the ends of the letter should be distinct from the loops of the S, but this is not always the case, and mintmarks that are slightly filled can be found for this version. Probably because of the limited nature of the improvement, a more squat and traditional serif S was put into use in 1982, making the 1981-S Clear S cent the only Lincoln cent to use this Type 2 mintmark.

Initially, the only way to get this cent was as part of the 1981 Proof set. The set was a big seller because the Susan B. Anthony dollar, included in the set, was not issued for circulation that year. Slightly more than four million sets were sold. Roughly one out of every six sets is said to contain a Clear S Lincoln cent, putting the estimated mintage of the variety at about 600,000. Although this does not make it truly scarce, it remains sought-after and widely collected. It is also still possible to pick out unattributed examples from original Proof sets. Finally, one should pay attention to the mintmark on Susan B. Anthony dollars, too, because a 1981-S Clear S dollar (number 58 on this list) is also worth a pretty penny.

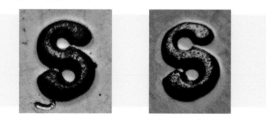

Pick-up point: Mintmark.

	Total Certified Population	Most Commonly Certified	
		Grade	No. in Grade
NGC	445	PF-68 UC	172
PCGS	915	PF-68 DC	324
Mintage: fraction of 4,063,083			
Retail value in most common certified grade (PF-68 DC): $125			

1979-S SUSAN B. ANTHONY DOLLAR, CLEAR S (TYPE 2), PROOF

Designed by Frank Gasparro. A bust of Susan B. Anthony faces right within an angular border. LIBERTY appears above her head and the date is below with 13 stars arranged on the left and right sides. IN GOD WE TRUST appears in small letters at the lower right. The reverse is a miniature version of the design on the regular Eisenhower dollar, also within an angular border.

Weight: 8.1 grams. *Composition:* Outer layers of 75% copper and 25% nickel bonded to an inner core of pure copper. *Diameter:* 26.5 mm. *Edge:* Reeded.

One of the great advantages of this variety is that it's relatively easy to attribute. Unlike with some other varieties, identifying this coin requires no reference material beyond the description here, as the two San Francisco mintmark styles seen on 1979 Proof Susan B. Anthony dollars are very distinctive indeed.

At the start of the year, the Filled S (or Type 1) mintmark was used. It has a rectangular shape from which the indistinct slither of the letter S seems to emerge. It is uncharacteristically rough and crude for a U.S. Mint product. Surprisingly, this style mintmark was used on all six denominations of Proof coins at the start of the year. The mark is less an S than it is a shapeless blob; while other coins display filled mintmarks, there are no other Proof issues where such a worn punch was used.

Later in the year, the Mint opted to make a change. They introduced a new S-letter punch. The letter in the new style has very small, almost-absent serifs, and is evenly weighted throughout the

curl. It is a more-modern letter style, called the Clear S or Type 2 mark by collectors. The easiest way to distinguish this mark is to examine the inset cuts where the ends of the S meet the loops. The letter shape does not emerge from a rectangular base, but from a fully S-shaped base.

This mintmark change occurs on all six denominations in 1979, although certain coins are found in more-even proportion between the two types, so their premiums are relatively modest by comparison (the 1979-S Clear S Kennedy half dollar is the exception). Some specialists have suggested that roughly one out of every eight Proof 1979-S Susan B. Anthony dollars are of the Type 2 variety, putting their estimated mintage at 460,000 of the 3.7 million struck. Since the Anthony dollar is such a short series, minted in just four years, this variety is considered a standard collectible coin to be included in the complete set, thus adding to its demand and price.

All 1979-S Proof dollars were sold as part of the 1979 Proof set, the case of which was jury-rigged with a clear plastic washer to fit the small Susan B. Anthony dollar into the oversized Eisenhower dollar slot. Because the differences are easy to spot, the variety is rarely sold unattributed. Collectors of original Proof sets will pay a premium for original 1979 Proof sets when all six coins possess the Clear S, Type 2 mintmark.

Pick-up point: Mintmark.

	Total Certified Population	Most Commonly Certified	
		Grade	No. in Grade
NGC	1,372	PF-69 UC	998
PCGS	3,487	PF-69 DC	2,560
Mintage: fraction of 3,677,175			
Retail value in most common certified grade (PF-69 DC): $200			

Designed by Frank Gasparro. The head of Dwight Eisenhower faces left on the obverse. LIBERTY arcs around the top of the obverse, and the date appears below the head. IN GOD WE TRUST appears at the lower left. On the reverse, an eagle with an olive branch in its talons alights upon the surface of the moon. A tiny earth can be seen in the background, and 13 small stars surround the eagle. UNITED STATES OF AMERICA and E PLURIBUS UNUM appear above the eagle; ONE DOLLAR appears below.

Weight: 22.68 grams. *Composition:* Outer layers of 75% copper and 25% nickel bonded to an inner core of pure copper. *Diameter:* 38.1 mm. *Edge:* Reeded.

The Mint saw lack of availability as a barrier to circulation for Eisenhower dollars. One cause of unavailability might be hoarding, and the Mint was determined to prevent speculators from hoarding the large dollar coins. The best way to do this was to produce such an abundant supply that the coin would be available everywhere. The coin was produced during 1971, but was not released until November of that year, giving the Mint time to strike some 115 million copper-nickel coins for circulation. In 1972, they again struck an unimaginable quantity: more than 168 million Eisenhower dollars were struck for circulation during that year.

Casinos welcomed the return of the dollar coin, which replaced their own dollar-sized tokens. But outside of that use, there was really very little need for such a large and heavy coin. Ultimately, it was impractical for commerce. It had been 36 years since the last dollar coin was issued in the United States, and, in the realm of daily commerce, it clearly was not missed.

In many ways, the Eisenhower dollar was made in a rush. It was approved for coinage in 1970, just as a five-year ban on production

of a dollar coin, imposed in 1965, was expiring. The impetus for the coin was, in part, public opinion. Many requests for this coin were made after Eisenhower, the soldier-statesman president, died on March 28, 1969.

In all the hurry, neither the Proof set nor the Mint set's packaging was ever refitted to accommodate the large dollar coin. Annual coin sets of one form or another had been issued continuously since 1947, but a dollar coin had never been made in this time. The 1971 and 1972 sets didn't include Eisenhower dollars. If anything, excluding them from the Mint set likely added hoarding pressure to the coin. There was simply no time to create new packaging and adjust the assembly-line machinery to accommodate these coins. When the Mint announced that the 1973 Proof set would include the dollar in an August 18, 1972, press release, they were still uncertain about the Mint set: "It is hoped that coins produced at both the Philadelphia and Denver Mints including the dollar . . . can be included in the 1973 Uncirculated coin sets. There are a few details still to be worked out before a firm commitment can be made."

When the Mint set went on sale, it did indeed include the Philadelphia and Denver Mint dollars. By this time, it was clear that the Mint's exuberant production had well-outpaced demand for the coin in circulation. Although the Mint could now include the coin in the annual coin sets, there was no need for additional 1973 Eisenhower dollars to be struck for commerce. The only Eisenhower dollars that were struck at the Philadelphia and Denver mints in 1973, therefore, were coined for inclusion in Mint sets.

Since no examples were struck for commerce, the mintage of the 1973 issues is very low. Adding them to the Mint set raised the set's issue price from $3.50 to $6. This increase had a devastating effect on the set's sales, and only 1,767,691 were sold, compared to 2,750,000 sets the year before in 1972. To meet this low demand, only two million Eisenhower dollars were struck at Philadelphia and Denver, compared to 76 and 93 million, respectively, during the previous year. While some of the silver-clad issues do have lower mintage figures, the 1973 issues are by far the lowest-mintage circulation-issue Eisenhower dollars. As a "Mint set only" issue, they are always in demand.

	Total Certified Population	Most Commonly Certified	
		Grade	No. in Grade
NGC	1,461	MS-65	690
PCGS	4,114	MS-64	1,788

Mintage: 4,000,056

Retail value in most common certified grade (MS-64): $75

1966 KENNEDY HALF DOLLAR, SMS, NO "FG"

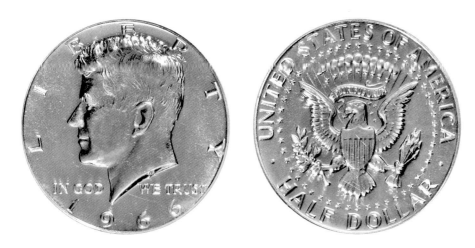

Designed by Gilroy Roberts (obverse) and Frank Gasparro (reverse). On the obverse, the head of John F. Kennedy faces left. LIBERTY arcs across the top of the obverse; the date arcs along the bottom of the obverse and IN GOD WE TRUST runs in a straight line beneath Kennedy's head. The reverse features a heraldic eagle, similar to that seen on the 1801 through 1807 and 1892 through 1915 half dollars, within a circle of 50 stars. UNITED STATES arcs around the top and HALF DOLLAR arcs along the bottom of the reverse.

Weight: 11.50 grams. *Composition:* 80% silver and 20% copper bonded to an inner core of 20.9% silver and 79.1% copper. *Diameter:* 30.6 mm. *Edge:* Reeded.

The name of this variety tells its story very straightforwardly. The first part of its name is SMS, indicating that it was issued in Special Mint Sets, the coinage sets that replaced Proof sets from 1965 to 1967 so that the U.S. Mint could focus its efforts on the transition from silver to copper-nickel-clad coinage. The No FG is an indication that the designer's initials, FG, do not appear on the reverse of the coin as they ought.

On all Kennedy half dollars struck from 1964 to date, the designer's initials are shown on the reverse of the coin. Those examples bearing the standard heraldic eagle design (all but the Bicentennial issue) have an FG placed between the eagle's left leg and tail. The initials stand for Frank Gasparro, the U.S. Mint chief engraver from 1965 to 1981. Gasparro designed the Eisenhower dollar, the Susan B. Anthony dollar, the Memorial cent reverse, and, of course, the reverse of the Kennedy half dollar. He is among the most influential coin designers of the latter half of the 20th century.

Some half dollars found in 1966 Special Mint Sets (SMS) do not show Gasparro's initials, or even any trace of them. Although there is no formal explanation for this omission, it is thought that

the initials were simply polished off the dies during their preparation for the production process. The coins in the Special Mint Sets did not receive the care and attention given to Proof coins, though they were struck from highly polished dies that give the coins a mirrorlike surface.

There is some history of coins missing initials. It happened previously and with a similar explanation on the Proof 1941 Liberty Walking half dollar, which can be found without its designer's initials. This exact variety of the Kennedy half dollar, without the designer's initials, was created twice more at the Denver Mint in both 1972 and 1982, but those times the mistake was on business-strike coins headed for circulation. This 1966 variety is the only time that the omission has occurred on a presentation version of the Kennedy half dollar.

The absent letters make this self-explanatory variety very easy to attribute. Even so, only a few hundred are known, and they can often be lower grade than the typical SMS Kennedy half dollar. Although the most-coveted SMS coins display cameo contrast between the mirrored fields and frosted design elements, this variety is not found with cameo contrast, and not a single cameo coin has been graded by a major service. Because the coins are highly sought-after, finding a high-grade example, or an example displaying cameo contrast, would yield the discoverer a nice return.

It is likely that many tens of thousands of 1966 SMS half dollars without designer initials were struck and can still be found in original sets. The 1966 Kennedy half dollar is an exciting issue for collectors because a doubled-die obverse also exists for this year, showing a doubled profile of Kennedy. Cherrypickers can examine the reverse of their coins to determine if it's missing the initials—the most desirable variety of the year—and if that disappoints, they can flip the coin over to examine whether it's a doubled die.

Pick-up point: Area between eagle's tail and leg on reverse.

	Total Certified Population	Most Commonly Certified	
		Grade	No. in Grade
NGC	116	MS-66	54
PCGS	84	SP-65	22

Mintage: fraction of 2,261,583

Retail value in most common certified grade (MS-66): $125

2005-D JEFFERSON NICKEL, "SPEARED BISON" VARIETY

Designed by Joe Fitzgerald (obverse) and Jamie Franki (reverse). The new portrait of Thomas Jefferson on the obverse was inspired by a 1789 marble bust by Jean-Antoine Houdon, and the inscription "Liberty" was based on Jefferson's handwriting. The reverse features an American bison in profile.

Weight: 5.00 grams. *Composition:* 75% copper and 25% nickel. *Diameter:* 21.2 mm. *Edge:* Plain.

In 2004 and 2005, the four-coin Westward Journey Nickel Series™ infused new interest into the staid Jefferson nickel series, which had not seen a design change in its 66-year history. The themes of the new coinage reflected the historic expedition undertaken by Meriwether Lewis and William Clark from 1804 to 1805 to explore the lands recently acquired from France in the Louisiana Purchase. The third coin released in the series, the first of 2005, featured a new obverse portrait of Jefferson and the bison on the reverse.

Reactions to the new enlarged, offset portrait of Thomas Jefferson were varied. For all collectors of current coinage, one of the most exciting moments is the first examination of newly minted coins. Many collectors of circulation issues go through rolls of new issues to select the best examples for their collection. Every now and then, this first examination can result in an exciting new discovery. Such was the case for East Texas collector Pamela Ryman-Moir, who discovered the 2005-D Speared Bison nickel in March 2005 while looking through bank-wrapped rolls of the recently released nickel.

This particular anomaly was a long, raised line running vertically through the bison's midsection and sticking out above

and below its torso. The bison was, indeed, speared, as the eponym suggests, looking like an insect that was pin-mounted for display. The likely explanation for the "spear" is a die gouge or flaw, an indent made unintentionally and inexplicably, that then presented on all the coins it struck. What was particularly unusual about this coin was the size of the die gouge: the flaw extended across nearly the entire reverse of the coin. In the annals of U.S. coinage, few die flaws are as large and as prominent as that on the Speared Bison nickel.

The value of the coin benefited from a speculative frenzy, such as many varieties experience initially after their discovery. The colorful and descriptive name that was almost universally applied to the variety helped it gain steam as well. Further, this new variety was discovered precisely when die-gouge varieties found among the 2004-D Wisconsin statehood quarters, the Extra Leaf High and Extra Leaf Low varieties (see numbers 18 and 19), had collectors already buzzing. Like the Wisconsin state quarters, the Speared Bison nickel was found to have a regional distribution, and most were found in East and Central Texas. Those lucky enough to find the coins were initially able to sell them in online auctions for hundreds of dollars. As a word of caution, it should be noted that this variety is often described by its more formal numismatic name as "Reverse Die Gouge." Other minor die-gouge varieties exist, but the long and dramatic Speared Bison variety should be unmistakable.

The variety continues to hold interest among collectors, and high-grade examples can require some effort to hunt down. This coin isn't always collected as a requirement for building a complete set and, unlike the Extra Leaf Wisconsin state quarters, it isn't referenced in all the major hobby guides, which together add a degree of uncertainty to the long-term prospects for this variety.

Pick-up point: "Spear" under bison's abdomen.

	Total Certified Population	Most Commonly Certified	
		Grade	No. in Grade
NGC	—	—	—
PCGS	641	MS-64	353

Mintage: fraction of 487,680,000

Retail value in most common certified grade (MS-64): $200

1996-D CENTENNIAL OLYMPICS (PARALYMPICS) DOLLAR COMMEMORATIVE

Designed by James C. Sharpe (obverse) and Thomas D. Rogers (reverse). The obverse features an athlete in a wheelchair competing in a track and field event. The Paralympic mark is to the right and the word "spirit" appears in Braille above the figure's upraised arms. Additional inscriptions read TRIUMPH OF THE HUMAN SPIRIT, IN GOD WE TRUST, PARALYMPICS, LIBERTY, and 1996. The reverse portrays the Atlanta Committee for the Olympic Games logo with torch and flame. The inscriptions read UNITED STATES OF AMERICA, ONE DOLLAR, E PLURIBUS UNUM, ATLANTA 1996, and CENTENNIAL OLYMPIC GAMES.

Weight: 26.73 grams. *Composition:* 90% silver and 10% copper (net weight .77344 ounces pure silver). *Diameter:* 38.1 mm. *Edge:* Reeded.

Athletes from around the world with physical disabilities have competed in the Paralympic Games since 1960. They are held immediately after the Olympic Games in the same host city and venues. The 1996 Atlanta Paralympics received mass-media sponsorship and played a significant role in the continued growth of this event. Two silver dollars, one in each year 1995 and 1996, were issued as part of the 1996 Atlanta Olympic Games coinage program to honor the Paralympics.

Unfortunately, the Atlanta Olympic Games coinage program included a glut of coins, which, along with other commemora-tive programs during the mid-1990s, found only limited enthusiasm among collectors. The 1995 Paralympics dollar had sold fewer than 170,000 of the 750,000 coins autho-rized. In order to boost the appeal for the second issue, the authorized mintage was dropped from 1,000,000 coins to 350,000. This seems to have had no effect on the sales effort, though, and just 98,777 sold, consisting of 84,280 Philadelphia Mint Proof-finish examples and a paltry 14,497 Uncirculated examples struck at Denver. Both the gross number and the Uncirculated number are the low-est since the first modern commemorative silver dollar was issued in 1983.

The coin's obverse, designed by artist James Sharpe, features a Paralympian in a three-wheeled racing wheel-chair in facing view. His arms are raised in apparent vic-tory. At the top of the obverse is the motto of the 1996 Paralympics, TRIUMPH OF THE HUMAN SPIRIT, and to the right of the figure are a word in Braille and the logo of the 1996 Paralympics. The reverse of the coin shows the common reverse seen on all 1996 Olympics commemora-tive half dollars, including a large torch—the logo of the games—and required legends.

The low mintage of the coin places the Uncirculated example among the most-valuable silver dollars in the series. Ironically, it garners this position because it was so undesirable at the time of its issue as a result of the ballooning commemorative-coinage program. A number of years of more responsible stewardship of the program have now swelled the ranks of collectors, who remain the primary source of support for this issue. With so much support for current issues, it's unlikely that mintages will fall to levels anywhere near the low seen for the 1996-D Paralympics dollar any time soon.

	Total Certified Population	Most Commonly Certified	
		Grade	No. in Grade
NGC	573	MS-69	469
PCGS	843	MS-69	734

Distribution: 14,497

Retail value in most common certified grade (MS-69): $500

1996-W CENTENNIAL OLYMPICS (FLAG BEARER) $5 COMMEMORATIVE

Designed by Patricia L. Verani (obverse) and William Krawczewicz (reverse). The obverse features an athlete bearing a flag followed by a group of athletes waving to an unseen crowd. The inscriptions include LIBERTY, IN GOD WE TRUST, and the date 1996. The U.S. Olympic logo appears in the right field of the coin. The reverse features the Atlanta Committee for the Olympic Games logo surrounded with laurel leaves. The inscriptions are UNITED STATES OF AMERICA, FIVE DOLLARS, E PLURIBUS UNUM, and ATLANTA.

Weight: 8.359 grams. *Composition:* 90% gold (.242 ounces pure gold). *Diameter:* 21.6 mm. *Edge:* Reeded.

While the silver and clad coins of the expansive Centennial Olympic Coin Program relied on individual sports for their themes, the gold coins chose more general subjects. The $5 gold coins of 1996 centered on ceremonial aspects of the games, including the lighting of the cauldron that holds the Olympic flame and the flag bearer who carries the flag in during opening ceremonies.

For all of the commemorative coins struck for the centennial games, an overabundance of issues met with a tepid response from collectors, and the coins sold poorly. The coin with the lowest mintage of all the 1996 Olympic commemoratives is the Flag Bearer $5 gold coin. It has one of the lowest mintage figures of any commemorative, with just 9,174 Uncirculated examples sold (supplemented by 32,886 Proof versions).

Designed by New Hampshire sculptor Patricia L. Verani, the U.S. team flag bearer carries the Stars and Stripes on the coin's obverse, while four athletes seen in line behind wave to the crowd and flash big smiles. Of tangential interest, the actual 1996 U.S. Olympic team entered the stadium wearing hats (not shown on the coin), and the flag bearer, wrestler Bruce Baumgartner, wears a recognizable moustache, while the flag bearer portrayed on the coin is clean-shaven.

With its strongly patriotic theme, the Mint and all those involved were certainly hoping for a coin that would sell successfully. The goal was for the Olympic commemorative coins to raise $180 million in surcharges to offset expenses from the games, and the Mint spent nearly $30 million to advertise and promote the coins.

Sales were slow from the start, and the Mint sought out new ways to promote their offerings. The low mintage figures were released to numismatic publications with the hope of enticing collectors. In early 1996, Mint Director Philip N. Diehl set out on a world tour to promote the Olympic coins. While stopping at the Vatican, he presented a set of the coins to the Pope (and the coins received a Papal blessing). The Mint also contracted with the National Science Foundation Polar Programs to make the Olympic coins available in Antarctica—a publicity-generating move, as now the coins would officially be available on all continents.

Despite these efforts, the sales figures remained disastrously low. The surcharges generated from sales totaled just $18 million, only 1/10 the desired amount. The result was so poor that the future of the entire commemorative program was in doubt. Legislative changes and independent oversight ultimately righted the commemorative programs, and today these programs have a very large collector following. This increased demand puts enormous pressure on issues like the Uncirculated 1996-W Centennial Olympics (Flag Bearer) $5 gold coin, of which fewer than 10,000 were struck.

	Total Certified Population	Most Commonly Certified	
		Grade	No. in Grade
NGC	587	MS-70	298
PCGS	1,231	MS-69	1,134

Distribution: 9,174

Retail value in most common certified grade (MS-69): $1,800

1979-P SUSAN B. ANTHONY DOLLAR, WIDE RIM

Designed by Frank Gasparro. A bust of Susan B. Anthony faces right within an angular border. LIBERTY appears above her head and the date is below, with 13 stars arranged on the left and right sides. IN GOD WE TRUST appears in small letters at the lower right. The reverse is a miniature version of the design on the regular Eisenhower dollar, also within an angular border.

Weight: 8.1 grams. *Composition:* Outer layers of 75% copper and 25% nickel bonded to an inner core of pure copper. *Diameter:* 26.5 mm. *Edge:* Reeded.

On October 10, 1978, President Jimmy Carter signed the Susan B. Anthony Coin Act into law. He stated that the smaller coin would be easier to handle, improve the coinage system, and lower production costs. The Eisenhower dollar was 38.1 mm in diameter and weighed 22.68 grams; comparatively, the Anthony dollar measured 26.5 mm and 8.1 grams. This dramatic difference in size and weight allowed the government to achieve significant cost savings by switching to the new coin.

Although the new dollar coin was certainly much easier to carry, it still faced a major barrier to circulation: it very closely resembled the quarter dollar, which was 24.3 mm in diameter and the same color as the Anthony dollar. In fact, the new dollar was only .25 mm thicker than the quarter. The potential for confusion between the two coins actually made using the small dollar a liability.

The legislation authorizing the coin only stipulated that the design include Susan B. Anthony on the obverse and an eagle landing on the moon (the emblem of Apollo 11). On the reverse, the Mint added a broad, 11-sided inner border to the circumference of the coin—a design element specifically intended to differentiate the new dollar coin from the quarter. Although the coin itself was round, the geometric hendecagonal shape was meant to be a distinguishing feature that would make the dollar coin easier to see.

Initially, the coins were issued with a comparatively narrow rim. When criticism emerged that the coin was still too similar to the quarter, the distinctive rim was widened. The mints in Denver

and San Francisco produced only narrow-rim coins in 1979 and implemented the change in 1980. In Philadelphia, however, the wide-rim version was put into immediate production, and thus the 1979-P dollar can be found with both narrow and wide rims. In 1980 and all subsequent years, the Anthony dollar would only be struck wide-rim.

The easiest way to tell the narrow-rim from the wide-rim dollar is actually to look at the date position. Because the rim is thinner on the narrow-rim, the date appears farther from the edge of the coin; this variety is sometimes called the *far-date* as well. On the wide-rim variety, the date nearly touches the edge of the coin, and this variety is therefore sometimes called the *near-date*.

Although the coin was issued just over 30 years ago, precise information about the wide-rim variety is surprisingly scant: the Mint did not record precisely how many coins of each variety were struck. Reports of die use seem to suggest that close to half the mintage may have been the wide-rim version, but the variety accounts for much less than half the coins known to collectors. While not a scarce coin, it is rather hard to come by in higher grades, making it far and away the most valuable Susan B. Anthony dollar in gem Uncirculated condition.

Virtually all recollections mention that the wide-rim version of the coin was first put into circulation late in 1979, but that information may be anecdotal as well. Striking of the Anthony dollar began in late 1978; to prevent hoarding, the coin was not released until July 2, 1979, after 500 million coins had been struck. Many companies and the U.S. Postal Service issued first-day covers, coins in envelopes with stamps canceled on the first date of the coin's release. Although seen less frequently, 1979-P Wide Rim dollars can indeed be found in first-day covers, suggesting that both varieties were available right from the outset. There are still many curious details of this modern coin that remain unanswered.

Pick-up point: Date.

	Total Certified Population	Most Commonly Certified	
		Grade	No. in Grade
NGC	879	MS-65	327
PCGS	2,287	MS-65	96

Mintage: fraction of 360,222,000

Retail value in most common certified grade (SP-69): $100

2003-W FIRST FLIGHT CENTENNIAL
$10 COMMEMORATIVE

Designed by Donna Weaver (obverse) and Norman E. Nemeth (reverse). The obverse features portraits of Orville and Wilbur Wright. The surrounding inscriptions read **LIBERTY, IN GOD WE TRUST**, the centennial dates 1903–2003, **ORVILLE & WILBUR WRIGHT**, and **FIRST FLIGHT CENTENNIAL**. The reverse features the Wright 1903 Flyer in flight with an eagle overhead. Inscriptions include **UNITED STATES OF AMERICA, E PLURIBUS UNUM**, and **TEN DOLLARS**.

Weight: 16.718 grams. *Composition:* 90% gold and 10% copper (net weight .48375 ounces pure gold). *Diameter:* 27 mm. *Edge:* Reeded.

The historic legislation that created the 50 State Quarters® Program and the Sacagawea dollar also created a three-coin commemorative program to honor the 100th anniversary of the first flight, the Wright brothers' successful airplane flight at Kitty Hawk, North Carolina, on December 17, 1903. The authorization was approved in December 1997, six years before the coins were to be issued. The lead time was far longer than many coins enjoyed, and suggested the austerity and importance of the occasion.

Uncharacteristically, the program consisted of a clad half dollar, a silver dollar, and a $10 gold coin, the first time commemoratives had been issued together in this arrangement. Normally, $5 gold commemorative coins are issued; this coin was only the second $10 gold commemorative since the resumption of the commemorative-coinage program in 1982 (or the third if the bimetallic Library of Congress issue is counted). But that wasn't the only peculiarity of the legislation. Another requirement stipulated that the First Flight Foundation would receive proceeds from the surcharges collected

upon the sale of the coins only if they had received a similar amount of donations from private sources. This condition was a first among coinage legislation.

In the wake of the terrorist attacks of September 11, 2001, and a modified, less-ambitious plan for the visitors' center at the site of the first flight, the foundation had trouble raising anything close to the predicted $9 million in surcharge receipts that the coin's sales would generate. Concerned that the foundation would receive nothing, North Carolina Senator John Edwards introduced a legislative fix just three months before the coin went on sale to make sure that at least $2.5 million of the funds raised from the coins' surcharges would go to the foundation. Ultimately, the foundation would receive more than $3.5 million in proceeds from the sale of the coins.

But sales were soft, especially for the $10 gold piece. Most previous issues of commemorative gold coins were of a $5 denomination and contained 7.5 grams of pure gold. These coins contained double the amount of gold of a $5 coin, and therefore were nearly twice as expensive. The 2002-W Salt Lake City Olympics $5 Uncirculated coins sold for $180 and the Proofs sold for $195. By contrast, the U.S. Mint priced the First Flight $10 coin at $340 for the Uncirculated and $350 for the Proof, and sold 10,009 and 21,676 examples, respectively. The mintage of 10,009 pieces makes the 2003-W First Flight $10 Uncirculated coin one of the most elusive in the series and also one of the most valuable today.

On the obverse, the coin shows side-by-side facing busts of Orville and Wilbur Wright wearing high-collared early-20th-century-style suits. The arrangement of two superimposed, three-quarters busts, created by U.S. Mint sculptor-engraver Donna Weaver, is somewhat atypical, giving the impression that the two men are standing very close to one another. The reverse shows their plane, the Wright Flyer, and an eagle soaring above it. Collectors will note that the soaring eagle resembles the bird that appears on the reverse of the American platinum eagle bullion coin. References and recast imagery occur numerous times in the annals of U.S. coinage design, especially when a commemorative can borrow a design element that has been implemented successfully elsewhere.

	Total Certified Population	Most Commonly Certified	
		Grade	No. in Grade
NGC	1,784	MS-70	1,339
PCGS	1,649	MS-69	1,254
Distribution: 10,009			
Retail value in most common certified grade (MS-70): $950			

1984-W LOS ANGELES OLYMPIAD
$10 COMMEMORATIVE

Designed by John Mercanti and James Peed (obverse) and John Mercanti (reverse). The obverse depicts two runners holding aloft the Olympic torch. Inscriptions include LIBERTY, IN GOD WE TRUST, LOS ANGELES, the date 1984, and OLYMPIAD XXIII at the base of the coin. The reverse features an adaptation of the Great Seal of the United States. Inscriptions include UNITED STATES OF AMERICA, TEN DOLLARS, and E PLURIBUS UNUM on two banners above the eagle.

Weight: 16.718 grams. *Composition:* 90% gold and 10% copper (net weight .48375 ounces pure gold). *Diameter:* 27 mm. *Edge:* Reeded.

The $10 gold coins struck to commemorate the 1984 Olympic Games were a collection of firsts. They were the first U.S. gold coins struck since 1933, and to conform to this earlier coinage, they were identical in composition to the circulating $10 gold coins made more than 50 years earlier. Further, this coin was the first and still remains the only commemorative issue in U.S. history to be struck at four different mints. Of significant note to collectors, the West Point issue was also the first U.S. coin ever to bear the W mintmark.

The obverse, designed by U.S. Mint artist James Peed and executed by engraver John Mercanti, shows a male and a female athlete gripping a torch that they run to the games. Mercanti also designed the great seal adaptation for the reverse. Originally, the $10 gold coin was struck only at the West Point Mint and offered in Proof and Uncirculated versions. Demand was robust through

the entire sales period, and when sales were closed at the end of 1984, a total of 381,085 of the Proof and 75,886 of the Uncirculated versions had been purchased.

Released mid-way through the coinage program, additional Proof versions of the $10 coin were also struck at Philadelphia, Denver, and San Francisco. As had been true during the classic commemorative programs of the past, these mintmark variants were offered to prompt additional sales specifically to collectors, and they foreshadow the abuses of the Olympic commemorative coinage that would come for the 1996 Atlanta games. These additional gold coins were greeted much less enthusiastically, and only 30,000 to 50,000 of each were sold, with the highest sales belonging to the San Francisco issue—no doubt buoyed by California residents enthusiastic about the locally held games. A unique feature of the sales effort for these coins was that banks and S&L's participated, receiving coins on consignment from the Mint to then sell to their customers. While institutions across the country participated, California led the sales effort.

Total surcharges received from the sale of the Olympic gold coin were $28,668,200. This places it third on the list of most-successful single commemorative issues in terms of surcharges raised; only the Statue of Liberty dollar and the Constitution Bicentennial $5 gold coin eclipse it. Counting the silver coins as well, the 1984 Olympic commemorative-coinage program raised more than $73 million to fund athlete training and offset costs of the games, and it was deemed a major factor in closing the games on budget.

Although some of the other mints' Proof coins are lower mintage and can carry a higher price premium, the Uncirculated West Point issue is the only coin of this format released. Of note to advanced collectors, this coin is found with two subtly different surface finishes: a heavy matte surface and a satin, semi-prooflike sheen. While researching these different surface characteristics in 2006, a doubled-die obverse variety was identified that can be found on the satin surface type. A surprise to many collectors, the doubled die took more than 20 years to be discovered.

	Total Certified Population	Most Commonly Certified	
		Grade	No. in Grade
NGC	1,380	MS-69	967
PCGS	2,004	MS-69	1,816
Distribution: 75,886			
Retail value in most common certified grade (MS-69): $750			

2004-P DOUBLED-DIE OBVERSE PEACE MEDAL NICKEL

Designed by Felix Schlag (obverse) and Norman E. Nemeth (reverse). The obverse features a bust of Thomas Jefferson facing left. IN GOD WE TRUST appears inside the left edge, and LIBERTY and the date appear inside the right edge. The new Peace Medal reverse was adapted from the reverse of certain of the original Indian Peace Medals commissioned for Lewis and Clark's 1803 expedition. Inscriptions include UNITED STATES OF AMERICA, LOUISIANA PURCHASE 1803, E PLURIBUS UNUM, and FIVE CENTS.

Weight: 5.00 grams. *Composition:* 75% copper and 25% nickel. *Diameter:* 21.2 mm. *Edge:* Plain.

D oubled dies hold a special status among variety coins, as there are some very dramatic and valuable doubled-die coins. In the Jefferson nickel series, an incredible doubled die occurred during the second year the coin was issued, 1939. On the reverse of these coins, the word MONTICELLO is fully doubled with strong separation. But despite the very long history of the Jefferson nickel series, there are few important doubled-die varieties, and this 2004 variety is the only one that makes the list of 100 Greatest U.S. Modern Coins.

This coin is, in fact, the most dramatic doubled die to occur thus far in the 21st century and the most significant since the 1995 Doubled-Die Obverse cent. Its significance derives from two aspects of the variety: First, it is easy to attribute due to the prominent doubling and extra thickness seen on the date, the mintmark, the motto IN GOD WE TRUST (most prominently),

and the word LIBERTY. Second, it occurred on a one-year design-type.

The Jefferson nickels of 2004 celebrated the 200th anniversary of the expedition of Lewis and Clark. Themes relevant to their journey were chosen as reverse designs for a set of four nickel five-cent coins, two issued in 2004 and two in 2005. The first of the nickels featured a design adapted from the Indian Peace Medals that Lewis and Clark carried with them to present to Native American leaders as they traveled westward. The design shows two hands clasped and forming a bond. Each hand emerges from decorated cuffs that symbolize, respectively, the U.S. government and the Native Americans.

This particular doubled die was first identified in summer 2004 in South Florida by an astute collector who received the coin in change. Other discoveries were subsequently made by collectors who acquired rolls of the coins from local Florida banks. Reasonably large caches turned up, and a few thousand examples have made their way into the marketplace. Since the initial interest in this coin quieted, few large finds have come to market and prices have stabilized.

As is typical of many modern coins that are found in rolls intended for general circulation, these coins are most frequently found in the MS-63 to MS-64 grade range and suffer from contact marks. Examples grading above MS-65 are rare. Additionally, specialists will try to locate early-die-state examples of this coin because as the die wore out from use, the separation became less pronounced and the later-struck examples of the variety consist primarily of extra thickness on the lettering.

Doubling evident in date and motto.

	Total Certified Population	Most Commonly Certified	
		Grade	No. in Grade
NGC	—	—	—
PCGS	21	MS-64	12

Mintage: fraction of 361,440,000

Retail value in most common certified grade (MS-64): $125

1964-D/D KENNEDY HALF DOLLAR

Designed by Gilroy Roberts (obverse) and Frank Gasparro (reverse). On the obverse, the head of John F. Kennedy faces left. LIBERTY arcs across the top of the obverse; the date arcs along the bottom and IN GOD WE TRUST runs in a straight line beneath Kennedy's head. The reverse features a heraldic eagle, similar to that seen on the 1801 through 1807 and 1892 through 1915 half dollars, within a circle of 50 stars. UNITED STATES arcs around the top and HALF DOLLAR arcs along the bottom of the reverse.

Weight: 12.50 grams. *Composition:* 90% silver and 10% copper. *Diameter:* 30.6 mm. *Edge:* Reeded.

This coin belongs to a class of varieties called *Re-Punched Mintmarks*, commonly abbreviated as RPM. This is an exciting type of variety because it provides insight into the manual process of die creation. Prior to the mid-1980s, the mintmark was added to all U.S. coin dies by hand. Coin dies were impressed with their design by a working hub that did not include a mintmark. In a subsequent step, the mintmark was punched onto the die manually. When something went awry during this process and a misaligned impression of the mintmark was punched into the die, a re-punched mintmark was created.

There are many RPMs among the modern coin series, and many collectors specialize in this class specifically. Kennedy half dollar RPMs are particularly sought-after by die-variety collectors, and this one is the most dramatic and easiest to spot of all modern RPMs. Specialists recognize as many as 21 different collectible Kennedy half dollar RPMs, and 11 of them are from the 1964-D issue. To distinguish them all, various numbering systems are used. The most important varieties are collected in Whitman's *Cherrypickers' Guide to Rare Die Varieties of United States Coins: Half Dimes Through Dollars, Gold, and Commemoratives*, where this specific variety is numbered as FS-50-1964D-501.

This particular coin is among the boldest and most-desirable of all RPMs in the modern series. It shows north-south re-punching, with the second D punched slightly below but nearly as strongly as the first D. It is common to describe the placement of each mintmark on an RPM by their relative compass coordinates (north, south, east, or west), the amount of spacing between them, and the relative strength of each mark. In common parlance, this coin will be referred to as a "D over D."

The best way to spot an RPM is to examine the mintmark under magnification; 10x magnification is enough to spot any collectible variety. If the mintmark appears doubled or unusual, check the surrounding lettering. If the lettering around the mintmark is also doubled, it's very unlikely that the coin being examined is an RPM. Instead, it's probably a strike-doubled coin. When one is looking for RPM coins, sometimes strike doubling or mechanical doubling can be misleading. Strike doubling occurs when vibrations during the manufacturing process leave shelves or steps on the sides of letters, created by the side-to-side movement of the coin or die during striking. It is very common, especially on San Francisco coins of the late 1960s, and never worth a premium.

Because mintmarks were added to the master die (which makes working hubs that then create working dies to strike coins) in the mid-1980s, this kind of variety is no longer being created. There are literally dozens of collectible RPMs and, in addition to this sought-after Kennedy half dollar, collectors can look for a 1968-D/D cent and a 1970-S/S Large Date cent. Both are among the most dramatic RPMs of the modern coinage era, just missing the 100 Greatest U.S. Modern Coins list, and both can be found in pocket change.

Pick-up point: Mintmark.

	Total Certified Population	Most Commonly Certified	
		Grade	No. in Grade
NGC	4	MS-64	4
PCGS	39	MS-64	19

Mintage: fraction of 156,205,446

Retail value in most common certified grade (MS-64): $150

2008-W ANDREW JACKSON $10 FIRST SPOUSE GOLD

Designed by John Reich (obverse) and Justin Kunz (reverse). The obverse features a reproduction of Liberty as originally used on the Capped Bust, Lettered Edge half dollar minted from 1807 to 1836. To provide for continuity of the First Spouse Coin Program, an image emblematic of Liberty was used for this issue, as Andrew Jackson was widowed shortly before he took office. Inscriptions include IN GOD WE TRUST, 7th PRESIDENCY, the year 1829 above the year 1837, Jackson's dates in office, and 2008. The reverse features an image of Andrew Jackson, the war hero of the Battle of New Orleans. Inscriptions include the president's nickname of OLD HICKORY, UNITED STATES OF AMERICA, E PLURIBUS UNUM, $10, 1/2 OZ., and .9999 FINE GOLD.

Weight: 15.55 grams. *Composition:* 99.99% gold.
Diameter: 26.49 mm. *Edge:* Reeded.

It is certainly fitting that when creating a new coinage series to honor the presidents, the first spouses should be similarly honored. That's exactly what happened when Congress passed the Presidential $1 Coin Act of 2005. That legislation also brought into being the First Spouse Gold Coin Program. Concurrent with the issuance of each Presidential dollar, the law stipulated that a $10 coin made of 1/2-ounce of .9999 fine gold was to be sold by the Mint honoring each president's respective spouse.

Many questioned the need for this program. It had its advantages, however; Congress was actively seeking to introduce .9999 fine gold (or 24-karat) bullion, as American eagles are only .9167 fine and many nations are now producing bullion gold coins of much higher fineness. The Presidential $1 Coin Act of 2005 also alleviated this need by creating the American buffalo gold coin, a bullion coin of .9999 fineness.

When the first coins in the series came out in 2007, honoring Martha Washington and Abigail Adams, they sold out their entire limit of 40,000 examples. The third coin in the series, Thomas Jefferson's Liberty, was even more popular. For program continuity, the authorizing legislation stipulated that a design emblematic of Liberty be shown on the obverse of the coin in the event that a president was not married while in office. For Jefferson, whose wife died before he became president, the Liberty design chosen was that used on the cent coins that circulated from 1800 to 1808.

As with Presidential dollars, Spouse coins for four presidents come out each year (more than four coins if a president had more than one spouse while in office). The fourth coin of the series, for popular First Lady Dolley Madison, only sold 30,896 of the 40,000 authorized, though. In 2008, interest in the coins really began to dwindle. The first two coins of 2008, for Elizabeth Monroe and Louisa Adams, saw sales of only 12,452 and 11,677 coins, respectively.

The third coin of 2008 was Andrew Jackson's Liberty. Jackson's wife died a few months before he was inaugurated as president. The obverse of the coin shows Liberty as borrowed from the Capped Bust half dollar that circulated from 1808 to 1836. The reverse shows Jackson as a general on horseback, leading troops against the British in the Battle of New Orleans in 1815. Jackson, nicknamed "Old Hickory" for his toughness, is a popular president, and the Capped Bust half dollar is a popular coin. But, alas, they did not make a popular coin in combination. Only 4,754 Uncirculated examples were sold and 7,806 Proofs. With less than 5,000 Mint State coins, they are already a bit tricky to come by in the secondary market.

For 2010 First Spouse coins, mintage limits have been cut from 40,000 to 15,000 coins, in hopes that lower mintage caps will motivate collectors. But there is little doubt that future First Spouse coins will see lower net mintage figures, with a few issues probably touching record lows for modern U.S. coins. Since Jackson is such a popular president, this coin's low mintage places it atop the list of First Spouse coins for the time being.

	Total Certified Population	Most Commonly Certified	
		Grade	No. in Grade
NGC	590	MS-70	454
PCGS	410	MS-69	234
Mintage: 4,281			
Retail value in most common certified grade (MS-70): $850			

1996-W CENTENNIAL OLYMPICS (CAULDRON) $5 COMMEMORATIVE

Designed by Frank Gasparro (obverse) and William Krawczewicz (reverse). The obverse features an athlete lighting the Olympic flame. The inscriptions include **LIBERTY, IN GOD WE TRUST, 1996,** and the U.S. Olympic logo. The reverse features the Atlanta Committee for the Olympic Games logo surrounded with laurel leaves. The inscriptions are **UNITED STATES OF AMERICA, FIVE DOLLARS, E PLURIBUS UNUM,** and **ATLANTA.**

Weight: 8.359 grams. *Composition:* 90% gold and 10% copper (net weight .2418 ounces pure gold). *Diameter:* 21.6 mm. *Edge:* Reeded.

The modern commemorative issues certainly brought a resurgence of artistry—and corresponding criticism—to U.S. coinage design. Chief Engraver Elizabeth Jones received abundant praise for the George Washington half dollar, the Statue of Liberty $5 gold coin, and the 1988 Olympics $5 gold piece, the last of which some critics claim to be among the finest designs ever to appear on any U.S. coin. Other artists contributed to this sudden infusion of high-caliber design, including medalist Marcel Jovine and U.S. Mint engraver John Mercanti. But dur-

ing the mid-1990s, one U.S. Mint engraver had achieved the status of a legend among U.S. coin collectors—former Chief Engraver Frank Gasparro.

Gasparro joined the Mint in 1942 and served as chief engraver from 1965 until his retirement in 1981. Among his design credits are the Memorial Reverse of the Lincoln cent, the reverse of the Kennedy half dollar, the Eisenhower dollar, and the Susan B. Anthony dollar. While in his mid-80s and having been retired from the Mint for more than a decade, Gasparro submitted designs for the 1991 Mount Rushmore commemoratives and the 1996 Olympic Games commemoratives. For the Olympic coins, three of his designs were selected, including the obverse for the 1996-W Centennial Olympics (Cauldron) $5 gold coin.

In some ways this coin is a companion piece to Gasparro's design for the 1995 $5 coin that featured a runner carrying a torch with the city in the background. In this 1996 coin, appropriately struck later in sequence than the torchbearer coin, the Olympic flame is transferred to its cauldron, where it would remain alight throughout the Games. The actual cauldron-lighting scene at the 1996 games was quite different from the image presented on the coin. The nature of the lighting remained a surprise until the very last moments, when the cauldron was dramatically lit by boxer Muhammad Ali, whose presence there evoked strong emotions at the ceremony's climax.

The work of a legendary coin designer and the power of this moment at the games provided little boost to the sales of the struggling Olympic commemorative issues. Just 9,210 Uncirculated examples were sold along with 38,555 Proof coins. Even though the Cauldron coin fared better than some of the other $5 gold coins of the era, the number of Uncirculated coins still ranks among the lowest mintage figures for any modern commemorative.

	Total Certified Population	Most Commonly Certified	
		Grade	No. in Grade
NGC	673	MS-69	403
PCGS	1,234	MS-69	1,159

Distribution: 9,210

Retail value in most common certified grade (MS-69): $1,900

Designed by Norman E. Nemeth (obverse) and Charles L. Vickers (reverse). The obverse features the Marines raising the Stars and Stripes over Iwo Jima as shown on the famous photograph by Joe Rosenthal. Inscriptions include LIBERTY, IN GOD WE TRUST, MARINES, and the dates 1775 and 2005. The reverse features an eagle, globe, and anchor—emblems of the Marine Corps. Inscriptions include UNITED STATES OF AMERICA, E PLURIBUS UNUM, SEMPER FIDELIS (the Marine Corps motto), and ONE DOLLAR.

Weight: 26.73 grams. *Composition:* 90% silver and 10% copper (net weight .77344 ounces pure silver). *Diameter:* 38.1 mm. *Edge:* Reeded.

Although a number of military-related themes adorn modern commemoratives, no individual branch of the military had been specifically honored on a coin before the issuance of the 2005 Marines dollar coin. It's surprising, in many respects, that all branches of the armed forces had not yet been recognized in this way—and yet the occasion for issuing this coin may still seem unusual. The coin commemorates the 230th anniversary of the Marine Corps; although an institution lasting for 230 years is an impressive feat, it's not a milestone anniversary that is routinely celebrated. But every commemorative coin needs an occasion, and the Marines had one in their 230th year. The Marine Corps Heritage Center was scheduled to open on November 10, 2005, the date of the Marines' 230th anniversary. Originally authorized by Congress in 2001, this Heritage Center was a new facility where researchers and the public could study, explore, and preserve the history of the Marines. Surcharge proceeds from the sales of the Marines dollar,

then, would be applied towards construction of the Marine Corps Heritage Center.

Based on research conducted by the Marine Corps Heritage Foundation (itself also being the beneficiary of the program) about the desirability of this coin, it was determined that the authorized mintage of 500,000 was too low to meet demand. In response, the secretary of the Treasury unilaterally increased the mintage limit to 600,000 coins, exercising this authority for the first time in history. As predicted, the coin was a super-seller. Coins first went on sale July 20, 2005, and all 600,000 were sold by September 21, 2005—even before the Mint's holiday gift catalog was mailed.

Why was this coin the bestselling commemorative in more than a decade? To start, there are approximately 200,000 active-duty Marines. The coin had a natural audience of every Marine—whether active, reserve, or retired—as well as their family members. Secondly, the design of the coin was phenomenal. Design requirements, per legislation, were to be "emblematic of the warrior ethos of the United States Marine Corps." Selected for the obverse design was perhaps the most famous image of Marine courage and commitment, the raising of the flag at Iwo Jima. The likeness, taken from Joe Rosenthal's picture, is thought to be the most reproduced image in the history of photography. The reverse of the coin simply shows the Marine Corps' eagle, globe, and anchor emblem as well as its motto, *Semper Fidelis,* which translates to mean "Always Faithful."

The coin's design clearly resonated with Americans. At the release ceremony for the Marines dollar, U.S. Mint Director Henrietta Holsman Fore said, "The coin design is simple and heroic. The Iwo Jima image is the storied symbol of the Marine Corps' heroism, courage, strength and versatility. It exemplifies Semper Fidelis to an appreciative nation every day around the world."

Today, this coin carries a significant premium to its issue price. The Proof version of the coin far outsold the Uncirculated version by more than 10 to 1, but it still continues to garner a higher price. This perhaps owes to the coin's popularity among Marines and other non-specialists; as many may be collecting on theme alone, they prefer more attractive coins to coins with a lower mintage.

	Total Certified Population	Most Commonly Certified	
		Grade	No. in Grade
NGC	10,927	MS-70	6,143
PCGS	3,801	MS-69	3,341
Distribution: 49,671			
Retail value in most common certified grade (MS-70): $100			

1996-D CENTENNIAL OLYMPICS (TENNIS) DOLLAR COMMEMORATIVE

Designed by James C. Sharpe (obverse) and Thomas D. Rogers (reverse). The obverse features a female athlete playing tennis. Inscriptions read LIBERTY, 1996, ATLANTA, IN GOD WE TRUST, and the U.S. Olympic logo. The reverse portrays the Atlanta Committee for the Olympic Games logo with torch and flame. The inscriptions read UNITED STATES OF AMERICA, ONE DOLLAR, E PLURIBUS UNUM, ATLANTA 1996, and CENTENNIAL OLYMPIC GAMES.

Weight: 26.73 grams. *Composition:* 90% silver and 10% copper (net weight .77344 ounces pure silver). *Diameter:* 38.1 mm. *Edge:* Reeded.

A s a recreational sport, tennis is enjoyed by millions of people. The U.S. Tennis Association (USTA), the sport's national governing body devoted to promoting and growing the sport, has more than 700,000 members and is the largest tennis organization in the world. The widespread popularity of the sport appears not to have translated into sales of the 1996 Olympic Tennis commemorative dollar coin, however, as a mere 15,983 Uncirculated dollars were sold along with 92,016 Proofs. The mintage figure for

the Uncirculated coins is the third-lowest silver dollar mintage figure in the entire commemorative program.

The poor sales are blamed on the glut of coins issued to commemorate the 1996 Atlanta Olympic Games, 32 in all counting Proofs and Uncirculated versions. Other sports that enjoy mainstream popularity, such as baseball and basketball, experienced slightly better sales because of specific promotions. Such was not the case with this issue, perhaps because the obverse design features a female player, which may have slightly limited the opportunity for promotion. The Proof coin does seem to enjoy a price premium a bit greater than its mintage might otherwise warrant, and this may be simply because this coin is often purchased as a gift to give to tennis-playing friends or family members.

When it comes to Olympic sports, tennis certainly isn't the first one to come to mind. In fact, during the 12 Olympic Games held between the 1924 Paris Olympics and the 1988 Seoul Olympics, tennis was either not offered or was played for exhibition only. Certainly the four major tournaments of the sport—the Australian Open, the French Open, Wimbledon, and the U.S. Open—are all more prestigious tournaments within the sport of professional tennis than the Olympic Games.

Interestingly, tennis at the Olympics is actually growing. Since 2004, results have counted towards professional rankings. At the upcoming 2012 London games, competition in mixed doubles will be offered for the first time since 1924. Furthermore, all matches will be held at the All-England Club, site of the Wimbledon Championships, in hopes that the austerity of the venue will contribute to athlete and fan enthusiasm for tennis at the games.

	Total Certified Population	Most Commonly Certified	
		Grade	No. in Grade
NGC	471	MS-69	402
PCGS	801	MS-69	677
Distribution: 15,983			
Retail value in most common certified grade (MS-69): $450			

Designed by Gilroy Roberts (obverse) and Frank Gasparro (reverse). On the obverse, the head of John F. Kennedy faces left. LIBERTY arcs across the top of the obverse; the date arcs along the bottom and IN GOD WE TRUST runs in a straight line beneath Kennedy's head. The reverse features a heraldic eagle, similar to that seen on the 1801 through 1807 and 1892 through 1915 half dollars, within a circle of 50 stars. UNITED STATES arcs around the top and HALF DOLLAR arcs along the bottom of the reverse.

Weight: 11.34 grams. *Composition:* 75% copper and 25% nickel bonded to an inner core of pure copper. *Diameter:* 30.6 mm. *Edge:* Reeded.

One of the interesting maxims in rare-coin collecting is that larger coins have a larger collecting base than do smaller coins. In other words, collectors just tend to like large coins. The obvious exception is collectors of varieties, who always look at coins through a magnifier and tend to prefer interesting varieties over big coins. Of the 10 doubled-die coins included on the list of 100 Greatest U.S. Modern Coins, this is the only half dollar. This also makes it the largest of all the coins on the list to display die doubling.

The relatively large size of this coin makes its doubling especially dramatic. Even without magnification, the stretching and doubling of the letters on the obverse legends are clearly visible. To the unaided eye, extra-thick letters on the word LIBERTY and the date are clearly visible, but on the motto, especially on the words WE TRUST, the letters become fully separated. The varia-

tion of doubling characteristics seen throughout the coin is caused by the location of the pivot point and the amount of offset between the two strikes from the hub to the die.

Doubled dies on larger coins are seen less frequently than similar varieties on smaller-denomination coins. Larger denominations are struck in smaller number than cents and other small-denomination coins, so fewer die pairs are used. Also, more significantly, the larger size of the coins makes such gaffes easier to spot and, therefore, less likely to leave the Mint unnoticed. This is, without question, the best Kennedy half dollar doubled die, and one of the most interesting in the entire modern series.

While as many as 150,000 coins are struck by a Kennedy half dollar obverse die, only a couple thousand of these coins are known and attributed. Although the most common source of this coin has been Mint sets, the variety's overall quality is not exceptionally high and most examples seen are lower- and mid-range Mint State coins (MS-63 and MS-64). Many Mint sets have been searched since this coin's discovery in the late 1970s, and examples are seldom located in original sets today. Roll finds of this variety do occur, but the grade of the coins tends to be lower still, and a number of lightly circulated examples are also known.

Because the total grade distribution of 1974-D Doubled-Die Obverse Kennedy half dollars is rather wide, condition plays a major factor in determining this coin's value. Higher-grade examples are worth significantly more than lower-grade examples, and professional certification is recommended when paying a premium for condition (as well as for attribution). No examples grading superb gem Uncirculated (MS-67) have ever been graded, and such a find would indeed be a significant discovery for specialists.

Pick-up point: WE TRUST.

	Total Certified Population	Most Commonly Certified	
		Grade	No. in Grade
NGC	—	—	—
PCGS	476	MS-64	271

Mintage: fraction of 79,066,300

Retail value in most common certified grade (MS-64): $125

1992-D XXV OLYMPIAD (BASEBALL) DOLLAR COMMEMORATIVE

Designed by John R. Deecken (obverse) and Marcel Jovine (reverse). The obverse features a pitcher about to throw a ball to a batter. Inscriptions read LIBERTY, IN GOD WE TRUST, USA with the Olympic logo, and 1992. The reverse features a shield, intertwined Olympic rings, and olive branches. Inscriptions include UNITED STATES OF AMERICA, E PLURIBUS UNUM on a scroll, ONE DOLLAR, and USA within Olympic rings.

Weight: 26.73 grams. *Composition:* 90% silver and 10% copper (net weight .77344 ounces pure silver). *Diameter:* 38.1 mm. *Edge:* Lettered on a reeded background.

The 1992 Olympic Commemorative Coin Act sought to raise money to support the training of athletes participating in the 1992 Olympic Games. Three coins were authorized: a copper-nickel-clad half dollar, a silver dollar, and a $5 gold coin. The only stipulation regarding the design of the silver dollar in the legislation was that "the design of the $1 coins shall be emblematic of the participation of American athletes in the 1992 Olympic Games."

Secretary of the Treasury Nick Brady openly solicited designs for the coins and selected the winners after consultation with the United States Olympic Committee and the Commission of Fine Arts. The winning design for the Olympic dollar featured a baseball pitcher firing a ball to home plate. Baseball isn't normally identified as an Olympic sport, and in previous games it had only been included as an exhibition. The 1992 Olympic Games in Barcelona were the first ever to include it as an official sport for which medals would be awarded. In light of this, it seemed fitting that the design selected for the dollar coin should highlight America's national pastime, baseball.

The coin's design was created by artist John Deecken, and it shows a right-handed pitcher in the midst of his motion. A maximum mintage of four million coins was authorized. Sales totals were 187,552 for the Denver Mint's Uncirculated version and 504,505 for the San Francisco Mint's Proof version. The Denver Mint coin is known for an unusual feature: it bore a lettered edge—the phrase XXV OLYMPIAD was impressed into its edge four times—and was the first edge-lettered coin to be issued in the United States since 1933. It was not this feature, however, that generated excitement among the numismatic press.

After the coin's release, collectors noticed an uncanny resemblance between the pitcher shown on the coin and the image on the Nolan Ryan 1991 Fleer baseball card. Every detail in the photograph of Ryan perfectly matched the pitcher's image on the coin, including the position of Ryan's arms, glove, and stride—even down to the crane of his neck and the wrinkles on his jersey. Ryan's unofficial depiction caused some controversy, and the coin's legality was even called into question. There was never any formal inquiry, however, because Mint officials and Deecken himself fervently denied that the resemblance was intentional.

For some time in the secondary market, the coin took on a nickname: the Nolan Ryan dollar. Since this dollar was produced, baseball has twice returned as a theme for U.S. commemorative coins. The sport is depicted on the 1995-S Olympic half dollar, struck for the 1996 Olympic Games, and on the 1997 Jackie Robinson commemorative dollar and $5 gold coins (see number five). Unfortunately, the sport has not fared so well at the Olympics. It was voted out of the Olympics for the 2012 London games, becoming the first sport to be removed from competition since 1936, when polo was eliminated.

	Total Certified Population	Most Commonly Certified	
		Grade	No. in Grade
NGC	2,836	MS-69	2,663
PCGS	1,918	MS-69	1,658
Distribution: 187,552			
Retail value in most common certified grade (MS-69): $65			

2008-W $10 AMERICAN GOLD BUFFALO

Designed by James Earle Fraser. The obverse and reverse designs are based on the original 1913 Buffalo nickel, with modified inscriptions on the reverse. The obverse features a portrait of a Native American facing right with the inscription LIBERTY and the date 2008. The reverse features a figure of a bison standing, facing left. The inscription reads UNITED STATES OF AMERICA, E PLURIBUS UNUM, IN GOD WE TRUST, $10, and 1/4 OZ .9999 FINE GOLD.

Weight: 7.776 grams. *Composition:* 24-karat (.9999) fine gold.
Diameter: 21.5 mm. *Edge:* Reeded.

When the Liberty Head nickel design was first released in 1883, a large V, signifying the Roman numeral for 5, was the only indication of its value. The word "cents" did not appear on the coin. There are stories that some miscreants plated the new nickels with gold, hoping to pass them off as $5 gold pieces. These gold-plated nickels are still sold as novelties today and are called "racketeer nickels." The dimensions of the nickel and the $5 gold piece, each a little more than 21 mm in diameter at the time, were similar enough to enable this illusion to pass.

Size is one of the features that make the 2008-W gold buffalo $10 coin so special. It is 22 mm and struck in 1/4-ounce of pure, .9999 fine gold. Its design faithfully replicates the design of the 1913 Buffalo nickel, making it a true representative of the original—a sort of racketeer nickel in reverse.

The gold buffalo coins were first authorized in 2005, and they were the first U.S. pure gold bullion coins. The design is nearly identical to James Earle Fraser's original composition for the Buffalo nickel that was struck from 1913 to 1938. The obverse shows a Native American chief in profile, said to be a composite of three models who sat for Fraser: Chief Iron Tail of the Lakota Sioux, Chief Two Moons of the Cheyenne, and a third whose identity Fraser could not recall. The American bison on the reverse is said to be modeled after Black Diamond, an animal kept at the New York Zoological Gardens.

Two years after the introduction of the one-ounce gold buffalo coin, fractional denominations were introduced. They were offered in the same weights and denominations as the coins in the American gold eagle series, only with the higher metal fineness of the buffalo. The coins were sold as bullion, in Proof versions, and also in Uncirculated versions. The Uncirculated coins had the same finish as their bullion counterparts but also included the W mintmark and were sold directly to the public. They were expensive, as the price of gold was high in 2008, and a surcharge was added. The Uncirculated varieties were also available only in limited quantities. The 1/4-ounce coin and the 1/2-ounce coins sold in the least numbers, 9,949 and 9,286, respectively.

To date, the 2008-W is the only 1/4-ounce Uncirculated version of the gold buffalo coin and, with fewer than 10,000 examples, it's an attractive scarcity. Because its size so closely mimics the Buffalo nickel that served as its model, the 1/4-ounce coin is in higher demand than the even-lower-mintage 1/2-ounce coin. The fractional gold buffalos were not issued in 2009. Based on the low sales figures in 2008 and the current high demand for bullion coinage, it's uncertain when collector versions of the fractional gold buffalo coins will be offered again.

	Total Certified Population	Most Commonly Certified	
		Grade	No. in Grade
NGC	3,220	MS-70	2,666
PCGS	817	MS-70	634
Mintage: 9,949			
Retail value in most common certified grade (MS-70): $2,500			

1976-S EISENHOWER DOLLAR, VARIETY 1, CLAD, PROOF

Designed by Frank Gasparro (obverse) and Dennis Williams (reverse). The obverse features the head of Dwight Eisenhower facing left. LIBERTY arcs around the top and the date reads 1776-1976. On the reverse, the Liberty Bell appears superimposed on the moon. The outer legends include UNITED STATES OF AMERICA above and ONE DOLLAR below. The motto E PLURIBUS UNUM appears in small letters to the lower right of the Liberty Bell.

Weight: 22.68 grams. *Composition:* Outer layers of 75% copper and 25% nickel bonded to a core of pure copper. *Diameter:* 38.1 mm. *Edge:* Reeded.

To celebrate the bicentennial of the Declaration of Independence, the reverses of the quarter, half dollar, and dollar coins were redesigned with images representing themes of symbolic significance. The long lead-up to the Bicentennial dollar coin's ultimate release in 1975 was markedly different from the release schedule of the original 1971 Eisenhower dollar issued just a few years before. For that coin, all of the design work was conducted by internal U.S. Mint resources. For the Bicentennial redesign, a public contest was held. The design selected for the dollar was submitted by Dennis R. Williams, a 21-year-old sculpture student at the Columbus College of Art and Design. He had been assigned the task of coinage design as a project for course

credit. For the dollar, the Liberty Bell was shown overlapping the moon. This image was selected for the coin before the end of 1973, and modeling work began right away.

The design as adopted for the coin was faithful to Williams' original rendering. The typeface on the reverse legends, which included both UNITED STATES OF AMERICA and ONE DOLLAR, was a thick, sans-serif letter type. The rather blocky letter style contrasted noticeably with the typeface used on the coin's obverse as well as that used on the reverse in previous years. Regardless of this unusual inconsistency, production of Proof Bicentennial coinage began early. In 1975, dual-dated 1776–1976 quarters, half dollars, and dollars were issued for circulation, in Mint sets, and in Proof sets. The 1976-S Bicentennial dollar coins with this original letter style are called Variety 1. All of the Proof copper-nickel dollars that were included in the 1975 Proof set were Variety 1.

For the 1976 Proof set, the Mint announced that, to improve the dollar's appearance, a new version would be used, the so-called Variety 2. This version featured lower obverse relief, softening the president's facial features. The reverse relief was raised and the lettering was restyled to conform to the obverse lettering. This last alteration constituted the most obvious change on the coin.

Among the special coinage issues for those years, a three-piece silver Proof set that included the Bicentennial quarter dollar, half dollar, and dollar was sold in 1975 and 1976. The entire mintage of the Proof silver Bicentennial dollars was Variety 1, and for this reason, the variety of silver coin is not as noteworthy.

The Variety 1 coin is more desirable than the Variety 2 largely because of the differences in their original mintage. Only 2.8 million Proof sets were sold in 1975 compared with more than 4.1 million in 1976. It's the slightly scarcer variety of the two copper-nickel-clad coins. The unusual appearance of the letter style also makes it somewhat of a standout as few such irregularities exist on modern U.S. coinage.

	Total Certified Population	Most Commonly Certified	
		Grade	No. in Grade
NGC	944	PF-68 UC	167
PCGS	9,286	PF-69 DC	8,552

Mintage: 2,845,450

Retail value in most common certified grade (PF-69 DC): $125

1986-S STATUE OF LIBERTY HALF DOLLAR COMMEMORATIVE

Designed by Edgar Steever (obverse) and Sherl Joseph Winter (reverse). The obverse features the Statue of Liberty standing before a ship of immigrants entering New York Harbor, with the New York skyline in the distance. The words LIBERTY / IN GOD WE TRUST appears above, and the date below. The reverse depicts an immigrant family with their belongings on the threshold of America, with the words UNITED STATES OF AMERICA / A NATION OF IMMIGRANTS above and E PLURIBUS UNUM and FIVE DOLLARS below.

Weight: 11.34 grams. *Composition:* 92% copper and 8% nickel. *Diameter:* 30.6 mm. *Edge:* Reeded.

Considering total mintage figures and surcharges levied, the Statue of Liberty commemorative program proved to be the most successful in the history of U.S. commemorative coinage. Although it was only the third modern commemorative-coinage program, it set a high-water mark that is yet to be surpassed. This achievement resulted from a perfect storm of factors that included a great theme, great designs, and great promotion.

The coins were struck to commemorate the centennial of the dedication of the Statue of Liberty, the symbol of American hope and opportunity that greeted so many immigrants upon their arrival to the United States. The coin's primary purpose was to raise money, in the form of surcharges, for the Statue of Liberty–Ellis Island Foundation. The Foundation was created to raise money for the renovation and preservation of the Statue of Liberty and had an aggressive goal of raising $265 million.

President Ronald Reagan appointed Chrysler CEO Lee Iacocca as the head of the Statue of Liberty–Ellis Island Foundation, which turned out to be ideal for both the coins and the foundation. Iacocca was a great champion of the coin, promoting it on television and at numerous press events. This was only the second commemorative-coinage program with a surcharge to benefit a specific agency. The alignment of the marketing efforts of the Mint and the foundation's fundraising goals helped enormously to promote the coin.

Still, others would argue that what contributed so much to the success of this program was that it included a "coin for the people," a copper-nickel-clad half dollar that was sold for only $7.50 (or $6.50 during the pre-release period). The brainchild of attorney and numismatist David L. Ganz—who also authored the legislation, according to an interview cited in David Bowers's *Commemorative Coins of the United States: A Complete Encyclopedia*—the affordable half dollar remains the best-selling U.S. commemorative coin in history, with more than 7.8 million sold. By far, the lion's share belonged to the San Francisco Proof issue, with a mintage of 6,925,627, and the balance were Denver Mint Uncirculated specimens.

One of the features contributing to the coin's success was its evocative, story-telling design. A perspective view on the obverse captures the Statue of Liberty, a steamship arriving, and a view of New York in the background. The reverse shows a family of four, having recently arrived in the country, waiting on the wharf for transport from Ellis Island to New York. Above the legend reads the caption, UNITED STATES OF AMERICA / A NATION OF IMMIGRANTS. This first copper-nickel commemorative half dollar was so successful that it has since been followed by 15 more.

In total, the half dollar, silver dollar, and $5 gold coin that comprised the Statue of Liberty commemorative-coinage program contributed $82.9 million to the Statue of Liberty–Ellis Island Foundation. The large issue-size of the half dollar means that it is readily available today and still not very expensive. What was true in 1986 remains true today—it's a coin for the people.

	Total Certified Population	Most Commonly Certified	
		Grade	No. in Grade
NGC	7,978	PF-69 UC	7,480
PCGS	4,646	PF-69 DC	4,197

Distribution: 6,925,627

Retail value in most common certified grade (PF-69 UC): $50

1999-W WASHINGTON $5
COMMEMORATIVE, PROOF

Designed by Laura Gardin Fraser. The obverse features a bust of President George Washington inspired by the bust modeled in 1785 by French sculptor Jean Antoine Houdon. Inscriptions include LIBERTY, IN GOD WE TRUST, and the date 1999. The reverse features a heraldic eagle with outspread wings and thirteen stars above. Inscriptions include UNITED STATES OF AMERICA, E PLURIBUS UNUM, and FIVE DOLLARS.

Weight: 8.539 grams. *Composition:* 90% gold and 10% copper (net weight .2418 ounces pure gold). *Diameter:* 21.6 mm. *Edge:* Reeded.

This coin was struck to honor the life of George Washington on the 200th anniversary of his death. Proceeds from a $35-per-coin surcharge went to the Mount Vernon Ladies' Association, which preserves the home of George Washington and educates people about his life. A similar coin, the Washington quarter, honors the 200th anniversary of the first president's birth and was first issued in 1932. Fittingly, these two coins are connected.

When a design competition was held in 1931 to select the design for the Washington quarter, 100 designs were reviewed. Overwhelmingly, the Commission of Fine Arts and the Washington Bicentennial Commission preferred above all others a design by Laura Gardin Fraser, who was married to Buffalo nickel designer James Earle Fraser. The final decision fell to Treasury Secretary Andrew Mellon, who preferred the design submitted by John Flanagan, which was then used without interruption on the Washington quarter from 1932 to 1998. His portrait of Washington

remains on the coin to this day, although the reverse design has changed.

When the time came to issue a second coin to honor the life of Washington, the Fraser design was resurrected. A U.S. Mint press release announcing the sale of the coin quoted U.S. Treasurer Mary Ellen Withrow: "I am particularly pleased that Laura Gardin Fraser's 1931 designs for a Washington quarter-dollar now adorn United States coinage." Like Flanagan's design, Fraser's obverse features a portrait of Washington in profile and the reverse shows the figure of an eagle. In the same press release, the portrait was described as "stunning," while the eagle is called "powerful" and "exquisitely detailed."

After the devastatingly poor performance of commemoratives issued during the mid-1990s, the Mint and Congress were getting back on track. They had learned that coin collectors could be good and loyal patrons if the commemoratives issued were indeed worthy. Coinage programs should be small and few in number. The George Washington Death Bicentennial program itself was small; it is, in fact, one of only two coinage programs that have consisted of just a single gold coin. Themes themselves also needed to be worthy, and the coin designs needed to have merit; both of these requirements were met with this Washington commemorative. This coin was the first to demonstrate this appreciation for the collector, especially as its design was steeped in numismatic history.

Collectors responded favorably. Both Proof and Uncirculated versions were struck at West Point, and 41,693 and 22,511 sold, respectively. While the numbers may not seem impressive, these figures represent 64 percent of the authorized mintage, making this the most successful gold issue by percentage of authorized mintage sold since 1987. The recirculation of an old design also resonated well with collectors, and other coins in future years would feature similar reprises to spur collector interest. For example, James Earle Fraser's design for the Buffalo nickel would grace the 2001 Buffalo dollar (see number 27) and Augustus Saint-Gaudens's 1907 design was featured on the 2009 Ultra High Relief double eagle (see number 16).

	Total Certified Population	Most Commonly Certified	
		Grade	No. in Grade
NGC	1,803	PF-69 UC	1,067
PCGS	1,500	PF-69 DC	425

Distribution: 41,693

Retail value in most common certified grade (PF-69 UC): $600

2009-W $100 AMERICAN PLATINUM EAGLE, PROOF

Designed by John Mercanti (obverse) and Susan Gamble (reverse). The obverse features a portrait of Lady Liberty. The reverse design is emblematic of the principle "To Form a More Perfect Union" as written in the Preamble to the Constitution, and features four faces representing the diversity of our nation.

Weight: 1.0005 ounces. *Composition:* 99.95% platinum.
Diameter: 32.7 mm. *Edge:* Reeded.

Ever since the American platinum eagle coins were first issued in 1997, they were available in four weights and in both bullion and Proof formats. This remained the case for 12 years without interruption. In 2009, however, the production of platinum coinage was suspended. The extreme volatility in both the metals markets and the broader financial markets caused demand for silver and gold eagles to swell unexpectedly, putting enormous pressure on the Mint to produce those issues. Platinum bullion coinage, a niche product in comparison, was put on hold. Only a single platinum coin was issued in 2009, the one-ounce Proof platinum eagle.

Beyond its being the only platinum coin issued in 2009, the coin was a departure in other ways as well. In that year, a new six-year design program was introduced for the Proof platinum eagle, with each year memorializing one of the six principles found in the preamble to the Constitution, beginning with "To Form a More Perfect Union" in 2009. The design selected for this issue shows four heads in profile—each of a different race—symbolizing the diversity of the United States. They form a circular arrangement, with their hair intertwined to suggest how different people have come together to create the nation. Within the circle is the legend A MORE PERFECT UNION.

Designed by U.S. Mint artist Susan Gamble and sculpted by Phebe Hemphill, this coin lacks something that all other platinum eagle reverse designs have had: an eagle. Although no law requires this coin to include an eagle, other coins are required to have this design element. Additionally, the coin forms part of the American Eagle Bullion program, and thus an eagle motif is appropriate, if not apt. To overcome the omission, the design includes a "privy mark," or small symbol of an eagle's head based on an original coin punch in the archives of the U.S. Mint at Philadelphia. This mark was simply meant to indicate that the coin is indeed an American eagle coin.

It is likely that future Proof platinum eagle issues will also include a small eagle mark, giving artists greater space and freedom on the coin. This is the first privy mark to appear on a U.S. bullion coin. The feature is employed routinely by a number of other countries, however, to produce special-purpose limited editions of their bullion coinage without requiring a separate commemorative program or incurring the costs of creating a whole new design. A similar design element appeared on the reverse of the Franklin half dollar: although the Liberty Bell is the prominent design feature, a small eagle appears beside it, as its inclusion was required by law.

A total of 8,000 examples of the 2009-W $100 platinum eagle were scheduled for sale, and the issue sold out despite the relatively high issue price of $1,792. Although this figure is comparable to earlier issues, the 2009 coin is both the only platinum coin issued for the year and the first coin in a six-part series. The emphasis on artistry and the freedom allowed in the allegorical representations should produce some exciting coins. The price of platinum metal and the quality of the designs will be the key elements in assessing future demand for the six-coin subseries.

	Total Certified Population	Most Commonly Certified	
		Grade	No. in Grade
NGC	2,003	PF-70 UC	1,689
PCGS	1,335	PF-69 DC	793

Mintage: 8,000

Retail value in most common certified grade (PF-70 UC): $2,500

1995-S KENNEDY HALF DOLLAR, SILVER, PROOF

Designed by Gilroy Roberts (obverse) and Frank Gasparro (reverse). On the obverse, the head of John F. Kennedy faces left. LIBERTY arcs across the top of the obverse; the date arcs along the bottom and IN GOD WE TRUST runs in a straight line beneath Kennedy's head. The reverse features a heraldic eagle, similar to that seen on the 1801 through 1807 and 1892 through 1915 half dollars, within a circle of 50 stars. UNITED STATES arcs around the top and HALF DOLLAR arcs along the bottom of the reverse.

Weight: 12.50 grams. *Composition:* 90% silver and 10% copper. *Diameter:* 30.6 mm. *Edge:* Reeded.

What's the lowest-mintage Kennedy half dollar? This question will stump a lot of numismatists, but modern coin specialists will arrive at the answer fairly quickly. It is the 1998-S Matte Finish specimen that was sold to accompany the Robert F. Kennedy commemorative dollar (see number 22). Ask again which coin is the second-lowest mintage Kennedy half dollar, though, and you'll likely be greeted by silence. It's not an easy question and it will stump a lot of numismatists.

The second-lowest mintage Kennedy half dollar is the Proof silver 1995-S issue. This coin was only sold in Silver Proof sets and Silver Premier Proof sets, and in 1995 these sets experienced their lowest sales ever. First issued in 1992, Silver Proof sets contain 90 percent silver versions of the dime, quarter, and half dollar. The occasion for the issuance of that first set was given as the 200th anni-

versary of the Mint, founded by an act of Congress in 1792. The set proved popular—and profitable—and the Mint has continued to offer Silver Proof sets each year since.

The Mint did not change its prices on the Silver Proof set from 1992 through 1998, offering the standard set for $21 and the Silver Premier Proof set for $37.50. The coins in both sets were identical, but the Premier set had a lush velvet and satin case and a parchment-style Certificate of Authenticity. That first year, more than a million of the two types were sold combined, but these figures slid to a low point in 1995, reaching just 549,878 for the standard silver set and 130,107 for the Premier Proof set. This put the mintage of the three silver coins at 679,985 each, which was an all-time low for the Kennedy half dollar until the 1998-S Matte Finish coin was released.

The reason for the slow sales isn't entirely clear. Silver prices were picking up, although the total value of silver in the set was only about $3.20 at the time of issue (the half dollar, quarter, and dime contained a combined 0.61 ounces of pure silver), so it should not have been a factor. Certainly these sales figures were following a general trend of slowing sales for Silver Proof sets. Most likely, the culprit was the poor performance of U.S. Mint products in the secondary market during the mid-1990s. With a glut of products and low demand in the aftermarket, most Silver Proof sets could already be bought for less than their issue price. Dealers' prices for the 1992 set, the highest-mintage issue, eventually fell to a low of about half of the U.S. Mint issue price.

This was never the case for the 1995 Silver Proof set. Only a couple of years after issue, its relative scarcity was already recognized and its value more than doubled the original issue price. The 1995-S silver Kennedy half dollar was the most-affected coin, becoming one of the most sought-after issues in the series. It has maintained this position for more than a decade, because in subsequent years Silver Proof sets sold better. In 1999, the Mint's offerings were reconfigured to accommodate the five statehood quarters, producing key issues in that series, but sales have always been above 1995 levels thus far.

	Total Certified Population	Most Commonly Certified	
		Grade	No. in Grade
NGC	1,053	PF-69 UC	892
PCGS	2,135	PF-69 DC	1,822

Mintage: 679,985

Retail value in most common certified grade (PF-69 DC): $125

1996-D CENTENNIAL OLYMPICS (ROWING) DOLLAR COMMEMORATIVE

Designed by Bart Forbes (obverse) and Thomas D. Rogers (reverse). The obverse features four men rowing. The inscriptions include XXVI OLYMPIAD, IN GOD WE TRUST, LIBERTY, 1996, and the U.S. Olympic logo. The reverse portrays the Atlanta Committee for the Olympic Games logo with torch and flame. The inscriptions read UNITED STATES OF AMERICA, ONE DOLLAR, E PLURIBUS UNUM, ATLANTA 1996, and CENTENNIAL OLYMPIC GAMES.

Weight: 26.73 grams. *Composition:* 90% silver and 10% copper (net weight .77344 ounces pure silver). *Diameter:* 38.1 mm. *Edge:* Reeded.

Rowing has been contested at every modern summer Olympics since the second games in 1900 in Paris. While scheduled for the first Olympics four years before, events were not held because of bad weather. The United States is the most-decorated country in Olympic rowing, having won 84 total medals over the years, including 31 gold medals. The next-closest nation is Great Britain with 54 total medals. Despite the impressive performance of U.S. athletes at the games, the sport has relatively limited participation in the United States. Just 4,000 high school athletes and 8,000 college athletes participate in rowing in the country, and USRowing, the national governing body for the sport, has just 14,000 members.

The coin nicely illustrates the sport of rowing. The design features a close-up section of a coxless four in mid-stroke. Designed by illustrator Bart Forbes, the composition makes for an attractive coin, although the upper legend XXVI OLYMPIAD is shifted left rather than centered above the rowers, perhaps to indicate a sense of direction or motion. The reverse uses the common design used on all 1996 Olympics silver dollars, featuring the logo of the games.

Sales of this coin were surprisingly strong in one sense. While the authorized mintage had been lowered from 1,000,000 pieces to 500,000 in an effort to spur collector interest, just 168,148 were sold of the Proof and Uncirculated versions, about a third of the revised authorization. Nonetheless, this coin is still the second-best-selling Olympic commemorative dollar of 1995 or 1996. In the absence of another explanation, this suggests that rowing enthusiasts supported the coin, even if they themselves are few in number. By a margin of nearly 10 to 1, the majority of coins sold were Proofs, leaving a net mintage of 16,258 of the Uncirculated 1996-D Centennial Olympics (Rowing) dollar. This figure makes it among the scarcest of all U.S. commemorative dollar coins ever issued.

Another interesting feature of the Uncirculated 1996-D Centennial Olympics (Rowing) dollar is that it has the lowest combined certified population of any modern coin. In other words, combining the figures of NGC and PCGS, the lowest total number of coins graded belongs to this issue. This information further supports the notion that sales were relatively strong outside of the traditional numismatic marketplace and perhaps went to rowers as well as collectors.

Any mintage figure below 20,000 pieces puts pressure on the supply. Dealers actively seeking such coins need to pay a premium, which keeps the price of this issue comparatively high—among the highest of all modern commemorative silver dollars. The coin is simply not available in large numbers on the marketplace; this trend is not changing, making this coin an enduring key of the modern commemorative series.

	Total Certified Population	Most Commonly Certified	
		Grade	No. in Grade
NGC	409	MS-69	329
PCGS	669	MS-69	580

Distribution: 16,258

Retail value in most common certified grade (MS-69): $400

1970-S LINCOLN CENT, SMALL DATE

Designed by Victor David Brenner (obverse) and Frank Gasparro (reverse). The obverse continues the design of 1909. The reverse shows a frontal view of the Lincoln Memorial with UNITED STATES OF AMERICA and E PLURIBUS UNUM appearing above and ONE CENT below.

Weight: 3.11 grams. *Composition:* 95% copper and 5% tin and zinc. *Diameter:* 19 mm. *Edge:* Plain.

Throughout the entirety of U.S. coin collecting, there are dozens of coins described as being Small Date or Large Date, a reference to the size of the digits used on the date of the coin. There are two principle reasons why the Mint might change the size of a coin's date. First, as the coin's design varies, there may be aesthetic reasons to modify this particular aspect of the design. More often with modern coins, though, modifying the date is a way to improve die life and production quality. Such was the case in 1960, when the date on the Lincoln cent was enlarged in the middle of the year because the small 0 was determined to cause breaking and wearing of the dies. To balance out a larger 0, the rest of the date was reconfigured in a larger size, creating two very collectible varieties, the 1960 Small Date and 1960 Large Date cents, each struck at both mints that produced Lincoln cents that year.

Ten years later, in 1970, coins struck at the San Francisco Mint were produced in two date styles, Small Date and Large Date. There is no record, though, of why or when this change occurred, and many simply believe that two different hubs with minor variations were by the Mint to create dies from the very beginning of the year. Coins of both the 1970-S Small and Large Date varieties were found early in 1970 and far from California in the Northeast and the South. Numismatic researcher and author David W. Lange suggests that these coins were widely distributed throughout the country to combat hoarding by speculators. It became clear right away that the Small Date variety was much

scarcer than the Large Date. Since then, the 1970-S Small Date Lincoln cent has emerged as one of the key Lincoln cents of the era.

The 1970-S Small Date Lincoln cent is rather scarce and valuable but is not as well known as other Lincoln cent varieties, including the 1960 Small Date and Large Date coins. One reason may be that this variety can be difficult to attribute. The size difference between the two date styles isn't significant enough to "eyeball" to determine whether a coin is Large or Small Date—though that technique is more than enough to attribute many of the gold coins from the 1840s and 1850s that are collectible by date size. Oftentimes, when a collector encounters either variety, he or she doesn't have an example of the other variety with which to compare it, either. Understanding Small and Large Date varieties is an essential skill for the collector of U.S. coins, and knowing how to accurately attribute varieties in isolation is very important.

The 1970-S Lincoln cent offers some attribution clues that make it possible to identify the Small and Large Date varieties with 100 percent accuracy. First, the position of the 7 should be examined. On the Small Date cent, the top of the 7 is aligned with the tops of the 9 and 0 that surround it. On the Large Date cent, the top of the 7 is lower than the 9 and 0. For this reason, sometimes these varieties will be referred to as the "High 7" for the Small Date and the "Low 7" for the Large Date. Additionally, on the Small Date variety the word LIBERTY is usually, but not always, indistinct and mushy, while on the Large Date the word LIBERTY will be crisp. Knowing these diagnostics makes easy work of attributing this elusive Lincoln cent.

Pick-up point: Date (left, normal date; right, small date).

	Total Certified Population	Most Commonly Certified	
		Grade	No. in Grade
NGC	460	MS-65 RD	179
PCGS	1,411	MS-64	603
Mintage: fraction of 690,560,004			
Retail value in most common certified grade (MS-64): $125			

1981-S SUSAN B. ANTHONY DOLLAR

Designed by Frank Gasparro. A bust of Susan B. Anthony faces right within an angular border. LIBERTY appears above her head and the date is below. Thirteen stars are arranged on the left and right sides. IN GOD WE TRUST appears in small letters at the lower right. The reverse is a miniature version of the design on the regular Eisenhower dollar, also within an angular border.

Weight: 8.1 grams. *Composition:* outer layers of 75% copper and 25% nickel bonded to an inner core of pure copper. *Diameter:* 26.5 mm. *Edge:* Reeded.

From all appearances, the new dollar-coin experiment was ready to be abandoned in 1981. Between the coinage issues of 1979 and 1980, nearly 850,000,000 Susan B. Anthony dollars had been produced for circulation, but only a third of this number had actually been dispersed. One last effort employed to boost circulation was to abandon the dollar bill in favor of the coin at overseas military bases, but when the coins began trading at a discount to the bills, soldiers objected. With this final option exhausted, Anthony dollars were not produced for circulation in 1981 and were only struck for collector sets.

Released in Mint sets only, the 1981-S Susan B. Anthony dollar had a mintage of 3,492,000 pieces to meet demand (2,908,145 Mint sets were sold in 1981). In addition to this San Francisco issue, around three million coins were also struck for Mint sets at Philadelphia and Denver. The mintage figure is low, which always makes a coin appealing to collectors. A second feature of the San Francisco issue, however, contributes significantly to the desirability of this coin over its counterparts from the other mints: it was very poorly made.

Because these coins are found in sets, one would assume that they are available in high grade. That is not the case. Even though these coins did not circulate, they exhibit numerous contact marks and other blemishes throughout the portrait of Anthony as a result of their handling at the mint. One explanation posited for this is that the San Francisco dollar coins were shipped to another mint, as they are packaged in the same cellophane as the Denver Mint coins. Jostling during transport may have contributed to their rough condition. Also, not all examples are well-struck, and some are produced from late-state dies. Fully lustrous high-grade examples are scarce, and only a handful of examples grading superb gem (MS-67) are known, making them very valuable. The finest examples graded by a major certification service are highly coveted and worth many thousands of dollars.

After 1981, Anthony dollar production was put on extended hold; more than 550 million Anthony dollars remained in government storage in 1981. The main uses of the coin were U.S. postal service and public transportation vending machines, which gave the coins in change; demand from these sources averaged between 40 and 50 million coins per year. After an 18-year hiatus, the Anthony dollar was struck again in 1999 for a final time, before the Sacagawea dollar was introduced in the following year.

	Total Certified Population	Most Commonly Certified	
		Grade	No. in Grade
NGC	395	MS-64	153
PCGS	1,184	MS-64	539
Mintage: 3,492,000			
Retail value in most common certified grade (MS-64): $50			

2010-D ZACHARY TAYLOR DOLLAR, MISDATED

Designed by Don Everhart. The obverse features a portrait of Zachary Taylor. The inscriptions include ZACHARY TAYLOR, IN GOD WE TRUST, 12th PRESIDENT, and the years 1849–1850. The reverse features a rendition of the Statue of Liberty with the inscriptions UNITED STATES OF AMERICA and $1. The date, mintmark, and mottos IN GOD WE TRUST and E PLURIBUS UNUM are incused on the edge.

Weight: 8.1 grams. *Composition:* Outer layers of 77% copper, 12% zinc, 7% manganese, and 4% nickel over a core of pure copper. *Diameter:* 26.5 mm. *Edge:* Lettered.

Dollar coins are much more cost-effective for the government than paper currency, but it has been many years since a dollar coin actively circulated in the United States. The legislation that authorized the Presidential $1 Coin Program sought to eliminate some of the barriers to circulation. One of the resulting initiatives was the U.S. Mint's Direct Ship program. To encourage the circulation of dollar coins, the Mint will send any customer up to two coin boxes of 250 dollar coins for their face value. The Mint will even cover all shipping costs. That means that anyone, anywhere in the United States, has easy access to dollar coins for use in general commerce.

In 2010, the U.S. Mint created five different dollar coins for circulation, all of which are edge-lettered with the date, year, and motto E PLURIBUS UNUM. There were four different Presidential dollars along with the Native American dollar coin. The Presidential dollars honor U.S. presidents in the order that they served, and four coins, each featuring a different president, are released throughout the course of each year. Usually, the first of the four Presidential dollars is released in mid-February, and subsequent issues come out in three-month intervals. One Native American dollar coin is released near the start of each year. In January 2010, the Mint began shipping rolls of Native American dollars under the Direct Ship program.

In 2010, one U.S. Mint Direct Ship customer made an astonishing discovery. In a roll of 2010-D Native American dollars, he spotted a Zachary Taylor Presidential dollar coin. The Taylor dollar was the last Presidential coin issued in 2009, coming out on November 19 of that year, so any correctly produced Taylor dollar should bear the date 2009. This coin, intermixed with new, 2010-dated Native American coins, was also dated 2010, making it the first time that the wrong date had been reported on an edge-lettered U.S. dollar.

In order to have dollar coins ready for their release, production begins early—well before the New Year. At the Denver Mint, production of the 2010 Native American dollar coin began soon after or concurrent with the production of Zachary Taylor coins in late 2009.

The date and mintmark on each circulating dollar coin appears on its edge and is applied by an edge-lettering machine after the obverse and reverse are struck with a blank collar. Current speculation is that machinery struck 2010-D Native American dollars soon after completing a run of 2009-D Zachary Taylor dollars. A Taylor dollar must have been left behind somewhere between striking and edge-lettering, and then accidentally became mixed with the Native American dollars headed for the edge-lettering process. As a result, the machine inscribed the edge of this particular Zachary Taylor dollar with the wrong date.

This coin's origin from a Direct Ship package firmly places it within the category of circulating coins, making it one of the great U.S. circulating coin finds of the decade. Thus far, only a single Zachary Taylor dollar with the wrong date has been reported. Because it was only first discovered in February 2010, it is still too early to say how significant or rare this error will prove in the long-term. More importantly, though, enthusiasts of modern U.S. coins received prima facie evidence that coins in circulation still offer great potential for exciting and valuable finds.

	Total Certified Population	Most Commonly Certified	
		Grade	No. in Grade
NGC	1	MS-66	1
PCGS	—	—	—

Mintage: unknown

Retail value cannot be speculated; due to recency of discovery, market not fully established.

1987-P AND D KENNEDY HALF DOLLARS

Designed by Gilroy Roberts (obverse) and Frank Gasparro (reverse). On the obverse, the head of John F. Kennedy faces left. LIBERTY arcs across the top of the obverse; the date arcs along the bottom and IN GOD WE TRUST runs in a straight line beneath Kennedy's head. The reverse features a heraldic eagle, similar to that seen on the 1801 through 1807 and 1892 through 1915 half dollars, within a circle of 50 stars. UNITED STATES arcs around the top and HALF DOLLAR arcs along the bottom of the reverse.

Weight: 11.34 grams. *Composition:* 75% copper and 25% nickel bonded to an inner core of pure copper. *Diameter:* 30.6 mm. *Edge:* Reeded.

Mint sets were first sold in 1947 as a way to acquire all the coins produced for circulation in a given year, and they have been issued almost every year since, with a few notable exceptions. They are a convenience to collectors who can keep current with all the coinage issues.

A couple of times in the past, the Mint excluded certain circulation-issue coins. When the Eisenhower dollar was first issued in 1971, the packaging equipment was not able to handle the larger coin, and the dollar coin was thus excluded from Mint sets until 1973, an omission that infuriated collectors. As if to make up for the exclusion, the 1973 dollars were included even though none were actually needed for general commerce; they were produced specifically for the 1973 Mint sets. In fact, a handful of Mint sets

include other coins that likewise would not be available any other way. This first occurred in 1970, when the Denver Mint Kennedy half dollar was included in the Mint set even though none were struck for general circulation that year.

This happened again in 1987. The Mint announced that no half dollars would be issued for circulation, but that they would be included in the 1987 Mint set. The advance notice led to a surge in orders for the set, with nearly 2.9 million sold, compared to only 1.2 million in the previous year. The net mintage figure of the 1987 Philadelphia and Denver Mint Kennedy half dollars is just 2,890,758 of each, low mintage figures that had not been seen since the 1970-D issue. Beyond the low mintage, these coins benefit from the special cachet of being "Mint set–only" issues; collectors know their provenance because there can be no uncertainty about their early history.

In truth, the Kennedy half dollar is no longer a circulating coin. It would be struck for commerce again from 1988 through 2001, and about 20 million coins were made at both Philadelphia and Denver each year. Beginning in 2002, the coin was only struck for inclusion in Mint sets and for sale to collectors in rolls and bags. Circulation demand is met by a supply of pre-2002 issues. As two of the earliest of the Mint set–only issues, the 1987 varieties possess a special status among Kennedy half dollar collectors.

One of the factors that separates the 1987 Kennedy half dollar from current Mint set–only issues is condition. During most years, coins included in Mint sets did not receive any special attention, meaning that, although the coins were not circulated, they were often regular, banged up, ho-hum-quality coins. Since 2005, however, the coins included in Mint sets have had a special satin finish. While their special handling still does not compare to that of Proof sets, they are receiving some extra attention, and it is noticeable in their appearance. It is much easier to find superb gem grade (MS-67) examples of 2005 and later Kennedy half dollars than it is for the 1987 issues. In fact, MS-67 is a much-better-than-average grade for the 1987 varieties.

	Total Certified Population	Most Commonly Certified	
		Grade	No. in Grade
NGC	425	MS-66	208
PCGS	1,162	MS-66	602
Mintage: 5,781,516			
Retail value in most common certified grade (MS-66): $50			

Scott Schechter is the son of a collector and has been involved in numismatics since childhood. In his early teens, he started traveling to numismatic conventions around the country and began collecting U.S. commemorative coins. This area of numismatics remains a core interest. While still in high school, he had his first formal job in numismatics as an intern at the Smithsonian's National Museum of American History, working with the National Numismatic Collection. Throughout college, he cataloged ancient coins at the Semitic Museum. After graduating from Harvard with a degree in history of science in 2000, he joined Pinnacle Rarities and became a dealer in U.S. coins.

In 2005, he began work at Numismatic Guaranty Corporation, where he is now vice president. He has worked extensively on the development of the NGC Registry and online collection-management tools. He is particularly proud of his role in the project to upgrade the preservation of the National Numismatic Collection, which involved the creation of a custom conservation-grade holder for the Smithsonian's coins, bringing his professional experience full circle. He has lectured on modern coins for the Professional Numismatists Guild, contributed to *Coin World* and *Coin Dealer Newsletter*, and written extensively for NGC. He has also spoken about coin certification at many conventions in the United States and abroad, including the Beijing International Coin Expo in China and the World Money Fair in Germany.

Scott's wife, Sonia, while not a collector herself, is very supportive of his seemingly endless fascination with numismatics. Together they live in Florida and enjoy traveling. Scott also plays tennis regularly.

Jeff Garrett began his coin collecting in 1969, when a family friend gave him a Lincoln cent board. Since then, coins have been the focus of his life. Growing up in the Tampa Bay area in Clearwater, Florida, Garrett became very active in several local clubs, serving as a junior officer of the Clearwater Coin Club in the 1970s. He was mentored at an early age by many of the area's dealers, among them Ed French and Jeff Means. Garrett attended his first American Numismatic Association convention in 1974 in Miami with Ed French and has not missed one since. He has been a member of the ANA for more than 25 years, with life membership number 3124.

At the age of 17, Garrett was offered a position with Florida Coin Exchange, one of the dominant firms of the day. Two years later, he became a partner. In 1984, Garrett founded Mid-American Rare Coin Galleries, which continues to operate today. He is also co-owner of the Sarasota Rare Coin Gallery. During the 1980s, he was a partner in Mid-American Rare Coin Auctions, which sold many important collections and earned Catalogue of the Year in 1986 from the Numismatic Literary Guild. Several years later, Garrett organized the Bluegrass Coin Club in Lexington, Kentucky. Because local coin clubs were so important in his early life, Garrett wanted to foster the same atmosphere of enthusiastic collectors that he enjoyed as a youth. Today, the club is very healthy, with more than 30 members in attendance each month.

Garrett describes his expertise as being a "dealer's dealer." With a network of professionals he has established over 25 years, he helps with financing, research, and acquisitions sales. Over the course of his career, Garrett has handled nearly every U.S. rarity. During the American Numismatic Convention in 2003, he was one of the experts called upon to authenticate the long-lost 1913 Liberty Head nickel. In 2004, Garrett handled one of the greatest gold collections ever assembled, the famed Dukes Creek set of Georgia gold, which sold for nearly $4 million.

Another important aspect of his career is his membership in the Professional Numismatists Guild, to which he has belonged since 1982. Today, Garrett is a former president of the prestigious organization. In 2003, the PNG awarded him the Abe Kosoff Founders Award, that organization's highest honor, for work promoting the hobby and organization. In 2003, the first edition of *100 Greatest United States Coins* was given the Best Book award by both the NLG and the PNG. Although he spends most of his time buying and selling coins, Garrett enjoys research and the study of rare coins. He is coauthor of *The Official Red Book of Auction Records* and of the award-winning *Encyclopedia of United States Gold Coins 1795–1933*, a project done in cooperation with the Smithsonian Institution. Garrett is currently valuation editor for *A Guide Book of United States Coins* (the Red Book), published annually by Whitman.

Living in Lexington, Kentucky, he enjoys golf, travel, and spending time with his family: his wife Mary Lynn, their daughter Morgan, and their son Ben, who works as a coin grader for NGC.

ABOUT THE FOREWORD AUTHORS

Kenneth E. Bressett has been involved in the hobby since the 1940s. He has written many numismatic articles and is author or editor of more than a dozen related books; has been a past governor, vice president, and president of the American Numismatic Association; and is a highly accomplished teacher, researcher, and student. He has served for many years as the editor of *A Guide Book of United States Coins* (the Red Book)—at more than 21 million copies, one of the best-selling nonfiction titles in American publishing. As a former consultant to the U.S. Mint, he was instrumental in originating the 50 State Quarters® Program and in selecting many of the coins' reverse designs. Ken is a recipient of the Numismatic Literary Guild's Clemy Award and is an inductee in the Numismatic Hall of Fame (at ANA Headquarters in Colorado Springs).

Q. David Bowers became a professional numismatist as a teenager in 1953. He has served as president of both the American Numismatic Association (1983–1985) and the Professional Numismatists Guild (1977–1979). He is a recipient of the highest honor bestowed by the ANA (the Farran Zerbe Award), was the first ANA member to be named Numismatist of the Year (1995), was given the Lifetime Achievement Award (2005), and has been inducted into the ANA Numismatic Hall of Fame. Bowers has received the PNG's highest honor (The Founders' Award) and more "Book of the Year Award" and "Best Columnist" honors of the Numismatic Literary Guild than any other writer. In July 1999, in a poll published in *COINage*, "Numismatists of the Century," by Ed Reiter, Bowers was recognized in this list of just 18 names. He is the author of more than 50 books, hundreds of auction and other catalogs, and several thousand articles including columns in *Coin World* (now the longest-running by any author in numismatic history), *Paper Money*, and, in past years, *The Numismatist*. He serves as co-chairman of Stack's (New York City and Wolfeboro, New Hampshire) and numismatic director for Whitman Publishing, LLC.

The most secure holder. The strongest guarantee.
The hobby's first choice for modern coins.

Trust your US moderns to the experts at NGC.

NGC employs the industry's most rigorous grading standards and the strongest guarantee. Our conservation-grade holder ensures your coins are secure for the long-term, without sacrificing the magnificent display they deserve. We're the only company that offers your US moderns variety attribution through VarietyPlus® — as well as popular release designations like Early Releases and First Day of Issue.

Discover why more collectors turn to NGC every day. Visit NGCcoin.com

NGC
Numismatic Guaranty Corporation

800-NGC-COIN (642-2646)
www.NGCcoin.com

Official Grading Service of

AMERICAN NUMISMATIC ASSOCIATION | P·N·G

ROBERT B. LECCE NUMISMATIST INC.

Boca Raton, FL 33498 • (561) 483-4744 • Fax (561) 483-2660
Rareusgold@aol.com • Artglass2000@aol.com

We supply many of the largest coin companies with Modern coins.
Let us supply your company with coins at wholesale prices.

We have one of the largest inventory of Gold,
Silver and Platinum Modern coins in the country.

Our coins are graded by both PCGS and NGC.

We can supply you with all of the inventory and the
knowledge you need to sell these rare coins of the future.

If your firm is thinking getting into the Modern Coin market please contact us!
(Sorry wholesale to dealers only.)

We also have an extensive inventory of Proof Gold, Silver and Platinum
Eagles in their original Boxes or Graded Proof 70 by NGC or PCGS.

P·N·G
Knowledge. Integrity. Responsibility.

AMERICAN NUMISMATIC ASSOCIATION

PCGS
The Standard for the Rare Coin Industry

NGC
AUTHORIZED MEMBER/DEALER

ICTA

"How Much Are My Coins and Collectibles Worth?"
Find out at the

WHITMAN
COIN & COLLECTIBLES EXPO

Four shows held annually in Baltimore and Philadelphia

Baltimore Convention Center, Baltimore

✳

Pennsylvania Convention Center, Philadelphia

BUY ◆ SELL ◆ TRADE

For more information:
404-214-4373

info@WhitmanExpo.com ✳ WhitmanCoinCollecting.com

STACK'S

A LEADER IN U.S. AND WORLD NUMISMATICS FOR 75 YEARS

Trusted Experts for Generations!

- **Financial Security**—Stack's has held continuous auctions since 1935 and each and every consignor has been paid on time.

- **Personal Service**—Stack's offers clients a good measure of old-fashioned personal service and warmth. We guarantee that you will be pleased with every transaction.

- **Expert Staff**—Stack's staff brings you world renowned, experienced numismatic experts. Put our unsurpassed expertise to work for you!

- **Record Prices**—Stack's has set many auction records, including the most valuable coin ever auctioned, the 1933 double eagle at $7.59 million (in partnership with Sotheby's).

- **Diverse Auction Offerings**—Our marvelous sales feature U.S., World and Ancient coins, tokens, medals, and paper money.

- **Auctioneer of the World's Most Valuable Collection:** Stack's sales of the John J. Ford, Jr. Collection realized nearly $60 million.

- **Internet Presence**—Stack's has a leading-edge Internet presence with a variety of bidding options including live audio and video feed. Hundreds of thousands worldwide visit our site at www.stacks.com.

Stack's

BUYERS, SELLERS AND AUCTIONEERS OF THE WORLD'S FINEST COINS FOR OVER 70 YEARS.

Visit www.stacks.com or call 800-566-2580

ANA MEMBER · P·N·G

Auctions, Appraisals, Retail · Since 1935

123 West 57th Street • New York, NY 10019 • 212-582-2580 • Fax 212-245-5018
P.O. Box 1804 • Wolfeboro, NH 03894 • 800-566-2580 • Fax 603-569-3875 • auction@stacks.com

www.stacks.com